HISTORY OF PRUSSIA

BY

HERBERT TUTTLE

———◆———

VOLUME II. — (1740–1745.)

MAP OF
CENTRAL EUROPE
TO ILLUSTRATE
THE FIRST AND THE SECOND
SILESIAN WAR.

HISTORY OF PRUSSIA

UNDER FREDERIC THE GREAT

1740—1745

BY

HERBERT TUTTLE
PROFESSOR IN CORNELL UNIVERSITY

BOSTON AND NEW YORK
HOUGHTON, MIFFLIN AND COMPANY
The Riverside Press, Cambridge

The Riverside Press, Cambridge:
Electrotyped and Printed by H. O. Houghton & Co.

PREFACE.

THE two volumes accompanying this preface are designed to be the second and third in a series, which began some time since with the work entitled "History of Prussia to the Accession of Frederic the Great." By themselves they also form the first half of what it is hoped will be a complete account, descriptive and historical, of the reign of the third king of Prussia. A fourth volume, to be issued in the near future, will cover the period of the Seven Years' War, including the measures which were taken to heal the wounds left by that bloody struggle. The fifth will bring the story down to the death of Frederic. Such being the plan of the work, it will be necessary to refer to the earlier volume all readers who may desire a fuller knowledge of the antecedents of the great king, and of the inherited forces and problems of his reign, than can be given in the limits of a mere introduction. But I have not the less aimed to make the nature and objects of Frederic's preliminary measures clear by a brief survey of the state of Prussia at the time of his accession.

After this account of their scope and connections the volumes might now be left to the general reader without any further explanation. But the critics and specialists would not be satisfied. The great name of Carlyle is associated so commandingly with the reign of Frederic the Great that any other writer, who ventures to treat the same subject, is bound to make good in advance his claim to a hearing. I am certainly not wanting in respect for those who suspect, or even resent, any attempt by an inferior pen to write upon a theme which has been touched by the hand of the master. But my own faith was shaken when during a residence of several years in Berlin I discovered how inadequate was Carlyle's account, and probably also his knowledge, of the working system of the Prussian government in the last century, — a system which it is absolutely necessary to understand if one desires to know as well why Frederic was able to accomplish what he did, as why his successors failed to accomplish what they undertook. A candid but indiscreet friend of Mr. Carlyle completed the disenchantment. Mr. Froude has shown that Carlyle was not called to the subject of Frederic by the imperative voice of duty, bidding him to erect a monument over one of the world's benefactors, but rather that, casting about for a topic on which to employ his professional pen, he fixed upon the third king of Prussia as the most available one which offered itself. This revelation destroys much of the romance which has hitherto connected Frederic with Carlyle's general scheme of social philosophy, and compels his work to submit to the tests imposed on all ordinary, uninspired productions. Is it, with all its peculiar merits as a work of art, a true and adequate picture of the Prussia of Frederic the Second?

The answer to this question I must leave to the judgment of readers who do me the honor to read my own account of the same reign. But I may properly explain wherein the present work differs in plan and treatment from that of Carlyle's, and what sources I have been able to use that were either not open to him, or being open were not consulted.

In regard to the first distinction it is enough to state

that I do not come forward as a biographer of Frederic. My task is rather to explain the part played by Frederic and his reign in the process by which Prussia became what she is to-day. That part was possibly determined more by the personal qualities of the king himself than by any other one influence, so that any history of his reign must be largely biographical in treatment. But there is still a distinction between the life of Frederic and the history of Prussia during his life. I have tried to give due attention to those personal details which throw light upon the character of the king, and lend interest to the narrative; but it is essentially the life of Prussia as a state, the development of polity, the growth of institutions, the progress of society, which I have made it my object to describe.

In this work I have been aided by a vast literature which has grown up since the time of Carlyle. The author of the " History of Friedrich II." studied most of the available printed material with great care; and, as one of the few persons west of the Straits of Dover who have plowed their way through that dreary field, I can testify that Dryasdust is a real personage, fully deserving all the reproaches that have been poured upon his phenomenal dullness, yet deserving also perhaps more praise than he has usually received for the fidelity with which, according to his light, he arranged the records of his time for the use of future historians. But it does not appear that Mr. Carlyle, though he made two visits to Germany during the progress of his labors, undertook any researches in the Prussian archives. The principal works in which he found original, official material were the sumptuous edition of the " Œuvres de Frédéric le Grand," published under the auspices of the Berlin Academy of Sciences; Dr. Preuss' " Friedrich der Grosse;" and the first editions of Ranke's masterly contributions to Prussian history. From Austrian and Russian sources he had little or nothing; from French, scarcely anything that laid claim to official authority except the careless and inadequate "Histoire de la diplomatie française" of Flassan. The English material had been more liberally used, especially in the various compilations by archdeacon Coxe, and these Carlyle himself supplemented by studies among the papers of the British Museum and the Record Office.

The subsequent publications which throw light upon the reign of Frederic represent nearly every national standpoint, and almost every variety of literature. Among the general histories at least two masterpieces must be named. The elaborate "Geschichte Maria Theresias," by Dr. von Arneth, director of the Austrian archives, not only derives a special value from the facilities which the author's official position gave him, and the faithful use which he made of them, but it is also written in a firm, clear, luminous style, shows great independence of judgment, and rarely sins against good taste. His views are of course sharply attacked by Prussian critics; and even Adolph Beer, who has examined the same material, dissents from some of his conclusions. But the work is by far the most complete and authentic account of Austria's great queen, and is in my judgment one of the best histories in the German language. The Prussian view of the relations between the courts of Berlin and Vienna from 1740 to 1756 is presented with great ability in the fifth part of Droysen's "Geschichte der preussischen Politik." The lamented death of the author two years ago left his work unfinished in the very portion which most needed his unrivalled skill in solving obscure diplomatic problems, and tracing the lines of complex negotiations through masses of bewildering correspondence; yet nobody will read

Droysen for entertainment, or for judicial opinions. The style is harsh, abrupt, forbidding. The book is that of an advocate. But the laborious researches that he made, and the firm grasp of his material that he everywhere shows, give his work a value which is only lessened, not destroyed, by its violent and sometimes cynical partisanship. These two comprehensive treatises are supplemented by a number of historical monographs, which describe special periods, events, or persons with more detail. The late professor Arnold Schaefer's "Geschichte des siebenjährigen Kriegs" is now the standard history of the third war between Frederic and Maria Theresa; and, notwithstanding slight errors which the critics have discovered, it may be followed with reasonable confidence. Dr. G. Grünhagen's "Geschichte des ersten schlesischen Krieges" deserves even warmer recognition. The author had become favorably known by several studies from the archives of Breslau before he published this learned, able, and candid work; and it is to be hoped that he will feel encouraged to apply his admirable method to the history of the later struggles for his native province. The list contains many other books of more or less importance, only a few of which can be mentioned, and those by little except the name. Count Vitzthum's "Maurice de Saxe et Marie Josephe, dauphine de France," throws incidentally some new light upon Frederic's Moravian campaign in 1742; Brückner's "Katharina die Zweite" is one of the few popular histories which may be consulted as an authority by the special inquirer; "Die erste Theilung Polens" by A. Beer is the most elaborate account, mainly from the Prussian standpoint, of a transaction which is not yet free from obscurity, and with it may be compared Ssolojof's "Geschichte des Falles von Polen" in the German translation of Spörer for the Russian version, and

Ferrand's "Les trois démembrements de la Pologne;" Saint-René Taillandier's "Maurice de Saxe," though laying little or no claim to originality, is a good critical sketch of the only general who during Frederic's time could be called his peer; in Desnoiresterres' "Voltaire et Frédéric II.," Keyserling's "Moses Mendelssohn," and Pröhle's "Friedrich der Grosse und die deutsche Literatur" may be found interesting facts and discussions bearing on one of the many sides of Frederic's activity; and the "Mémoires" of the duke de Luynes are the contribution of an unusually well informed observer to the history of the court of Versailles during many years of the reign of Louis the Fifteenth.

A second and still larger class of works consists of special studies, diplomatic and political, from the different archives of Europe. Isaacsohn's "Geschichte des preussischen Beamtenthums," though ill-arranged, unreadable, and abruptly terminated by the author's death after it had only reached the early part of Frederic's reign, is an invaluable guide to the early history of the Prussian civil service; and Bornhak's "Geschichte des preussischen Verwaltungsrechts" discusses the same subject from a slightly different standpoint, yet with equally useful results. In his "Geheimnisse des sächsischen Cabinets," count Vitzthum sets forth the Saxon view of the relations between Berlin and Dresden down to the close of the Seven Years' War. The duke de Broglie has published two sets of studies from the French archives, under the titles "Frédéric II. et Marie Thérèse," and "Frédéric II. et Louis XV.;" these are piquant, readable, and full of interesting revelations. From the Hanoverian archives, now in the possession of Prussia, Dr. Borkowsky has compiled "Die englische Friedensvermittlung in Jahre 1745." To the same class of works belong also Arneth's "Joseph

II. und Katharina von Russland ; " several monographs by
A. Beer, such as " Holland und der oesterreichische Erb-
folgekrieg," " Aufzeichnungen des Grafen Bentinck," and
" Friedrich II. und von Zwieten ; " Schlözer's "Friedrich
II. und Katharina II.," and many others.

There remains finally a third class of authorities, and
the most important of all, the recent and numerous publications from the various archives of Europe. The place
of honor here properly belongs to the " Politische Correspondenz Friedrichs des Grossen." This great enterprise,
begun several years ago under the auspices of the Academy
of Sciences, and the general supervision of professors
Droysen, Duncker, and von Sybel, has now proceeded as
far as the fourteenth volume, which extends to the year
1757. The mechanical execution of the work leaves
nothing to desire. The successive editors, Dr. Reinhold
Koser and Dr. Albert Naudé, both pupils of Droysen,
and among the most promising of the younger historical scholars of Prussia, have done their work with industry, discrimination, and impartiality. Though the
term " political " is narrowed down, in accordance with
Droysen's example, to mean practically diplomatic, the
editors have not confined themselves in their search for
material to letters actually written or dictated by Frederic,
but have incorporated everything which, proceeding directly or indirectly from him, casts light upon his foreign
policy. To the authors and conductors of this generous
scheme historical students owe a debt which cannot be
too gratefully acknowledged. The liberality with which
the Prussian archives are administered under their present
director, professor von Sybel, has also led to two other
enterprises, scarcely less welcome. The first of these is
the series called " Publikationen aus den königlich-preus-
sischen Staatsarchiven," in which over a score of volumes

have already appeared. Several of these concern the policy or the personality, or both, of Frederic. Of the three which bear the title "Preussens Könige in ihrer Thätigkeit für die Landescultur," the second is devoted to his reign, and gives, in the form of edicts, decrees, ordinances, and laws, together with an introductory essay by R. Stadelmann, a complete view of his efforts to improve the national agriculture. Five volumes, compiled and edited in the same excellent manner by Max Lehmann, are on the subject "Preussen und die Katholische Kirche seit 1640. Still another volume contains the conversations of Frederic with Henry de Catt, the reader and amanuensis who accompanied him through several campaigns, the recipient of his literary confidence, the faithful chronicler of his frank, free, and unreserved opinions on a great variety of topics. As the series proceeds it will doubtless open up many other sides of the king's busy life. The third set of publications is exclusively friderician, its title being "Preussische Staatsschriften aus der Regierungszeit Friedrichs des Grossen." Only two numbers have as yet been published, and these reach only to the year 1756. The documents, too, are, with few exceptions, reprints of controversial material, which had already seen the light. But many of them are now first published from the authentic official text, and the notes of the editor, Dr. Koser, make the volumes an extremely valuable repertory for one side of the history of the period. Successive issues will, it is presumed, continue the series throughout the reign of Frederic. These three works are the ones on which, so far as Prussian sources are concerned, and in addition to earlier publications, I have chiefly depended for my knowledge of Frederic himself, his foreign policy, and his system of government. I have tried to describe his reign as it is drawn by himself in his own writings and his own official acts.

In the mean time, at opposite corners of Europe, the archives have been opening their secrets to the historian. In France have appeared M. Boutaric's two volumes, " Correspondance secrète de Louis XV.," and the duke de Broglie's " Le secret du roi," two works which describe, with an abundance of documentary material, the private diplomacy of madame de Pompadour's lover, the original ally and final enemy of Frederic. A cordial acknowledgment must also be made to the series known as " Instructions données aux ambassadeurs et ministres de France." Two volumes have already appeared, one devoted to Sweden and one to Austria, that is to say, to the successive ministers of France at these courts. Their value is, of course, lessened by the fact that the ostensible instructions issued to French representatives abroad did not always agree with their secret orders, and partook more of the nature of academic essays than of practical rules of conduct for all emergencies. But, with this limitation, the volumes supply official information of an undoubted value. While historical specialists have thus been mining in the cabinet records of their own countries, the Russian Imperial Historical Society, with a zeal which deserves the warmest recognition, has taken the archives of nearly all Europe into its service. The " Sbornik," which is the title of the volumes issued by it from time to time, is the most comprehensive of all sources for the diplomatic history of the eighteenth century. In the main, the series consists of collections of the correspondence between the principal European governments and their agents at St. Petersburg, arranged by periods and countries, and accompanied by a Russian translation. The editorial parts are also in Russian, which renders them useless, of course, to

the larger number of inquirers. But the general scope
and conduct of the enterprise are such as the scholars of
Western Europe might well make their model.

The use of both the older and the newer material for
the history of Frederic's reign has been made easy for me
by the kindly assistance of many persons. First of all I
must name Andrew D. White, one of the founders and for
many years the president of Cornell University. When,
on the completion of my first volume of Prussian history,
he learned that the continuation of the work might be made
difficult, or at least be delayed, by the scarcity of material
in America, he generously offered me what was in effect
an unlimited authority to order in his name any books
that might be necessary; so that I was enabled to obtain a large and indispensable addition to the historical
works already present in Mr. White's own noble library,
and in that of the university. It is proper that I should
take this opportunity publicly to express my profound
thanks for the substantial support which he thus gave to
my labors.

The various public libraries to which I have had occasion to apply for books have met my requests with uniform courtesy and promptness. At Harvard College Mr.
Justin Winsor gave me free access to the books presented
by Mr. Carlyle, and the loan of others from the large and
rapidly growing collections under his efficient charge.
The director of the Boston Public Library, Mellen Cham-
berlain, esq., secured me in the same way special facilities
for consulting the books which private and corporate
generosity have put upon the crowded shelves of that
noble institution. From the library of the State Department at Washington I obtained the loan of what, so far
as I know, is the only copy in America of the Russian
" Sbornik: " the admirable management of Mr. Theodore

F. Dwight keeps this library easily the first in the country for the student of diplomatic history. The Cincinnati Public Library readily sent books on my application, and my thanks for the favor are due to the librarian. At the Astor Library in New York I was enabled to consult the Hardwicke Papers, recently purchased in England by a wise outlay of considerable money. If I found little new material in a collection which had already been used by archdeacon Coxe and others, I was at least enabled to verify the statements made by them, to convince myself that the resources of these MSS. have been by no means exhausted, and that the example set in their purchase might well be followed by other American libraries. The kind permission of Mr. Francis Parkman gave me an opportunity to examine the voluminous material collected by him in the archives of Paris and London, and now deposited with the Massachusetts Historical Society. The fruitful use which the owner himself has made of this material renders it forever unlikely that another writer will undertake to cultivate the same field ; but the papers, which with rare unselfishness he has thus thrown open to the public, will always help special students to find light upon many obscure points in the colonial history of North America, and its relations to the general history of Europe. To all the gentlemen who have thus aided me in their public or private capacity, and to many others, who, in one way or another, have rendered willing and useful service, my grateful acknowledgments are made.

In the spelling of proper names I have tried to avoid the appearance of pedantry which would follow a rigid adherence to any one system, and the anarchy which would result from the neglect of all systems. Where there are established English forms for geographical terms I have usually employed them; in other cases I have used sometimes the local spelling, and sometimes the spelling of that language which offers the most intelligible words. Thus I write Regensburg and not Ratisbonne or Ratisbon, but I also write Munich and not München. The same rule, if rule it may be called, has been applied to the names of persons. Where there is a conflict of usage, as between Seckendorf and Seckendorff, or between Bestuschew, Bestuscheff, and Bestuschef, I have generally chosen the shorter and simpler form.

The references to authorities will, it is hoped, present little difficulty. Such letters as are contained in published collections I have usually cited by day, month, and year, not by volume and page, for the latter method would involve much useless repetition, and add little in point of clearness. Thus the letters of Frederic referred to in the notes will be found, if no other place is indicated, either in the academy edition of his works, or in the " Politische Correspondenz." Voltaire's correspondence is also contained in every complete edition of his writings; I have used that of 1820–1822, in sixty-six volumes.

H. T.

ITHACA, N. Y., *October*, 1887.

CONTENTS.

———◆———

CHAPTER I.

THE KING AND THE KINGDOM.

CHAPTER II.

THE NEW FOREIGN POLICY.

CHAPTER III.

THE FIRST SILESIAN WAR.

CHAPTER IV.

THE DIPLOMATIC INTERLUDE.

CHAPTER V.

FREDERIC'S SECOND CAMPAIGN.

CHAPTER VI.

THE PEACE OF BRESLAU.

CHAPTER VII.

THE UNION OF FRANKFORT.

CHAPTER VIII.

THE SECOND SILESIAN WAR.

FREDERIC THE GREAT.

CHAPTER I.

THE KING AND THE KINGDOM.

AT the death of Frederic William the First, in 1740, the kingdom of Prussia held nearly the fore- The kingdom most place among European states of the second of Prussia. rank. It was, indeed, inferior to Holland in extent and variety of resources. It wanted the associations of past grandeur, the influence of a surviving magnificence, the prestige of vast colonial possessions, which still made the name of Spain imposing and formidable. The military annals of Sweden were more brilliant; the social fabric of Saxony was older and finer; and even Hanover was raised nearly to the grade of a rival by the connection with England. And in that public estimation which often plays a decisive part in fixing the relative rank of states Prussia was still little more than one of several princi-palities, which competed for influence and authority in the councils of the German Empire. But in a compact political organization and an efficient civil service, in a thrifty administration patiently laying by an annual surplus, and a large army brought to the highest point of perfection, the young kingdom had elements of strength which, though long unperceived by its neighbors, far sur-passed those of any other except three or four of the greatest powers. With such resources at his command an enterprising and ambitious prince could easily overthrow the accepted classification of states.

This flattering position, or rather these means for as-
serting a position, had been acquired by the
patient labor of over three hundred years.
From the time at least of the first Hohenzollern, the electors of Brandenburg, before and after they added the
further title of king of Prussia, pursued a fairly uniform
policy of conquest and aggrandizement. Now and then,
indeed, there arrived one who, instead of increasing the
common stock, seemed fitted only to squander what his
predecessors had accumulated. Thus history points re-
proachfully to Joachim II., to George William, to Frederic
I. But while the natural weakness of the second of these
was aggravated by the anarchy of the Thirty Years' War,
in the midst of which his lot was thrown, Joachim rendered
his state a striking service by espousing the cause of the
Reformation, and Frederic won for his house the crown
and prerogatives of royalty. These were not the less durable triumphs of policy because the motive in each case was
perhaps vanity and ambition rather than an unselfish desire to serve the interests of the public. But the ordinary
and more characteristic measures by which the electors
urged onward the fortunes of Brandenburg-Prussia were
not dramatic or picturesque, seldom appeal to the imagination, and fill no large place in recorded history. They
suggest rather the thrifty, prudent, faithful economy of
the wise father of a family. A sharp eye for profitable
investments, a skilful use of marriage contracts, the
steady increase and improvement of an estate originally
small and ill-favored by nature, and zealous efforts to
refine the agents and methods of civil discipline, — these
were the quiet and unobtrusive arts by which a dozen
generations of Hohenzollerns built up the kingdom of
Prussia. Territorial growth went hand in hand with
political consolidation. A few ambitious schemes were
indeed baffled, others delayed; and there were many frictions which checked for a time, and even threatened for

Method of its growth.

ever to arrest, the march of progress. But the general course of development was little affected by such incidents. Year by year the frontiers of the state were enlarged. Year by year the several provinces were knit more closely together into a common frame, and a more efficient unity was given to all other forms of concentration. The increase of revenue, the growth of the army, the perfection of the administrative system, and the centralization of authority were features of a policy which, pursued as it was for several generations, left Prussia in the middle of the eighteenth century with one of the firmest and strongest political organizations in Europe.

Yet the king who had the merit of bringing the machine of state to such a point of perfection was unfitted by his tastes and his talents to employ it in enterprises of conquest. Frederic William I. was the master of a large force and a large fund, both of which his own measures had more than doubled; but in foreign politics he trusted mainly to the power of his voice, which finally ceased to have any terrors for Europe, and left him little more than the name of a common scold. It was only at home, and among his own people, that he was feared as much as he was hated. The early years of his reign had displayed, indeed, a manly public spirit, and witnessed the triumph of wise practical reforms, which atoned for many faults of manner and method. The first and only foreign enterprise of the king, the acquisition of Stettin, was creditable to the arms, and, if not judged by a stern morality, to the statesmanship of Prussia. The example of the palace taught the humblest citizen the great lesson of thrift and industry. Marital infidelity was shown to be no necessary part of the royal character, and a pompous ceremonial was seen to disappear without any loss to the dignity of the state. But as time went on the severe yet wholesome virtues of the king had been obscured by violent and intol-

erable vices, either developed with the progress of years
from latent germs, or called into being under the influence of disease, intemperance and disappointment. Many
of these vices, too, were public and political; and even
those which were by nature personal passed over into the
conduct of official relations, and affected every department
of state. The officials in all grades of the service trem-
bled before the violence of their manifestations. Foreign
powers, even while utilizing them for their own ends,
chafed under the extraordinary vicissitudes of temper and
policy which they made possible. And yet if the diplomacy
of Frederic William's later years was not characterized by
that stability which could have procured him useful allies
abroad, it wanted at the same time that firmness which
would have made it respected at home. It was his misfortune and his fault to lose the esteem of nearly every
class of persons with whom his policy came in contact.
The diplomatists whose treaties were thwarted by his rude
caprices, the ministers who had an equal dread of his cane
and his tongue, the professors who fled from his presence,
the judges whose verdicts he reversed, the members of
his own family who were schooled to nearly every kind
of evil, and the great mass of the toiling, suffering, un-
complaining Prussian people whom the burdens of state
tortured in every relation of life, were all prepared to
welcome a change of reign as an auspicious and beneficent
event. For it seemed impossible that the system of government, which vexed them all alike, could survive the
king who had brought it to such cruel perfection.

Frederic the Second, the successor of this rugged
Accession of tyrant, had thus the good fortune to receive, on
Frederic II. ascending the throne of his fathers, a welcome
such as has been granted to few of the princes of history.
Hatred of the old system which was now expected to pass
away, and confidence in the new system which was expected to take its place, combined to greet the young king

with a generous and widespread enthusiasm, most intense, indeed, in Prussia, yet felt in some degree in every part of Europe, and scarcely marred by a note of dissent.

It is true that the hopes of a general reform rested on little except the supposed characteristics of Frederic himself. He nowhere appears as an enemy of his father's system of government. The treatment which he himself had suffered at the hands of his father was purely a domestic grievance; and the court-martial, which sat in judgment upon his attempt to escape by flight from the paternal tyranny, refused to include it in the category of public offences. This was not, indeed, the attitude of Frederic William. Founding his whole scheme of parental discipline upon a quaint, stern theory of public duty, he naturally regarded the prince's insubordination as a military crime. But Frederic could have had little difficulty in choosing between the view of his father, which might have sent him to the scaffold, and the view of the court, to which he possibly owed his escape. This distinction might, again, have been carried much farther. Other cases of individual hardship might have been treated, not as necessary consequences of a system of government, but as outbursts of temper on the part of the man who happened to be at the head of the system; and there is no evidence that this was not the line along which Frederic had always reasoned.

Popular expectations.

Even the character of Frederic was, it now appears, grossly misunderstood by his buoyant and sanguine subjects of 1740. But it was from his character as they understood it, and from his history, that they drew all their hopeful conclusions; and the materials which they had for forming a judgment could hardly lead to any other results. It was known that he had been exposed from an early age to the insults and blows of his royal father; that an attempt to escape had cost him a term in a felon's cell; that he had been released from prison with the loss of his military rank, and only to pass to the drudgery of a government office ; that he had espoused, to please his father, a woman to whom his heart was not engaged ; that he was fond of the higher music, and found in his flute solace for many an hour of anguish ; that he had patiently, if not successfully, cultivated the muses ; that his controlling tastes were not for soldiers and tobacco, but for art, science, and letters ; and that he courted with singular ardor the wise, liberal, and elevated spirits of his generation. A few intimate friends also knew that the crown prince of Prussia had written lines which expressed, in French somewhat below the literary standard of Voltaire, sentiments not at all below the moral standard of Marcus Aurelius. It was not unreasonable, then, to regard his accession as the dawn of an era of enlightenment, toleration, liberality, and reform. It can cause no surprise that Prussia expected him to lessen the rigor of the existing system ; to reduce the army ; to renounce oppressive taxes ; to give responsible ministers some share in the power of the state ; to consult the people upon schemes which concerned their own fortunes ; and, scorning a microscopic passion for details, to raise himself into that higher sphere whence a broad and liberal statesmanship could survey the larger interests of the commonwealth.

Yet it soon appeared that he intended to assert, even more strenuously than his father, his own absolute, undivided authority. Frederic William was always under the influence, though without knowing it, of two quite different classes of men. The one class was represented by ministers like Ilgen, the secretary for foreign affairs, whose special attainments made him indispensable to a king with little diplomatic knowledge and no diplomatic tact. There was, again, a small knot of personal favorites who, even when they had ability, kept their places by flattery and intrigue. The gifted, dashing, unscrupulous

Grumbkow may stand for this group. But Leopold of Dessau, known familiarly as the "Old Dessauer," had in some degree the characteristics of both these schools. He was a specialist in the profession of arms, and a boon companion of the second king of Prussia.

No other general of the army had had more experience, or had rendered greater service, than this ruler of Leopold of the principality of Anhalt-Dessau. He fought Dessau. with Marlborough and Eugene of Savoy at Blenheim; with Eugene at Turin ; and as a volunteer he was present at the battle of Malplaquet. He invented the iron ramrod, which gave the Prussians a vast advantage on many a desperate field. His reforms in the practical discipline of troops were such that he is often called the founder of the modern system of military tactics. A rough, rude, uncultured son of nature, a soldier above and before all things, he was not deficient in the arts of the courtier, and his credit with Frederic William is not hard to understand. But the son of Frederic William had little respect for persons. When this veteran soldier, who had entered the Prussian army half a century before Frederic ascended the throne, ventured to express the hope that he and his sons would continue to enjoy their authority, he was sharply told that there was no intention of disturbing them in their places, but the only authority in the state was that of the king.[1]

An equally rude reception was given to the cavalry general Schulenburg. His personal claims to favor were even stronger than those of the "Old Schulenburg. Dessauer," for he had presided over the court-martial which, by a courageous verdict, saved Frederic from the vengeance of his father. Hence the new reign had no

[1] Baron Pöllnitz, in his unpublished memoirs of the reign of Frederic, is the authority for this incident, of which he describes himself as an eye-witness. The accuracy of the account has, however, been challenged.

sooner begun than he hastened up to the capital to offer his congratulations. But Frederic acknowledged his homage by bluntly ordering him back to his regiment, which he was enjoined not to leave again without permission. To other officious persons, who presumed on past service or former intimacy, and obtruded themselves, their claims, their advice upon the young king, the same stern lesson was taught. In every case the reproof left a sting behind.

Frederic was thus resolved to govern as well as to reign. But the maxims of government which he announced, while revealing no disposition to sacrifice any part of the prerogative, seemed to give assurance that the prerogative would be exercised in an enlightened manner, and with an eye single to the welfare of the people.

Frederic's views of government.

The views of Frederic in regard to the spirit in which a prince ought to administer his office had been set forth two years before in the " Anti-Machiavel." This was a treatise written in an outburst of real or well-affected indignation at the precepts of the wise Florentine, and sent to Voltaire for revision and publication.[1] The ideal prince of this work is accordingly very different from the prince of Machiavelli. He has all the virtues and none of the faults of his class ; he is thrifty, industrious, unselfish, moderate, and just; he keeps faith with his people and his neighbors. And it is, above all things, his duty to regard his kingdom, not as a possession, but as a trust, and to make the prosperity and happiness of his subjects his supreme concern. The king is only the first servant of the state. The model government is that

As crown prince.

---

[1] It is in vol. viii. of the Academy edition of the *Œuvres de Frédéric.* The editor explains that on the king's accession it was thought desirable to revise the MS. still further, but the printer, Van Duren, at the Hague, refused to return it. His edition appeared in September, 1740, the Berlin authorized edition a little later.

of England, where "the parliament is the arbiter between the people and the king, and the king, though having plenty of power for doing good, has none for doing evil." [1]

Some of the principles laid down in this and other youthful essays were reaffirmed by Frederic after his accession in the most solemn official As king. form. To the generals who came in a body on the first of June to express at once their condolence and their felicitations, the king frankly said that, while he had no doubt they would serve him as faithfully as they had served his father, he was compelled to remind them that the army ought to be serviceable rather than showy, and ought not to be oppressive to the people. The following day the ministers presented themselves to take the oath of office. The young king at once announced, with philosophical cynicism, his contempt for such idle forms, but said he would offer no objection to a ceremony which custom and superstition seemed to exact. Then he proceeded to deliver a species of allocution. He frankly recognized their services to his father, but announced also his own expectations in regard to the future. Hitherto, he said, they had made a distinction between the interests of the land and the interests of the king. The late king had approved this, and they were therefore blameless. But such a distinction was no longer to be observed. The interests of the people ought also to be his own, and wherever there seemed to be a conflict between them, those of the people were always to be preferred. [2]

[1] Anti-Machiavel, c. xix.

[2] Ranke, *Sämmtliche Werke*, xxvii., xxviii. 279 ; *Helden- Staats- und Lebensgeschichte Friedrichs des Andern*, Frankfort and Leipsic, 1746– 1764. I shall follow the example of other writers in citing this labored and anonymous compilation as *Heldengeschichte*. The editor was, it appears, one Christian Frederic Hempel, a publicist of Jena. Cf. R. Koser in the introduction to vol. i. of *Staatsschriften aus der Regierungszeit Friedrichs II.*, Berlin, 1877.

Frederic's first measures were quite in harmony with the principles thus announced. The use of torture was restricted to a small class of cases.[1] The costly regiment of giants at Potsdam was promptly disbanded. The corn magazines, or public granaries, filled by the foresight of Frederic William, were thrown open to the people, the grain sold at a moderate price, and great hardships caused by the severe winter of 1739–40 thus relieved.[2] Another edict permitted the free importation of foreign grain.[3] It was ordered that fines should no longer be exacted, or the royal dispensation required, in case of marriages not clearly within the forbidden degrees of consanguinity.[4] The alarm of certain Protestants, which found expression in a formal representation to the king, about the freedom of teaching accorded to the Catholics, was sharply rebuked: "In this country," it was declared, "every one shall get to heaven in his own way."[5] On the other hand, the Lutherans were authorized to restore their ritual, which Frederic William, under a puritanical impulse, had abruptly simplified. These and similar measures show the manner in which Frederic took up his work. Yet one might, perhaps, inquire, in a critical though not a captious or belittling spirit, whether, in the rush of enthusiasm caused by this

Preliminary reforms.

[1] Such as "crimen læsæ majestatis und Landesverrätherei, auch den grossen Mordthaten wo viele Menschen ums Leben gebracht, oder viele Delinquenten, deren Connexion herauszubringen nöthig, implicirt sind," etc. Preuss, *Friedrich der Grosse,* Berlin, 1832, i. 140.

[2] Edicts of 31 May and 16 June 1740.

[3] Mylius, *Corpus Const. March. Cont.* i. p. 341.

[4] Ibid. i. p. 342.

[5] Preuss, i. 138. But Ranke, xxvii., xxviii. p. 287, observes that it was by no means Frederic's purpose to encourage every person to set up a church of his own, which would have led only to religious anarchy. The order was, besides, a private rescript, addressed to officials, and not intended for the public.

rapid series of enactments, especially in the minds of a
people to whom any relaxation of governmental rigor was
novel, the real merit of the king was not unduly exaggerated. Prisoners continued to suffer the lash, and other
forms of corporal punishment, which were hardly dis-
tinguishable from torture, and which the higher courts
had frequent occasion to condemn.[1] And, in view of the
unfilial aspersions cast by Frederic upon his father in the
address to the ministers, justice requires that another
qualification be made. Frederic William had himself
advised his son to abandon so expensive a luxury as the
tall grenadiers,[2] and had even consented, in the spring of
1740, that the widespread distress should be relieved from
the royal corn magazines, although the concession was
reluctantly made, and was carefully guarded as to its
extent.[3] But, these exceptions being made, it must be
conceded that Frederic approached all problems of this
kind in a spirit vastly different from that of his father;
that he was freer from prejudice and pedantry; and that
he formed and executed his resolutions far more promptly.

These reforms were, however, only changes of detail,
not of substance and spirit. The leading features, like
the leading principles, of the governmental system were
retained as they had been received by Frederic: it is
doubtful if he had ever reflected on the wisdom of a
radical reorganization. The decorations of the edifice
would be different, he said just before his accession, but
the foundations and the walls would remain unchanged.[4]

This edifice was one of the most novel triumphs of
political architecture which could be found in The Prussian
Europe. It differed not less from the system of system.

---

[1] Stenzel, *Geschichte des preussischen Staats*, Hamburg and Gotha,
1830–1854, iv. 49, who gives cases and authorities.

[2] Droysen, *Geschichte der preussischen Politik*, Theil V. vol. i. p. 45,
note 2.

[3] Ibid. p. 43; Stenzel, iv. 46.

[4] Droysen, V. i. 45.

England, where ministers controlled a central parliament by bribes, bargains, and intrigues, while surrendering local administration to the dissolute but brave and spirited rural gentry, than from that of France, where the absolute king was robbed of his revenues with equal impunity by intendants and farmers-general on the one hand, and by court favorites of either sex on the other. The Prussian system aimed to avoid at once the anarchy of England and the demoralization of France. It was a clumsy device for securing honest administration without exposing the royal authority to any species of control, either on the part of the people or of powerful and ambitious statesmen ; of parliaments such as those of England, or of ministers like Richelieu, Mazarin, or Fleury. The predecessors of Frederic had become, in fact as well as in name, the supreme rulers alike in legislation and in administration. The first position they acquired by crushing the representative diets. They secured the second by the bureaucratic organization of the public service.

The highest advisory body in the state was the privy council, which, however, rarely met in general session. Some of its leading members, representing such departments as justice and foreign affairs, formed the cabinet ; but the term was an indefinite one, and did not invariably comprise the same persons, or describe the same classes of functionaries.[1] The general directory was, as a college or board, the most important in the state. Its relative dignity and estimation are now, indeed, somewhat difficult to ascertain ; but in the eighteenth century, and in a state where every thaler was scrupulously weighed, a council which directed the entire collection of the revenues must have been a very useful if not a very ornamental body. Its functions included many charges, too, only indirectly connected with revenue.

The governing boards.

[1] Cf. Klaproth and Cosmar, *Der geheime Staatsrath*, Berlin, 1805, p. 236.

It had to report on the ravages caused by a swollen stream, and to propose measures for checking the spread of the cattle plague ; to recommend bridges, dikes, and highways ; to lease the crown domains; to introduce improved methods of agriculture; to provide quarters for the troops; to prevent the exportation of wool, or the importation of woollens ; and, in short, to exercise a general yet minute supervision over a comprehensive class of social and political relations. But the whole system was strictly centralized. The head of the privy council, of the cabinet, of the general directory, was the king. To him was referred every case which raised a new question or involved a new expenditure ; everything which went beyond the most formal, mechanical execution of existing laws. The various officials could make reports and recommendations, which, however, derived very little weight from their own names or functions. Their power to decide was drawn within the narrowest limits.

It was not, however, by personal intercourse between the king and his officials that the public service was conducted. The act of 1723, by which Frederic William organized the general directory, seems to have had such direct relations in view, but even in his time nearly everything came to be reduced to writing. Frederic carried the practice to its extreme lengths. The great mass of government business, submitted in writing, was considered by the king in the presence of his cabinet secretaries; and his decisions were returned through the proper channels, or promulgated as decrees, edicts, and laws. The Prussian government was thus a gigantic writing-machine. The affairs of three millions of people were administered by an army of dull, plodding, pedantic clerks; sitting year after year behind paper, ink, and quills, sealing-wax and red tape; slavishly obeying formula and routine ; and spreading an impenetrable veil of secrecy over all the processes of a despotic government. And this formidable instrument was wielded by a single man, whose will no person, however high his rank, dared to question.

Yet the king who presided over this system was himself The king as not less its slave than its master. It required bureaucrat. of its head, if it were to serve its purpose with the best success, the virtues of industry, patience, penetration, promptness, and endurance; the will to master details, and the power to generalize conclusions; the petty application of a clerk, and the sweeping eye of the statesman. Such a combination of qualities is of course rarely found in perfection. Frederic William the First had no little aptitude for the more minute clerical part of his duties, but was deficient in breadth of grasp and view. His son, who had an active mind and much speculative temerity, seemed fitted for adventurous general measures, rather than for unattractive details. Yet it was soon discovered that the young dilettant of Rheinsberg, the patron of music, poetry, art, and letters, the friend of Voltaire and Algarotti, excelled his father alike in the qualities of the drudge and those of the statesman, and that the duties of the one character would be performed as conscientiously and efficiently as those of the other.

The personal changes were few. The last favorite of the old king, Eckhardt, who as the head of the inquisitorial fiscalate had become the most odious person in Prussia, was at once dismissed from office and banished from Berlin. But Frederic showed no disposition to take revenge upon those officials who, through excess of zeal toward his father, had contributed to his own misfortunes, and, it must be added, no great alacrity in rewarding those who had befriended him in his hour of trial. Both his likes and his dislikes were kept under excellent control. It is true that the absence of strong resentments and strong partialities is highly desirable in a prince, for their gratification may imperil the interests of the state itself. But it is not possible to ascribe to a sense of duty alone Frederic's neglect, or inadequate recognition of men who were languishing in poverty and exile because they had adhered to him when his friendship was a species of crime. The most that public duty forbade was a reckless dismissal of old servants in order to provide places for the companions of his youth. This, indeed, would have been fatal. A system of such intricate mechanism as the Prussian civil service obviously required that a large part of its members should at all times be trained and experienced men.

In the general directory the minister Boden had distinguished himself not more by his skill in administration, than by the firmness of his resistance to the extravagant schemes of the courtiers. As chief of the third department he was in form, indeed, only one among several equals. But his superior talents gave him a great ascendency over his colleagues, and he was popularly regarded as the main controlling force, under the king, in the conduct of the public revenues. All plans, too, based upon his expected dismissal by Frederic soon fell to the ground. An unauthenticated story represents Boden as forcing himself into the royal presence early in June to protest against a proposed increase of the army, which the state of the finances did not warrant; and ascribes to the king some impatience under this outspoken advice. But he soon recognized the motives which inspired the conduct of the fearless minister. By his ability, his zeal, his fidelity, and, above all, his inflexible integrity, Boden soon won the complete confidence of Frederic; and for several years the treasury had the benefit of his firm and prudent guidance.[1]

For Marschall, another survivor from the previous reign, a new department, that, of manufactures, was added to the general directory. The title

[1] Cf. Isaacssohn, *Geschichte des preussischen Beamtenthums*, vol. iii. p. 240.

of the department suggests its duties. It was to promote
the growth of manufactures, and especially, by a characteristic extension of the term as understood by Frederic
William, the finer branches of industrial art. The
instructions issued to Marschall directed him to take
measures, first, for improving the condition of existing
industries ; second, for introducing such as were not yet
established in Prussia ; and, third, for encouraging the
immigration of skilled foreign artisans.[1] For these objects he was to open correspondence with other countries ; to consider the expediency of founding public ware-
houses for the exhibition and sale of manufactured cloths ;
to provide remunerative investments for foreign capital ;
to offer to desirable immigrants privileges, exemptions,
and even pecuniary support. Two assistants were assigned to the new minister, and the fifth department was
soon in working operation.

The chief advisor in diplomacy and foreign affairs was
count Henry von Podewils. In the history of
the first years of this reign his name appears so
frequently that a careless reader might at times imagine
that he had before him a responsible minister in a free
state. But in fact Podewils' activity, which the complex
foreign relations of the first twenty years made so conspicuous, was little more than the activity of a confidential clerk. That he was capable of something better may
be inferred from the wisdom with which he used such discretion as was accorded him. He was apparently not too
firmly wedded to bureaucratic formalism ; was capable
now and then of turning his back on precedents ; was less
rigidly straightforward and more flexible than Boden ;
yet was governed by a cold, cautious, conservative judgment, which often led him to feel distrust about the reck-

Podewils.

---

[1] Instruction of 27 June, 1740, in Rödenbeck, *Beiträge zur Bereich-
erung und Erläuterung der Lebensbeschreibungen Fr. Wms. I. und Fr.
II.*, Berlin, 1838, vol. ii. pp. 116–119.

less enterprises of his master. Of European politics and diplomacy he had a sufficiently full though perhaps somewhat technical knowledge. But his great value lay in his possession of two usually irreconcilable virtues. It would have been difficult for Frederic to find another man who, like Podewils, could be trusted to conduct safely and skilfully a difficult negotiation, and who was at the same time willing to obey orders with the docility of a copying clerk.

Other ministers, like Cocceji in justice, Thulemeier and Borcke in foreign affairs, may be passed over at this time without special notice. A word at least of commiseration must, however, be said for the cabinet secretaries. There were at first three of these unfortunate men, — Eichel, Lautensack, and Schumacher ; but though they occupied positions of great trust, only one of them, Eichel, ever acquired the complete confidence of the king, and all alike were compelled to a life of the most appalling drudgery. Their daily work, which had to be completed with unfailing punctuality, left them rarely time for their midday dinners. They were required to live in the strictest seclusion. Even wives were denied to them, lest the weakness of conjugal affection and confidence should imperil the secrets of state, of which under the king they were the principal guardians.[1]

Such was, in respect to its leading members, the organization of the political household. A domestic household in the ordinary sense Frederic never possessed. There was, indeed, a somewhat numerous royal family, of which he was by law the head ; and three brothers, August William, Henry, and Ferdinand, made it unlikely that, even if the king himself should have no children, the succession would pass out of the direct line of Frederic William the First. Two unmarried sisters

Cabinet secretaries.

The royal family.

[1] Thiébault, *Mes souvenirs de vingt ans de séjour à Berlin*, 2d ed., Paris, 1805, vol. i. pp. 314, 315.

still formed part of the court of Berlin; a third, the princess Wilhelmina, was unhappily married to the margrave of Bayreuth. For all these Frederic had a warm attachment, but the favorite was Wilhelmina. She had been the companion of his youth. Their common sufferings under a cruel father formed an early tie of sympathy between them; and the strong, masculine nature of the sister made her, as long as she lived, the chosen recipient of Frederic's fraternal confidence.

The mother of Frederic, the queen dowager, who still survived, was fitted out with an elaborate, not to say sumptuous, establishment, and treated with the utmost respect. The queen consort, Elisabeth of Brunswick, was also comfortably installed in quarters of her own; had maids of honor, to whom was given, as the chroniclers are careful to record, the title of madame; had her carriages, her footmen, her pages. But she rarely saw her husband, and in stately solitude observed the proprieties required of a queen of Prussia.

The intimate family circle of Frederic wanted, then, the grace, tact, and refinement of virtuous and culti-

The king's friends.

vated women. It was made up exclusively of friends of his own sex, and, in his earlier years, of friends whom he had known in his retreat at Rheinsberg. Such were Kayserling, an officer who had read and travelled, had a winning disposition, and enjoyed the royal friendship in as pure a form as it ever took; Jordan, a reader, critic, and correspondent; Algarotti, the Italian scholar, who had been recalled to renew with the king an intimacy begun with the crown prince; and Camas, another soldier recommended by his culture. To these were afterwards added others, but it was especially with these that the social side of Frederic's reign began. They were generally invited to sup with his majesty, and their evenings were always expected to be at his service.

Frederic thus actually assumed the government, performed many official acts, and settled his own habits of life, in apparent indifference to the solemn ceremonies which usually emphasized the succession to a throne. It was, however, deemed expedient to permit the ceremony of homage in each of the several territories. A coronation the king, like his predecessor, rejected as a costly and useless show;[1] and even the formality of homage was directed to be as simple and unostentatious as possible. In Preussen, Cleves, and Brandenburg, Frederic consented to gratify his subjects by appearing in person. For all other places deputies were chosen to represent him.

Homage.

The choice of Preussen for the first act of homage was in strict accordance with precedents. It was the province which gave the king his title, and it was the only part of his dominions in which he was sovereign in law as well as in fact. But it was also the province where the spirit of local independence was the keenest, where the traditions of parlimentary control had the most vitality, and where franchises and charters most narrowly circumscribed the powers of the crown. Some consultations were therefore held in regard to the attitude to be taken at Königsberg, the capital.

In Preussen.

The liberties of Preussen were guaranteed in the bill of rights and the charter of 1663.[2] These had never indeed been observed. But they had also never been repealed; and even Frederic William the First had practically confirmed them by an assecuration issued in 1713. It is, then, not surprising that Frederic, who on taking the oath of office from the ministers had pronounced it an idle form, should have had few scruples about giving pledges in Preussen, such as had never proved to be the least restraint upon ancestors far more conscientious than himself. The office

---

[1] "Cérémonies inutiles et frivoles, que l'ignorance et la superstition ont établies." Frederic to Voltaire, 27 June, 1740.

[2] See Tuttle's *History of Prussia*, vol. i. pp. 190–193.

of landrath, which had been so important to the former autonomous institutions of the duchy, but had fallen into decay under Frederic William I., was revived on the advice of the crown jurists at Königsberg. A diet was summoned in the usual form. The complaints of the estates in regard to the grievances of the past were embodied in an address, which the speaker presented to the king. Frederic received it in good temper, although it contained some strong expressions ; and, without expressly renewing in words the constitution of 1663, returned answer that no prejudice should be done to any of their rights. On the twentieth of July the act of homage was performed. It was observed that on the medal struck to commemorate the occasion, appeared for the first time the title " King of the Prussians," an innovation which gave no little offence at Warsaw; for West Prussia was still a province of the republic of Poland.[1]

The ceremony at Berlin, which took place on the second of August, gave rise to fewer constitutional frictions. Complaints were indeed uttered ; the nobles referred to the arrogance of the military, and mildly denounced the excise, which they said was ruining their peasants ; the burgomaster of Berlin pleaded for the violated franchises of the city ; and the town of Rathenow asserted an eternal right to hew timber in the royal forests for the repair of its bridges.[2] But no collective remonstrance was made; and the jurists were not forced to find, as at Königsberg, a method by which the king could observe constitutional forms while evading the fulfilment of constitutional duties. Yet the proceedings at the capital did not fail to move the imagination, and perhaps the conscience,

At Berlin.

---

[1] For the transactions at Königsberg I have compared Droysen, V. i. 49, 50 ; Ranke, xxvii., xxviii. 295, 296 ; Rödenbeck, *Tagebuch aus Friedrich's des Grossen Regentenleben,* Berlin, 1840, vol. i. p. 17 ; *Heldengeschichte,* i. 386–393, etc.

[2] Ranke, xxvii., xxviii. 296, 297.

of the leading actor. It is related that, when Frederic appeared on the balcony of the castle, and looked down upon the surging mob of human beings before him, he was so affected by the sight that he remained standing many minutes, silent and buried in thought. This was a moment at which the young king's feelings, if they could be known, would have a strong dramatic interest. It is possible that the spectacle only awakened recollections of the past, of his childhood and his youth, of his alienation from his father, of all the trials and all the pleasures of his early life. But it is more probable that he was thinking of the future; that in the midst of the acclamations of his loyal Berlin subjects the thought of his own vast responsibilities shot across his mind; that there rose before him the picture of bloody struggles for power; of brave men in the agonies of death; of widows clad in rags and orphans begging for bread. But this emotion, whatever its cause, was soon conquered. Recovering himself, the king bowed to the multitude, and rode off to attend a military review.

It only remained to receive at Wesel the homage of the Rhine provinces. But the route which the king chose, by way of Bayreuth and Frankfort-on-the-Main, was a circuitous one, and he even lengthened it by a singular digression. He was accompanied by his brother August William, the younger prince Leopold of Anhalt-Dessau, Algarotti, and two or three military officers. At Bayreuth Wilhelmina was visited; she seems to have been charmed with Algarotti, but somewhat disappointed in Frederic, whom she describes as putting the charracter of king too conspicuously before that of brother.[1] There may have been policy, however, in this, as in the rebuff early given to the Old Dessauer and others. But once at least during the journey Frederic laid the royal dignity aside in a remarkable manner. At Frankfort-on-

Frederic in Strasburg.

[1] *Mémoires de . . . Wilhelmine, margrave de Bareith*, Brunswick, 1845, vol. ii. p. 291.

the-Main, the next resting-place, the boyish desire seized him to set foot on French soil, and Strasburg was chosen for the adventure. With two or three companions, all under assumed names, he boldly crossed into the city, alighted at the principal hotel, and invited some of the young officers of the garrison to dinner. Marshal Broglie, the commandant, hastened to offer courtesies to the distinguished strangers. Their real characters were, however, soon suspected; and when a private soldier, who had served at Berlin, made it positively known that the leader of the party was no other than the king of Prussia, a hasty flight across the Rhine was all that remained. Frederic himself sent a rollicking account of this adventure to Voltaire.[1]

The journey down the river was then resumed. At Wesel the ceremony of homage passed off without incident. Interest is rather first given to Frederic's visit in this part of the Prussian dominions by a number of personal events, which gratefully open up to view one of the better sides of his nature, that of the ardent lover of letters and science. For one of the most praiseworthy ambitions that the king brought with him to the throne was to rescue those noble charges from the degraded state into which his father had suffered them to fall. It is not indeed clear that the cause of literature was served in the same degree as that of publicity through the two periodicals which by Frederic's order were called into life soon after his accession. The Journal de Berlin, of which the French chaplain Formey was editor, wooed the muses in vain. Its German contemporary, The Berlinische Nachrichten für Staats und Gelehrten-

The cause of letters.

---

[1] *Œuvres de Frédéric*, xiv. 156 et seq. Dr. Preuss boldly puts this doggerel among the literary works, and not in the correspondence with Voltaire. For an account from the other side, yet not greatly different except in form, see *Mémoires du duc de Luynes*, Paris, 1860-1865, vol. iii. pp. 248, 249.

sachen, was even less likely, and in spite of the promised collaboration of the king himself, to find a hearing for its crude and awkward addresses. But in both these journalistic experiments there was shown a certain respect for the interests of free publicity, and for the usefulness of the press as an agent of influence upon literary progress and opinion.

In a similar spirit of toleration, Frederic promptly reinstated in his old place at Halle the well-known philosopher Wolf, whom Frederic William had foolishly banished. But the universities pursued science in a manner too unostentatious for Frederic's purpose. The favorite institution was rather the academy at Berlin, which not only made discoveries, but proclaimed them in loud tones to the world, and was thus better adapted to gratify the pardonable vanity of a young prince. To obtain great men for the academy was accordingly as earnest an object as it had been in the previous reign to find tall recruits for the army. All Europe was scoured for them. Euler, s'Gravensande, Muschenbroek, and especially Maupertuis, were early courted, and two of them were in fact captured, Euler somewhat later, but Maupertuis as one of the first prizes of the reign.

The Academy of Sciences.

This eminent mathematician had just crowned his scientific labors by an expedition to Lapland, where his observations established the fact that the earth was flattened at the poles. Flippant rivals tried to belittle the achievement; and there were not wanting serious men who still continued to believe that the author was more of a charlatan than a philosopher. But the solid merit of the work could not be attacked successfully because Maupertuis himself was pompous and vain ; nor could the privations and even dangers amid which it was performed be wholly denied because he possibly magnified them in his own account. His reputation was therefore great in spite of his enemies, and even of himself. He

Maupertuis.

seemed to Frederic an almost unrivalled prize. "As soon as I ascended the throne," he wrote, "my desire was to have you here in order that you might reorganize the academy. Come, then, and engraft the branch of true science on that rude trunk, and make it flourish. You have shown mankind the figure of the earth; show a king how sweet it is to possess a man like you." [1] To this plan Maupertuis, vexed by rivals and enemies at Paris, and flattered by the notice of a king, readily assented. The philosopher and his patron met by appointment at Wesel. The terms of the engagement were soon settled, and Frederic fetched his captive back with him in triumph to Berlin.

On this same journey the king had his first interview with Voltaire. They had been correspondents since 1736, when Frederic, from Rheinsberg, introduced himself to his literary hero in a letter full of fervid yet not unmanly sentiments of admiration.[2] Voltaire replied in the same spirit, but with a finer flattery.[3] From that time began an exchange of letters between these strangely dissimilar friends, which, though now and then interrupted, was only terminated by Voltaire's death in 1778. The communications range over all the topics that a common literary interest could suggest, from the evils of despotism to the folly of religion, from the virtues of Socrates to the " Henriade " of Voltaire, the poems of M. de Scudéri, the simple substances of Wolf. They flatter each other atrociously.[4] They drop without provocation into verse ; and if Frederic's lines often halt, Voltaire's are full of ease, elegance, vivacity, and wit. The

Frederic and Voltaire.

---

[1] Frederic to Maupertuis, Berlin, June, 1740.

[2] Frederic to Voltaire, 8 August, 1736.

[3] Voltaire to Frederic, 26 August, 1736.

[4] The term "flattery" may perhaps be applied to the observation of Frederic that one canto in the Henriade was worth all of the Iliad. See the " Avant-propos sur l'Henriade de M. de Voltaire." *Œuvres de Frédéric*, viii. 52 ; also ii. 37.

king sighed for the poet as a lover for his mistress, and his presence in Cleves gave an opportunity for a meeting. Voltaire was at the time in Holland, wrangling with the printer Van Duren about the manuscript of the "Anti-Machiavel." It was easy for him to run over to Wesel; and near Wesel, at the castle of Moyland, Frederic had the pleasure of worshipping his idol face to face during three days.

In the mean time Frederic, with the infinite capacity which he had for blending the pleasant and the serious, was attending to a vexatious problem in this neighborhood which his father had left unsettled.

This concerned the little barony of Heristal, familiar to the historical student through its connection *Affair of* with Pepin, the famous mayor of the palace. *Heristal.* In 1732, on the final settlement of the estate of the house of Orange, it had passed to Frederic William I. of Prussia. His jurists held that it was an immediate fief of the empire; and, supported by this opinion, which was doubtless easily obtained, the king had undertaken to exercise the full rights of sovereignty, including the administration of justice. But two rival princes contested this claim. The duke of Brabant and the bishop of Liège each pretended to a mediate lordship; and the effect of this claim, if admitted, would be to overthrow the theory of direct subordination to the empire, to force the king to seek the investiture at the hands of the minor lords, and to leave the appellate jurisdiction in their hands. And the case was still further complicated by the fact that the duke of Brabant was the emperor Charles VI. himself, and that he, without giving up his own pretensions, had guaranteed those of the bishop. The Prussian rule was unpopular with the democratic and turbulent people of Heristal. The judges sent thither were mobbed and driven out of the country; taxes were refused; and it was supposed that the resistance was secretly encouraged by the neighboring prelate. Frederic William was unequal to the solution of this problem, and by the time of his death the province had nearly passed out of his grasp.

It is needless to say that the matter engaged the earliest attention of Frederic. The ministers pointed out that an attempt to suppress the revolt by force would require two or three thousand men, and might embroil Prussia with the emperor, for which reasons they urged further negotiations. Frederic's reply was characteristic. "When civil officials discuss negotiations," wrote he, "they act rationally; but when they give advice about war, they are like an Iroquois talking of astronomy. I shall go to Cleves this year, and try gentle means, but if I am denied justice I shall find a way to get it. The emperor is the old phantom of an idol" — the figure is Frederic's — "which formerly had some power, but which is now nothing; he was a robust man, but the French and the Turks gave him a fatal shock, and he has no longer any nerves. Let things rest until I go to Wesel, where I can adopt the course which circumstances point out." [1]

At Wesel, then, Frederic took the matter seriously in hand. He sent the privy councillor Rambonnet to Liège with instructions to give the bishop forty-eight hours in which to answer categorically the question whether he would abandon his own claims, and cease to encourage the people of Heristal in acts of rebellion. The bishop replied that the period was not long enough for a proper consultation with his officials. On receipt of this reply general Bork led twelve companies of grenadiers, a squadron of cavalry, and some artillery into the territory of Liège, levied a heavy contribution, and again demanded a reply. Resistance was useless, and as a result of further negotiations the bishop formally bought up the claims of Prussia, so that Heristal passed completely into his hands.

[1] Frederic to the department of foreign affairs, (16) June, 1740.

The Prussian treasury cleared one hundred thousand thalers from this thrifty transaction.[1]

[1] These facts are drawn from Ranke, xxvii., xxviii., and Droysen, V. i., and the contemporary histories. Droysen gives a strong partisan coloring to his discussion of the case, but Ranke is as usual more judicious. Voltaire was employed to draw up an exposition of Frederic's case.

CHAPTER II.

THE NEW FOREIGN POLICY.

THE lesson thus sternly administered to the bishop of
Lesson of Heristal. Liège was not without effect upon other and
greater potentates. It showed, as Frederic had
intended, that the blustering and arrogant, yet essentially
feeble, policy of Frederic William I. had given way to a
firmer and prompter resolution, and that a dangerous
element had suddenly thrown itself into the relations of
the European states.[1]

Frederic's views on the character of these relations, as
he saw them just before and at the time of his
Frederic on the state of Europe. accession, may be found in many parts of his
writings. The earliest of these essays was
written in 1736.[2] The subject was again treated in 1746
as an introduction to the king's history of the Silesian
wars, and the original version of this work was recast
and enlarged in 1775. Between these several discussions
of the same subject there are slight differences of detail,
but the general line of thought is the same in all, and one

[1] " Dans ce changement de règne," he says, " il était plus convenable
de donner des marques de fermeté que de douceur." *Œuvres*, iii. 53.

[2] Considérations sur l'état présent du corps politique de l'Europe.
Cf. Preuss, *Friedrich der Grosse*, i. 77. This essay was first published
in 1788, and now forms part of vol. viii. of the *Œuvres de Frédéric*.
For an elaborate attempt to prove that it was not a mere academical
treatise, but a serious work, intended to confirm the naval powers in
their aversion to France, see, in Max Duncker, *Aus der Zeit Friedrichs
des Grossen* etc., Berlin, 1876, the article, Eine Flugschrift des
Kronprinzen Friedrich.

tone prevails throughout. They show some force of insight, but add little to the world's knowledge of the epoch; indeed, the statements are often extremely reckless, and now and then curiously inexact. The general tone is, however, coldly if not cynically frank. The personal portraits are often cleverly if maliciously drawn. But the most important lesson from these treatises, especially from that of 1746, is that, if they correctly represent Frederic's views, he came to power singularly free from sentimental feelings for or against any of the leading states of Europe, certain that honor counted for nothing in diplomacy, and convinced that the essential thing for a statesman was to make himself so familiar with the strength or weakness of his neighbors that he could promptly decide at any time where opposition would be dangerous and friendship profitable.

The relations of the leading states at this time were defined in an infinite number of treaties; some old, some recent; many of them crossed by others of a contrary tenor; a few thrown in doubt by pending disputes; and one at least suspended by actual war. To observe all, or to violate all, would alike have plunged Europe into anarchy. Some of these treaties were, indeed, secret; but secret treaties, like the hypocrisy of private life, are the homage which vice pays to virtue. They imply that the ends in view are improper in themselves, or that they are inconsistent with others publicly yet insincerely announced. But they also recognize in a measure the existence of a code of morality, which it is inexpedient wantonly to violate. Now it is the fashion to say that in the eighteenth century the standard of this code was deplorably low. It may be that in this century the standard is higher; that in respect to political virtue there has been progress. But since comparisons of this kind may be too lightly made, the conclusions drawn from them are to be scrutinized with the greatest care, for they are often fallacious, and are usually too broad even when not positively false. The strenuous efforts which were made to conceal engagements likely to arouse an offended morality show that there was even in the last century such a thing as a European conscience. That, in spite of this, immoral compacts were formed, proves not that the statesmen of that age were more depraved than the statesmen of this; it proves only that, the risks of detection being slighter, the restraints of a decent integrity were less powerful. Then it must be remembered, as a mitigating though not decisive consideration, that the most flagrant cases of international perfidy which had occurred up to 1740 were in the interest of peace, not of bloodshed and conquest. The defection of England in 1710 practically ended the war of the Spanish succession. The selfish treachery of France in 1735 closed the contest for the throne of Poland. And in the treaty of Belgrade in 1739 the emperor, while disgracefully abandoning his more successful ally, the empress of Russia, and making an ignominious peace with the Turks, at least put an end to the prodigal and useless sacrifice of life. To sir Robert Walpole this thought was profoundly significant. When in 1733 he made his famous declaration, " Fifty thousand men have fallen in battle this year, but not one in England," a few lips doubtless curled with contempt, but the great minister struck not the less surely the keynote of contemporary politics, and the politics of the continent as well as of England.

For the contrast which he drew, so greatly to the advantage of his own policy, was not strictly supported by facts. The period after the treaty of Utrecht was everywhere one of peace rather than of war. There were destructive battles on the Danube, indeed, and all along the shifting frontier that marked the limits of the Ottoman conquests. But, with slight and reluctant exceptions, the powers of central and western Europe fought out their quarrels in the cabinet rather than the field.

This was due in part to the exhaustion left by the long wars of Louis the Fourteenth; in part to the pacific or timid character of princes and statesmen; in part to the rapid growth of Indian and American commerce, with its visions of boundless wealth, and its attractions, rivalling those of arms, for the ambitious and the energetic. Such a state of things was little fitted to nourish the virtues of chivalry and heroism, the love of arduous achievement, the passion for leading gallant men into the jaws of death. It could not foster the broadest and noblest conception even of peace itself. The spirit of the age was simply mercenary; and the relations of the powers down to 1740 show accordingly no warmth either of enmity or friendship. They were governed rather by a cold, indolent, selfish timidity; a dread of war, because war required effort and money; a love of peace, because peace was the servant of wealth, tranquillity, and enjoyment.

Of the class of statesmen who represented this spirit in European politics, cardinal Fleury was perhaps Cardinal the most striking example. Louis XV. was not Fleury. a prince whose favor was often bestowed from the highest motives, or with the greatest wisdom; but his affection for his old tutor enabled Fleury to maintain himself in power, against all the intrigues of his enemies, to the last day of his life. The cardinal's love for office rose, indeed, to the height of a passion, the more singular since as an ecclesiastic he ought to have had no passions, and as an octogenarian ought to have outlived ambition. In ability and force of character, Fleury cannot indeed be ranked in the same class with the other two cardinals who in the previous century ruled the affairs of France. If he had some of Mazarin's suppleness, and was not wanting in expedients for solving certain kinds of problems, he was essentially timid, procrastinating, and evasive; fond of indirect and tortuous methods; more skilful in making plans plausible than in carrying them into effect by energy and firmness. Yet he possessed many qualities which made him extremely useful to France. He represented the allied policies of peace and economy; was a person of winning social manners; could extort the secrets of others while keeping his own; and, holding all the threads of European diplomacy in his hands, had a unique position of authority in all the negotiations of his time. But at the point which we have now reached the cardinal's power had become somewhat weakened through the persistent intrigues of various rival favorites at court, and the seductive eloquence of political adventurers.[1]

In England a situation in many respects similiar presented itself. Sir Robert Walpole was indeed, in nearly all personal qualities, the exact opposite to Fleury; but he long wielded the same powerful influence at court, was equally fond of office, and had an aversion no less strong to rash foreign enterprises. But Walpole, unlike Fleury, had to reckon with a parliament, and by 1740 his hold upon the houses had become so weak that his fall was already foreseen. He reluctantly consented, in 1739, to war with Spain, but his compliance added nothing to his strength. He held the singular position of a minister who, dreading both the cost and the risk for England of constant activity on the continent, served a king full of warlike impulses, and, as elector of Hanover, impatient under the narrow insular policy of his cabinet.

At Vienna there had been, since the death of prince Eugene in 1736, no person of such commanding eminence, either in the field or in the cabinet. The nominal chief minister was count Sinzendorf. But his ability and industry were not equal to his ambition,

Sir Robert Walpole.

Austria.

[1] What the king of Prussia thought of Fleury may be seen in *Œuvres de Frédéric,* ii. 8. In 1746 he wrote in his own peculiar style that the cardinal " aliait un peu La timidité et les Ruses de la prétaille dans les Negotiations, patlin, Souple, adroit, aimant les Intrigues, Les Supterfuges, les Soutairains, et haisant l'odasse et la Demarche Vigoureuse des entreprises hardies."

and among his colleagues one especially, Bartenstein, an obscure adventurer from Alsace, had risen to great influence by force of energy, audacity, and complete devotion to the state which he served. The state itself had just issued from a war with the Turks, which left its good name in disgrace, the army dispirited, the leading generals in prison. The treasury was nearly empty. Territories like the Netherlands and the Milanese, which were remote from the seat of government, yielded little to the common state. The older dominions were various in character, race, language, and institutions; in some, local rights crossed the efforts of administration; a fierce spirit of discontent reigned in others. There was hardly another country in Europe whose resources were so poorly developed, or so loosely conducted.

The early part of the eighteenth century saw Russia fairly enter the family of European nations. Its influence was feared and its alliance was courted. ^{Russia.} But while the foreign, and especially the German element was largely represented in its administration and its councils, the representatives themselves seemed to take on the Oriental type which they found, more easily than they imparted the Western type which they brought. The social morality and the political methods were those of Constantinople. The reigning empress, Anne, had been called to the throne by a palace revolution. The powerful favorite, Biron, had enjoyed the pleasure of seeing the heads of his rivals, the brothers Dolgorouki, roll from the same scaffold. But in count Ostermann, and marshal Münnich Russia had two men of the highest order of talent, fitted to cope with the best intellects of western Europe.

Of the lesser states three, Spain, Sweden, and Holland, had fallen from their former position of _{The lesser states.} influence and power to one in which, though their friendship was still desirable, their enmity was not greatly feared. Bavaria was ruled by a weak though ambitious elector; Poland and Saxony decayed alike under the sceptre of August III.; and the princes, as well secular as ecclesiastic, along the Rhine, were completely subservient to France.

But even these do not exhaust the list. In the complex family of European states, holding some entirely in its feeble grasp, stretching its arms in certain directions across the frontier of others, and having points of contact with nearly all, stood the tottering frame of a once great commonwealth, the Holy Roman Empire. For the house of Austria the imperial title was a convenient make-weight in current politics, but little more; a source of prestige rather than of power. The division into circles, which had once been the basis of military levies in the name of the Empire, no longer had much significance. Imperial armies were raised with great difficulty, and more often by treaties between the territorial lords than by formal summons from the head of the state; for to these nobody now paid any regard. The same rule prevailed in the case of the revenues of the federal treasury. With the emperor, as representatives of the confederation, stood three venerable bodies, the aulic council at Vienna, the diet at Regensburg, the court of justice at Wetzlar. But these, like the Empire itself, had no vitality. The council was made up of creatures of the emperor; the diet consumed its time in quarrels between the Protestant and Catholic members; the federal tribunal was the horror of suitors who desired an end of litigation. In verse and song the old mediæval commonwealth was still a popular and imposing figure; something on which the imagination liked to dwell; a memory which roused a certain kind of enthusiasm. But as a political body it was ill beyond hope of recovery. Foreign states preyed upon its weakness. The election for emperor had hardly been contested for centuries. The Empire was, in truth, little more than the house of Austria, with the prestige which an empty title added, and such aid as it could obtain by threats or bargains from other independent members.

Yet it is not always the case that the importance of a state is determined by its population or its area, by the form of its institutions or the nominal strength of its armed forces. A prince whose weakness excites the cupidity of his neighbors, and provokes wars of aggression, may often furnish the real key to an epoch in history. In endeavoring to fix the motives of action it is, therefore, possible to distinguish between states which are prominent by reason of their power, and states which, independently of their power, are prominent on account of their situation or their connections, their interests or their enterprise.

From one point of view, the prelate who was bishop of Liège in 1740, and whose name posterity has not very carefully guarded, was, in September of that year, a person of no little consequence. The elector palatine was clearly a prince of European importance. He was the last male survivor of the house of Neuburg, and his death, which any day might announce, seemed likely to set Europe in flames. The two leading candidates for the inheritance were, indeed, of vastly different degrees of strength and influence. The head of the house of Sulzbach, heir-presumptive to the Palatinate, with the electorship, and claimant to Jülich, Berg, and Ravenstein, held one of the lower grades in the great army of German princelets. The other suitor for the three prin- _{Jülich-Berg} cipalities was the king of Prussia. But, by a _{question.} paradox not unusual in politics, the power of the king was really the weakness of the claimant. For every increase of this power was viewed with suspicion, delayed by prevarication and technicalities, and peevishly conceded when it could no longer be prevented. Even the justice of Prussia's cause was not always a security against this policy. But in the Jülich-Berg dispute there was room

for doubt; and the great powers could pretend to serve
equity while they also served their own interests in giving
their encouragement to the weaker party.

It is true that Frederic William I. had succeeded, after
long and stubborn negotiations, in procuring from Austria
and France a partial recognition of his claims. The
emperor had formally ceded to Prussia his own right —
which was itself disputed — to Berg and Ravenstein, and
agreed to appoint a special commission to examine the
rival claims of the house of Sulzbach.[1] In 1739 France
had promised Frederic William, also by a secret treaty, to
use its influence to procure the assent of the elector palatine to an amicable partition not essentially different.
But doubts had arisen about the value of both these engagements.   Reports, more or less authentic, reached the
court of Berlin of secret negotiations between France
and Austria,[2] and between each of these powers and Pfalz-
Sulzbach, so that Prussia was at no moment sure of its
inheritance.   But the treaties were still legally in force.
They had never been formally terminated; and so long as
the casus fœderis, which alone could test their value, had
not yet arisen, there was no decent pretext for measures
of force.

This was the situation when Frederic took up the subject.   It is characteristic of his methods that,
while sounding the powers about the reality of

Taken up by
Frederic.

---

[1] Secret treaty of Berlin, 23 December, 1728, Articles 7 and 9. It
is commonly stated that by this treaty Charles VI. absolutely guaranteed the claim of Prussia as an equivalent for the guaranty of the
pragmatic sanction.   Frederic himself, *Œuvres*, ii. 48, even includes
Jülich among the territories thus assured to his father.   The real
facts are as I have given them, as will appear from the text of the
treaty, Förster, *Friedrich Wilhelm I.*, Potsdam, 1834, vol. ii. p. 314
et seq.

[2] In 1739 they agreed to guarantee Sulzbach in the provisional
occupation of the disputed duchies for two years after the death of
the elector palatine.

existing compacts, he also made prompt efforts to enlarge their scope at the expense of the house of Sulzbach. He decided to send a colonel of the army to each of the three courts, Paris, London, and Vienna. Nominally the mission of these special envoys was to make formal announcement of his accession. But they were also privately instructed by Frederic himself to bring up the Jülich-Berg question, in order that he might learn from what quarter to expect the most support for his pretensions.[1]

Colonel Münchow received at Vienna a friendly and even flattering reception. The emperor himself, Maria Theresa his daughter, and the grand-duke Francis of Lorraine, her husband, spoke in the most complimentary terms of the young king, and agreed in expressing the desire for the maintenance of the most cordial relations with Prussia. The ministers assured both Münchow and the permanent resident, Borcke, of the emperor's intention strictly to carry out the treaty of 1728. No more favorable engagement was offered, and none solicited.[2]

To Louis XV. and George II. were sent respectively Camas, the king's literary friend, and count Truchsess, a discrimination which provoked some angry comments at Paris. Camas, the descendant of a Huguenot family which had found an asylum in Prussia, was a plebeian by birth, and revived disagreeable memories of French religious intolerance. Truchsess was a member of the aristocracy. But it was explained that both alike were colonels in the army, and that in Prussia military rank alone was recognized. These two envoys had more explicit instructions than Münchow. They were especially to play upon the jealousy of England and France, each of the other; and thus to institute a species of auction, at which the alliance of Prussia could be sold to the highest bidder. Each was charged, therefore, to exalt the importance of the other's

---

[1] *Œuvres de Frédéric*, ii. 48.
[2] Droysen, V. i. 67, 68.

mission.[1] But this transparent policy was easily penetrated by cardinal Fleury, and the English ministers who
were in attendance upon George at Hanover. France acknowledged the treaty of 1739 with Prussia, but nothing
more.[2] In behalf of England Lord Harrington, the
secretary of state, made vague propositions for a general
alliance, but parried the demand for specific pledges in
regard to Jülich-Berg.[3] This elaborately contrived plan
did not, therefore, meet with the ready success which its
author had perhaps expected.

At this point the Heristal incident began to awaken
new reflections in the minds of statesmen. A similar
method of settling the Jülich-Berg dispute was feared.
There were rumors of a Prussian army of observation,
forty thousand strong, of a camp of instruction, of new
fortresses on the frontier, — in short, of preparations for
a prompt seizure of the disputed territory on the death of
the elector palatine. It is certain that Frederic carefully
inspected his troops and fortifications during the tour of
the Rhine, and otherwise examined the conditions of a
possible war. But his measures continued to be diplomatic rather than military.

The situation of affairs was, however, such that the
question of Berg soon lost itself in the graver
issues which hung in acute suspense over Europe. The war between England and Spain
was taking on new dimensions. But the Bourbon family
compact of 1733 required the courts of Versailles and
Madrid to make common cause in all political questions,
and it was the policy of France to prevent the spread of

England and
the Bour-
bons.

---

[1] Droysen, V. i. 76, 82 ; Frederic to Camas, 14 June, and to Truchsess, 18 June, 1740.

[2] " C'était trop peu pour contenter les désirs d'un jeune roi am-
bitieux, qui voulait tout au rien." *Œuvres de Frédéric*, ii. 48.

[3] See the correspondence of Frederic and Truchsess, July to
October, 1740.

hostilities to the colonial possessions of her ally.[1] When, therefore, England began to collect a fleet for an expedition against the Spanish West Indies, French ships were assembled in the harbor of Brest, and new fortifications were begun near Dunkirk, in the place of those which had been razed under the provisions of the treaty of Utrecht. The war feeling was daily rising both in France and in England. Fleury in the one country and Walpole in the other still struggled manfully for peace; but the flood was too violent even for strong and expert swimmers like themselves.

This state of things was regarded by Frederic as singularly advantageous to him. He had vast designs of his own, and eagerly desired allies; but he conceived that the more urgent needs of France *Frederic's negotiations.* and England would enable him to bid for their support while seeming only to receive bids for his own. This hypothesis is the key to his diplomacy for several months.

The plan of an English alliance did not present a favorable outlook, and the French connection was taken up more seriously. Camas was sent back to Paris to reënforce Chambrier, the Prussian resident. Renewed efforts were made to extract from the wily cardinal some greater concession in respect to Jülich-Berg, the promise of more territory in the eventual partition, or at least a more explicit declaration of fidelity to the treaty of 1739.[2] The

---

[1] When Ranke first called attention to this secret " pacte de famille " of 1733 in his English history, he supposed, and it was long afterwards supposed, that its existence was unknown to the English ministers. Otherwise why did it not produce such an explosion of anger as happened in 1761 on the discovery of a similar compact? But Professor J. R. Seeley shows, in the *English Historical Review*, vol. i. No. I., January, 1886, that its existence and provisions were thoroughly known to Walpole and his colleagues, who apparently regarded it with indifference.

[2] See Camas' new instructions in the *Politische Correspondenz Friedrichs des Grossen*, vol. i. p. 43, and Frederic's letter of 25 October, 1740.

declaration was obtained, but at the time nothing more. That there was any impropriety in thus soliciting the interference of France in a purely German affair, which was besides pending in the imperial courts, seems never to have occurred to Frederic.

The truth is, however, that there has been much idle France and declamation about the evils of the long influence the Empire. wielded by France in the politics of the Empire. It had undoubtedly been the policy of that court since the time of Richelieu to prevent Germany from becoming too strong by preventing it from becoming united; and this had frequently led to measures which morally are inexcusable. Nowhere has this policy been more vigorously denounced in recent times than in Prussia. Yet it is in no small degree to the traditional hostility of France to German unity that is due the present position of Prussia as an independent nation. The long duel between the Bourbons and the Hapsburgs was ruinous indeed to the Empire, but it saved the various states which composed the Empire. For at any time before 1866, and in spite of the victories of Frederic, the union of Germany meant the subjection of the other states, including Prussia, to the house of Austria. It meant the repetition of the process which had destroyed the identity of Castile and of Burgundy, which had built up the monarchies of Spain and France, which had swept away the last restraint upon the will of a Philip II. or a Louis XIV. An argument for a similar course of centralization in Germany might perhaps have been made. It might have been shown that the strong, compact French monarchy was a far more imposing object than the anarchical federation which called itself the German Empire; that it appealed more strongly to patriotism; and, when governed in the right spirit, was far more efficient for good. But such an argument would have served only the interests and the ambition of Austria.

There was then nothing new or indefensible in Frederic's efforts to obtain French support in the Jülich-Berg controversy. But with a view to gaining an additional guaranty for Berg, as well as to secure his eastern possessions from danger in case of war, he took the far more questionable step of inviting Russia also into the litigation of the Empire.[1]

A slight coolness had marked the relations of the two powers since the year 1733. England was negotiating actively at St. Petersburg for help in the impending struggle. But Frederic attached a high degree of importance to the Russian alliance and was ready to make great concessions to obtain it: communications were therefore opened for a treaty. The Prussian overtures looked to an offensive alliance, for the desired guaranty of Jülich-Berg amounted in effect to that. But this guaranty the empress refused. She could not interfere, it was explained in terms which nearly conveyed a rebuke, in a purely German quarrel.[2] She merely gave the assurance in a secret declaration that she had not formed, and would not form, any engagement in that matter prejudicial to Prussia, and with this Frederic was forced to be content. By the middle of October the treaty was signed. It contained reciprocal promises of help to the extent of ten thousand men. Russia was to protect the province of Preussen against attack from Frederic's enemies, and Prussia was to support Biron in Courland, where the Russian arms had installed him as duke at the same time that they made August III. king of Poland.

[1] In the " Considérations sur l'état présent," etc. *Œuvres*, viii. 12, Frederic reproaches the emperor for having called in a Russian army corps as an auxiliary in the war of 1734 against France. But that was the war of the Polish succession, which was not a German affair ; in fact it was on this ground that Frederic William I. hesitated to furnish his own contingent.

[2] *Œuvres de Frédéric*, ix. 187 ; Frederic to Mardefeld, Prussian envoy at St. Petersburg, 6 September, 1740 ; Droysen, V. i. 113.

With the exception of this treaty, which however was never ratified, the king's diplomacy had as yet little to show in the way of positive results. It is true that he had skilfully avoided both the grand alliance which France was anxious to form against England, and the counter-alliance which England aimed to complete against France. This, though a negative advantage, was one of considerable value. But he had purchased it at the cost of an efficient guaranty for Jülich-Berg, which either of the rival powers might have consented to give in return for his alliance against the other. And while he had offered to assume the new obligation to support the usurper Biron in Courland, he had not reduced in any degree the older obligations which he had inherited with his crown.

The most important of these was the guaranty of the pragmatic sanction. This, as the reader knows, was the famous instrument by which in 1713 the emperor Charles VI., the only living male representative of the house of Hapsburg, had provided that in case he should die leaving daughters, but no son, his hereditary possessions should descend to them and their heirs in the order of primogeniture. Two princes of the Empire, August III. of Saxony and Charles Albert of Bavaria, had married daughters of the emperor's older brother, Joseph I.; but the brides had solemnly renounced, at the time of their marriage, any rival claims which they might possess. August III. had repeated this renunciation in 1733, when the support of Charles VI. raised him to the throne of Poland. But the elector of Bavaria had another claim. He asserted an older title to the Hapsburg succession based on his descent from a daughter of the emperor Ferdinand I., and an alleged disposition of that prince to the effect that, in default of male heirs at any subsequent time, the succession should be continued in the line of this daughter. A renunciation by his wife could

Pragmatic sanction.

not, it was maintained by Charles Albert, abridge earlier rights which the house of Bavaria derived by direct descent. Against this protest the emperor could, however, cite the acceptance of the pragmatic sanction by the estates of all his hereditary dominions, its recognition by the Empire, and its guaranty by nearly every great power in Europe.[1]

One of the earliest of these guaranties was that of Prussia, given in the secret treaty of 1728. The second article of that compact contains the solemn pledge of the crown of Prussia, not only to renew earlier and more general pledges, but also especially " to guarantee the order of succession established by his imperial majesty in 1713 in respect to all his hereditary possessions within or without the Empire; in such a way that his majesty, the king of Prussia, shall be bound to render aid whenever the order of succession thus established shall be questioned, and to maintain the descendants of his imperial majesty in the peaceable possession of each and every part of his lands, without any exception, against all powers whatsoever." The stipulated aid was a Prussian corps of ten thousand men, liable for service in any part of the Austrian dominions except Italy. The only condition of this guaranty was the general provision that the emperor should sacredly observe the duties which the treaty imposed upon him. What those duties were, and to what extent they had or had not been performed, will already have been learned from the earlier pages of this chapter.

To meet this obligation when the crisis should arise, Frederic had resources which excited the envy even of more imposing states. He had an army

Guaranteed by Prussia.

Resources of Prussia.

---

[1] Spain in 1725 ; Russia, 1726, renewed in 1733 ; Prussia, 1728 ; England and Holland, 1731 ; France, 1738 ; the Empire, 1732. See J. C. Adelung, *Pragmatische Staatsgeschichte Europens,* Gotha, 1762–1767, vol. ii. pp. 126–129.

not indeed the largest, but the best in Europe. The equipment was good, the officers intelligent, the discipline perfect; it was deficient only in cavalry, to which neither Frederic William nor Leopold of Dessau had given adequate attention. Frederic had not changed the general organization of this force, but he had increased its strength by some sixteen battalions of foot and six squadrons of horse. In October, 1740, it must have numbered not less than ninety thousand men.[1]

The organization of the civil service was such as to form a strong support to the operations of the army, and to insure during its absence the unbroken activity of the public functions. Finally, the material conditions of the state were favorable. A treasure of eight or nine million thalers lay in the public vaults, ready for use. The annual revenues had not fallen below six millions since 1722, and for the last fiscal year were seven millions, with a surplus of eight hundred thousand.[2] The scanty harvest of the season just closing was indeed a cause of some anxiety. But the people were fairly prosperous, and, still sanguine about the blessings of the new reign, looked forward hopefully into the future.

While the country was thus enjoying a profound and Frederic at grateful calm, Frederic retired with a few chosen Rheinsberg. friends to Rheinsberg. He had hoped to renew his devotion to the muses, but his system also needed rest and attention. The malarial fever, which had attacked him at Wesel, was again troublesome; and on the twenty-sixth of October he lay prostrate with a severe attack of ague.

But on that day a momentous announcement was made Death of the at the castle of Rheinsberg. A swift courier emperor. from Vienna brought the news that the emperor

[1] Frederic to Voltaire, 27 June, 1740. A battalion was about 675 and a squadron 150 men.

[2] A. F. Riedel, *Der Brandenburg-Preussische Staatshaushalt*, Berlin, 1866, Beilage XI.

Charles VI. had died suddenly in the early morning of the twentieth of October. With him ended the male line of the house of Hapsburg. For five centuries the family had been prominent in Germany; for three centuries it had held the imperial dignity almost as a hereditary possession. Since the year 1718 Charles had labored to secure the descent of his hereditary estates to his daughter, Maria Theresa, and, after her marriage, to make her husband the successor to the title of emperor. He had guaranties in abundance for both these cherished aims, and now it remained to see what such guaranties were worth.

Maria Theresa was then twenty-three years old, and in the full bloom of her bewitching beauty. In the days of chivalry this alone would have won the heart, and commanded the support, of every brave and honorable man, whether he sat as a prince on the throne, or toiled as a peasant in the fields. The touching position of a wife about to become a mother appealed, even in an unromantic age, to the sympathy of the generous. And the young queen had, besides, those qualities of mind and heart which, even in the absence of physical charms, are accepted by the serious and discriminating of the other sex as just objects of respect and admiration. Her natural gifts were good, and her education, though careless and unsystematic, had given her various light accomplishments, and facility, if not correctness, in the use of the leading European languages, and even of Latin. The tongue of scandal had never touched her. Through all the temptations of a court not distinguished for austere morals or manners, the young princess had maintained a spotless purity of life and reputation; a native ingenuousness, never more attractive than in maidens of her rank; and a sincerity uncorrupted by the heartlessness and cynicism with which she daily came in contact. In her marriage to Francis of Lorraine her heart followed its own impulses, and her affection for her husband was an example for the humblest wife throughout the broad dominions of Austria. She was indeed proud. But it was the pride of a virtuous woman and a patriotic queen, resolved to insist on the respect due to her sex, and the obligations pledged to her state. The purity of her domestic life, her romantic attachment to her husband, her piety, her frankness, her affable manners, her conscientiousness, her excellence in all the qualities of the woman, the wife, and the ruler, seemed to assure the certain and peaceful enjoyment of her inheritance. It was indeed a striking event, the accession of a young, ingenuous, inexperienced woman to the ancient throne of the Hapsburgs. But Europe had seen an Isabella in Spain, an Elizabeth in England, a Catherine in Russia, taking and holding their places among the most powerful rulers of their times; and Maria Theresa rested with confidence on the loyalty of her people, and the good faith of her neighbors.

The elector of Bavaria acted in a prompt, honest, and Rival claim- consistent manner. He at once lodged a protest ants. against any disposition of the hereditary estates to the prejudice of his own rights; insisted on the will of Ferdinand I. ; and demanded the production of the original text. It was promptly produced. But it was found to convey the succession to the heirs of his daughter, the ancestress of the elector, not, as he contended, on the failure of male heirs, but in the absence of more direct heirs born in wedlock.[1] Maria Theresa could, however, trace her descent through nearer male heirs, and had, therefore, a superior title. Charles Albert was in any event only one of several claimants. The king of Spain, a Bourbon, presented himself as the heir of the Hapsburg

[1] Ehelich, not männlich, as the Bavarian copy read. Charges of forgery were, of course, made and retorted. The documents are given by Olenschlager, *Geschichte des Interregni*, Frankfort, 1742, vol. i. pp. 45–125, and in many other publications.

emperor Charles the Fifth. The king of Sardinia alleged an ancient marriage contract, from which he derived a right to the duchy of Milan. Even August of Saxony claimed territory by virtue of an antiquated title, which, it was pretended, the renunciation of his wife could not affect. All these were, however, mere vultures compared to the eagle which was soon to descend upon its prey.

The great news which the messenger brought to Rheinsberg was, after some hesitation, communicated to Frederic. It was the occasion of a marvellous cure, described by the king himself. The physicians, he says, infatuated with old prejudices, were unwilling to give him quinine; but he took it, nevertheless, because he proposed more important work for himself than nursing a fever.[1] And on the same day he wrote to Voltaire that he feared he would soon be more occupied with powder, guns, and soldiers than with actresses and plays.[2]

Podewils and field-marshal Schwerin were at once summoned to Rheinsberg. On their arrival, two days later, the king declared to them that in his judgment the best use to make of the fortunate situation in which the death of the emperor had placed him would be to seize Silesia. That would be the happiest contribution to the aggrandizement of Prussia and the glory of his house which had offered itself for a long time; and for it he could afford to sacrifice the far less valuable expectancy to Jülich and Berg. They were then invited to submit their views upon the best policy to adopt toward this end. Their reply, handed in on the twenty-ninth of October, describes and discusses two alternative lines of action.[3]

Action of Frederic.

[1] *Œuvres de Frédéric*, ii. 54.

[2] Frederic to Voltaire, 26 October, 1740.

[3] The paper is in the *Polit. Corresp.*, i. 74–78. Cf. Grünhagen, *Geschichte des ersten schlesischen Krieges*, Gotha, 1881, vol. i. pp. 48–52.

The first was what may be called the plan of negotiable friendship. It proposed in effect to offer to support the

His plans.

pragmatic sanction, to give the grand-duke Francis Prussia's vote for emperor, thus far, then, to fulfil the obligations of the treaty of 1728, and also to re-convey to Austria the ceded claim to Berg, on condition of the surrender of the province of Silesia. If the queen assented to these terms, which it was to be explained could alone save her from ruin, Prussia would join in alliance with Russia and the naval powers for her defence. The opposite scheme was one of open hostility. The leading features were a union with Bavaria and Saxony supported by France, the transfer of the principality of Berg to Sulzbach or Bavaria, the election of Charles Albert as emperor, and, to hold Russia in check, a friendly connection with the kingdom of Sweden.

Of these two plans the diplomatist and the soldier agreed in preferring the first. But they also submitted a third, somewhat different from either, and which Podewils thought " could be justified after a certain fashion." This was that Saxony should be incited to assert its own claims by invading Bohemia or Silesia, thus furnishing a pretext on which Prussia could also interfere to maintain her interests, not as against Maria Theresa, but as against other parties.

This third plan Frederic seems never to have considered. Of the other two, which he himself had proposed, he preferred the second; but that which he adopted was a combination of both. He resolved to act first and negotiate afterwards, but to negotiate with Austria, not with Bavaria.[1] What decided him, he says, was the death

[1] See the *Historische Zeitschrift*, vol. xxxvii., for an article " Friedrich am Rubicon," in which the author, Grünhagen, maintains that Frederic had already announced his intention to occupy Silesia at once. He thinks Frederic had had his eye on the province since the middle of August.

of the empress Anna of Russia.[1] On her death the
crown fell to the young grand-duke Ivan, son of
prince Ulric of Brunswick-Wolfenbüttel, his The decision.
own brother-in-law. The appearances were that during
the minority of the young prince Russia would be more
occupied in maintaining tranquillity at home, than in
sustaining the pragmatic sanction. This event, an army
ready to act, a full treasury, and perhaps the desire to
make a name, formed the cause of the war which the king
declared against Maria Theresa of Austria, queen of
Hungary and Bohemia.[2]

In fact, however, a declaration of war formed no part of
the king's policy. His assurances to the grand-duke, to
whom he wrote a letter of condolence, to Maria Theresa,
to whose notification of her accession he replied by ac-
knowledging her as queen of Hungary and Bohemia, were
all to the effect that there need be no doubt about his desire and purpose to give assistance, provided — and this
vague clause was the only reserve — he was first put in a
position for making that assistance effective.[3] This clause
did not indeed pass unobserved, but the general tenor of
the letters seems to have given satisfaction ; and the grand-
duke even felt encouraged to write an autograph letter
soliciting Frederic's support for himself in the imperial
election. The marquis Botta was the bearer of this communication.

Not less security was felt about the conduct of France.

[1] 28 October, 1740.

[2] *Œuvres de Frédéric*, ii. 55, 56. Voltaire states that in the original draft, which was sent to him for correction, this passage included
the words, " l'ambition, l'intérêt, le désir de faire parler de soi,
l'emporterent, et la guerre fut résolue," but that he advised the king
to strike them out. *Œuvres de Voltaire*, lxiv. 198.

[3] Frederic to Borcke at Vienna, 31 October, 1740. Cf. the dispatch
of Robinson, English ambassdor at Vienna, of 9 November, 1756, in
Raumer, *Beiträge zur neueren Geschichte*, Leipsic, 1836, vol. ii. pp. 74,
75.

Louis XV. was not only solemnly pledged, in the treaty of
Austria and
France. 1738, to sustain the pragmatic sanction, but
it was expressly stated that the guaranty was
given as an equivalent for other concessions made by the
emperor. The first of these was, of course, the assurance
of the eventual succession of France to the duchy of Lorraine.[1] As late as January 26, 1740, Fleury had written
the emperor that the king would observe the engagements
which he had made, with the most inviolable fidelity.[2]
Nothing could be clearer, or seem to be surer, than the
duty of France. In November the cardinal was indeed
less emphatic. He detained the envoy who announced the
queen's accession, with the excuse that it was necessary to
find in the archives some form of title by which she could
be addressed, but this and some other suspicious circumstances were attributed apparently to the cardinal's well-
known love for evasion and mystery. It was enough for
the time that he announced his master's intention to fulfil
his engagements.[3]

Yet the court of France was even then embarking on
a career of duplicity. While Fleury was scrupulously
seeking a title by which to recognize the new queen, he
privately assured the envoy of Bavaria that nothing in
the treaty required France to prevent the elector from com-
peting for the imperial crown, or to sustain the pragmatic
sanction against the rights of third parties.[4] This last
distinction was one of the choicest bits of casuistry that
the astute cardinal ever produced. At this time it was

[1] See the account of the preliminaries of 1735, and the treaty of
1738 in Garden, *Histoire des traités de paix*, iii. 189–196, and especially the guaranty article, pp. 194, 195, or in Schoell, *Abrégé de
l'histoire des traités de paix*, vol. ii. c. xv.

[2] Duc de Broglie, *Frédéric II. et Marie Thérèse*, 3d ed., Paris, 1884,
vol. i. p. 82 ; Arneth, *Geschichte Maria Theresias*, Vienna, 1863–1879,
vol. i. pp. 98, 99.

[3] Luynes, iii. 269.

[4] Broglie, *Frédéric II. et Marie Thérèse*, i. 87.

thrown out somewhat tentatively, for Fleury was not yet sure of his ground, and, still hoping to make the policy of peace and good faith prevail in the councils of his master, felt it advisable only to lay down a preliminary formula, on which he could afterwards, if necessary, base a scheme of perfidy. In this kind of ingenuity he had no superior.[1]

The first fortnight of the young queen's reign, though not without certain vague solicitudes, was then, on the whole, not discouraging. She did not hesitate, therefore, to name the grand-duke, her husband, co-regent in all the hereditary dominions; the estates did homage; the old ministers were confirmed in their places; and the slow political machine of state resumed its usual functions. There are few more pathetic figures in history than this young and inexperienced queen, calmly trusting the plighted faith of princes and statesmen who were already plotting her destruction. The earliest and most active of these was the king of Prussia.

Confidence of Maria Theresa.

On the day after the conference at Rheinsberg Podewils returned to Berlin. It was necessary to have somebody at the capital to keep up relations with the foreign ministers, and Podewils was not unskilful in the art of meeting their inquiries with vague answers, which excited

---

[1] I may perhaps here condense into a note the substance of the cardinal's logic, although the full syllogism was only developed somewhat later. He made a distinction between a claim and a lawful possession. It was the latter alone that France had guaranteed. But such guaranty did not of itself create a right; nor did it become operative until the right had been otherwise established. If then there were other parties, who had a better right to the Hapsburg inheritance than Maria Theresa, the provisions of the treaty of 1738 did not apply, for France had never accepted the iniquitous engagement to defend her in possessions to which she was not lawfully entitled. This ingenious sophism destroyed, of course, the whole force of the guaranty.

yet baffled curiosity. But scarcely a day passed in which
Activity of he was not overwhelmed with political conun-
Frederic. drums from the busy hand of the king. Thus,
on the first of November Frederic gave him a problem
to solve : When a man had an opportunity, ought he to
utilize it, or not? He was ready with his troops and
everything ; if he failed to act, he would be like one who
had a fortune which he neglected to use ; if he acted, it
would be said that he was clever enough to take advantage
of his superiority over his neighbors.[1] Two days later,
having received reports from Borcke, the resident at the
court of Austria, he gave a commentary on the situation.
In Vienna they were all pride ; they flattered themselves
that they could defend their own possessions. Vanity,
folly, ridiculous illusions![2] Podewils was evidently bewildered by this jaunty treatment of grave political questions ; and, although he tried dutifully to imitate it, he
evidently was not wholly at ease. He interposed no moral
objections to the problem, but offered some serious practical considerations. The king replied at length, and invited
further observations. Podewils then sent in a categorical statement of the views of his situation, and of the
obstacles which an adventurous policy was likely to meet.
Only one of these is now of historical interest. The minister admitted that the house of Brandenburg once had
such and such rights in Silesia. There existed, however,
solemn treaties, which, although they might have been obtained treacherously, would be appealed to by the court of
Vienna. But means could be found to revive these old
rights. The question of law thus raised Frederic abruptly
referred to the jurists.[3] The reflections which were drawn

---

[1] Frederic to Podewils, 1 November, 1740.

[2] Same to Same, 3 November, 1740.

[3] " L'article de droit est l'affaire des ministres, c'est la vôtre, il est
temps d'y travailler en sécret, car les ordres aux troupes sont
donnés." Frederic to Podewils, 7 November, 1740. This was two

from the relations of the European powers were, however, examined article by article ; and the acuteness of perception, the accuracy of calculation, which the king displayed, must be pronounced in the highest degree admirable. And at the end, brushing away all of Podewil's elaborate deductions, he announced that since there was nothing to restrain him he had issued orders to the regiments on account, first, of the Bavarian protest; second, of the armaments in Sardinia ; third, of the armaments in Hanover. The Bavarian protest was an act which furnished a casus fœderis, under the treaty of 1728. The Sardinian armaments affected only disputed territories in Italy.[1] The armaments in Hanover had in view the defence of the electorate against the French.

The sudden military activity which followed this resolution of Frederic could not fail to arouse the keenest curiosity. Even before that it had become an object with the diplomatists to learn what, in view of the new situation created by the death of Charles VI., was likely to be the course of Prussia. From Paris, from Hanover, came anxious inquiries. All these efforts were in vain ; and the only foreigner who had dangerous connections at the Prussian court, the baron Manteuffel, a friend of Frederic, was ordered to retire to his estates in Saxony.[2] But the military preparations could not be long concealed. Fleury, feeling his way cautiously as usual, not only charged the count Beauvau, sent by the king to congratulate Frederic on his accession, to examine the political situation, but also accepted the services of Voltaire, who had volunteered to probe the intentions of his royal friend.

days before the receipt of the news of the death of the empress Anna, which the king says decided him to act. Supra, p. 49.

[1] Cf. Frederic to Podewils, 15 December, 1740, where he admits that he himself had sent Algarotti to Italy to encourage the king of Sardinia to "lever le bouclier."

[2] Frederic to Podewils, 5 November, 1740.

This, the first visit of Voltaire to Prussia, was a brief,
and not wholly a pleasant one. The poet showed
the king an empty purse; and estimated that
three thousand thalers would replace the sum which it
had cost him to publish the Anti-Machiavel, and to make
a long journey to Rheinsberg on the invitation of an opulent royal friend. But Frederic was planning an enterprise which would severely test his opulence. He afterwards ordered the money to be paid, indeed, to the miser,
as he called Voltaire in a letter to Jordan, — adding that,
as the miser was with him only six days, it amounted to
five hundred thalers a day, — but it is evident that the
unliquidated claim must have been a troublesome spectre
at the festivities of Rheinsberg. The diplomatic part of
Voltaire's mission was, moreover, a complete failure. On
his return to Berlin he met Beauvau, the special envoy,
and Valori, the French resident, for an exchange of
views. But views proved to be all they had to exchange.
Voltaire had learned nothing even from Frederic's doggerel; and he seems to have shared the opinion of Beauvau that the king's purposes were not friendly to France.
Valori could not quite affirm the contrary. But he described Frederic rather as an ambitious young fellow,
ready to turn in any direction toward which his interest
seemed to incline him. " You are right," said Voltaire,
"he is equal to any kind of adventure, and if he fails —
he will return to philosophy." [1]

The English envoy, captain Guy Dickens, whom Frederic felt to be personally somewhat below the dignity of
his position, and whose recall he soon afterwards effected,
was more persistent but not more successful.

The military preparations were meantime continued,
and, of course, soon became visible to the whole
world. But their exact object remained a mystery. The diplomatists were in despair. One

[1] Broglie, *Fr. II. et M. T.*, i. 104.

held that they contemplated an alliance with England against the Bourbons; another that France was to be the beneficiary; now Maria Theresa was to be supported, now despoiled; while the majority of suffrages seemed to concentrate upon the theory that Frederic was preparing to make himself emperor of Germany. And there were grave discussions upon the consequences which would follow the election of a Protestant as head of the Holy Roman Empire.

Of all the diplomatists who were charged at Berlin to watch the policy of the king, only one, baron Demerath, the Austrian envoy, seems to have had a correct insight into the situation. He reported very early to his court that Silesia was in danger.[1] For a time his warnings were disregarded; but when the military movements became more open the optimism of Vienna gave way to a reluctant anxiety. The marquis Botta was therefore charged to inquire into the matter.

In the interval before his arrival, the veil of mystery, which had covered the Prussian preparations, was partially lifted. The order for putting the army on a war footing was made known in Berlin on the tenth of November. But Podewils' explanation, that the king aimed only to be ready for any emergencies which might arise out of the death of the emperor, or the approaching death of the elector palatine, found no belief:[2] the conviction spread

[1] Arneth, i. 104. In this connection it may be interesting to cite some opinions of prominent persons at Vienna. "The grand duke Francis said 'the king of Prussia is the one prince who most regards his honor. He can have no evil intentions toward the queen of Hungary.'" Raumer, *Beiträge*, ii. 80. But Bartenstein, inclining to a French alliance, had less confidence in Frederic. "There was never such a character," he said, "as the king of Prussia. I foresaw it, and gave the warning at the time when Charles VI. ordered me to write the letter which saved the prince's life. . . . The queen has no enemy to fear except the king of Prussia." Robinson, 10 December, 1756, apud Raumer, *Beiträge*, ii. 87.

[2] Droysen, V. i. 154.

that Frederic had already found or created the emergency, and was prepared to act. Dickens, and even Brackel, his Russian colleague, began to share Demerath's conviction that Silesia was threatened.[1] But the policy of deception was still kept up not unsuccessfully for some days longer. Two or three regiments were ostentatiously marched toward the southwest.[2] The garrisons in Cleve were strengthened. Podewils was ordered to hear all questions, and return no answers. The envoys abroad were to consult the tone of feeling, each at the court to which he was accredited, and to present the explanation most likely to be acceptable, giving no positive assurances, yet leaving everything favorable to be inferred.[3] The arrival of Botta was awaited with the greatest curiosity.

On the twenty-ninth of November the special envoy finally arrived, and brought the solution of the secret with him. For all the way between the Prussian frontier and the capital he had met troops on the march towards Silesia. Their destination could no longer be in doubt.[4]

The next day Frederic himself returned to Berlin. The diplomatists, to whom at Rheinsberg he had firmly closed his doors, were then received in special audiences. To Guy Dickens Frederic frankly declared that he had no intention of maintaining the pragmatic sanction ; and as to Berg, which the envoy had intimated might be guaranteed by England, he replied that he did not attach much importance to that acquisition. It would arouse the jealousy of Holland, while

Frederic at Berlin.

[1] Dickens to Harrington, 15 November, 1740. "The general opinion is that his Prussian majesty must have some designs upon Silesia."

[2] Frederic to Podewils, 15 November, 1740.

[3] "à chaque cour d'une façon différente ;" to England one thing, to France another, etc. *Polit. Corresp.*, i. 99.

[4] On that day, accordingly, Dickens wrote, "The project of invading Silesia is now as good as avowed."

there was another quarter in which he could make conquests without causing any uneasiness to the naval powers.[1] The marquis Botta had his audience on the 6th of December. Intervening events had rendered the mission on which he was originally sent a mournful farce, but it was executed to the letter. The communication of the grand-duke requesting Prussia's vote in the electoral college, and one from Maria Theresa, innocently seconding her husband's request, were solemnly handed to the king. Then Botta observed significantly that he had come by way of Silesia, and that on account of the rain the roads were almost impassable. Frederic, feigning not to comprehend, replied that the only disadvantage was that a traveller would arrive with muddy boots.[2] In later audiences the marquis tried threats and tried entreaties; neither made any impression.

The regiments continued their march to the rendezvous at Crossen, near the Silesian frontier. By the thirteenth of December the main force, some twenty-two thousand strong, was concentrated there; and a rear guard of ten or twelve thousand more were on the way from Berlin.[3]

The march to the frontier.

The first officer in command, field-marshal Schwerin, was an admirable choice. A native of Pomerania, he had been a roving soldier of fortune for many years; had fought in the war of the Spanish succession; had visited Charles XII. at Bender; had boldly led the troops of Mecklenburg against an army commissioned to chastise that principality in the name of the emperor; until, in 1720, when Pomerania fell to Prussia, he accepted an invitation from Frederic William

Schwerin.

---

[1] Dickens, 6 December, 1740, apud Raumer, *Beiträge*, ii. 82 et seq.

[2] *Œuvres de Frédéric*, ii. 57.

[3] This is the estimate of Droysen, V. i. 164, n., and is some five or six thousand lower than those which had previously been current. But Grünhagen, i. 152, admits only 19,000.

to join the Prussian army. A man of culture, wit, and social experience, he was often employed in diplomatic as well as military services, and acquitted himself not less creditably in the one part than in the other. In war he was preëminently a fighting general. He lacked the power or the patience for strategical combinations; and on occasions which required caution and watchfulness was not unlikely to prove either reckless or negligent. But in battle he was brave as a lion. His impetuosity made him the admiration of the soldiers; and yet, as his self-control was never lost, they followed him with perfect confidence in the most desperate charges. This was the man whom Frederic selected for his lieutenant. He had at first frankly given his counsel against the enterprise, but took it up after it had been adopted with perfect loyalty, zeal, and intelligence.

A final measure of preparation was to dispatch count von Gotter on a special mission to Vienna. Borcke, the resident, had well acted his part, which was to give cheerful pledges, scarcely tempered by certain vague reserves, and thus gain time for the completion of the Prussian armaments. But Gotter was to conduct a bolder diplomacy. The nature of his instructions was communicated to Botta on the 9th of December.[1]

Mission of Gotter.

The old prince of Anhalt-Dessau looked upon the Silesian enterprise with an evil eye. Living in the traditions of the war of the Spanish succession, his sympathies were strongly Austrian; and he had on all occasions spoken openly in opposition to the scheme.[2] When he failed to change the king's plans he urged with much persistence that he, as the oldest general in the army, should have an active part in their execution.

Leopold of Dessau.

[1] Arneth, i. 114, 115.
[2] Orlich, *Geschichte der schlesischen Kriege,* Berlin, 1841, vol. i. pp. 36–39.

But this did not suit Frederic's purposes. In a letter which gave full credit to the veteran's merits, and promised to use his services whenever needed, he declared that he reserved the present expedition for himself alone ; the world must not suppose, he said, that the king of Prussia marched with a tutor at his elbow.[1] Then to counteract, as he himself says, any disaffection which the Old Dessauer might have awakened in the army, the king addressed at the palace a short speech to the assembled officers. He was about to undertake a war, he said, in which he had no other allies than their valor and their good will ; his cause was just, and his resources were in his good fortune. Let them remember the glory which their ancestors won on the plains of Warsaw, and at Fehrbellin. Their future was in their own hands ; distinctions and rewards awaited those who should merit them. But he had no need to excite them to glory ; they had nothing else before their eyes ; it was the only object worthy of their efforts. They were going to meet troops which under prince Eugene had enjoyed the finest reputation ; so much greater would be the honor if they should defeat them.[2]

The French diplomatists were the last to open their eyes to the situation. Their theory of Frederic's intense aversion to France had a natural tendency to circumscribe their views, and it does not appear that either was a man of great penetration, although Valori perhaps concealed under a coarse exterior more ability than has usually been ascribed to him. It was, however, Frederic's policy not to commit himself too far with the French, and to avoid an alliance with them if he could achieve his purpose without it. He did

The French diplomatists.

[1] Frederic to Leopold of Dessau, 2 December, 1740.

[2] *Œuvres de Frederic*, ii. 58, 59. In the earlier draft of the "Histoire de mon temps," a shorter and terser version of this address is given.

not, indeed, share the opinion of Podewils that Maria Theresa would yield Silesia without a struggle. He understood more correctly than his minister the temper of the court of Vienna. But he also understood the unpopularity which French support gave to any cause in Germany; and preferred to accept it only as a last resort. It was, however, deemed not less desirable to leave an opening through which the French alliance could be admitted in case of need; and the method of treatment best adapted to this end the king correctly called cajolery. But if by cajolery he intended to arouse false, hopes the policy was a complete failure. The French envoys persisted in their scepticism, and after Botta's stormy interviews still treated his indignation as part of a play, of which a Prusso-Austrian alliance formed the main feature. They adhered to this opinion even after Frederic had assured Beauvau, in the audience of leave, which was given him on the twelfth of December, that he was about to play a great game, and that if he should draw the ace he would divide with France.

The evening of that day there was a grand masked ball at the royal palace. The king himself was present; wore his domino like the rest; smiled affably on the ladies; and chatted from time to time with the foreign envoys. At nine o'clock the next morning he set out to join the army.

CHAPTER III.

THE Austrian, or more strictly speaking the Bohemian, province which was called Silesia comprised a number of distinct and once semi-independent principalities. Until the middle of the twelfth century it was one of the great duchies of the republic of Poland. But on the expulsion of the tyrannical Wladislaus it was practically severed from the parent state and divided among his sons, the progenitors of the great piast families in the aristocracy of Silesia. Their heirs made further partitions, until the entire territory was parcelled out into a multitude of small baronies, too feeble to maintain their independence, or even to preserve order within their own limits. Implacable feuds arose between the petty lords, and were conducted with the peculiar ferocity which often marks the quarrels of kinsmen. In the fourteenth century the whole province was in a state of anarchy. The distracted princes were at length forced to solicit foreign protection, and, one after another, commended themselves as vassals to the crown of Bohemia.

With the progress of the Reformation, two centuries later, the doctrines of Luther were widely diffused throughout Silesia, especially among the German part of the population, and tenaciously maintained themselves through all the trials of the Thirty Years' War.

In 1537 the duke of Liegnitz, one of the most powerful of the surviving piasts, formed with the elector Joachim II. of Brandenburg a family compact, which made the two houses eventual heirs, each of the other, in respect to possessions held in fee of Bohemia. But Ferdinand, king of Bohemia, denied the power of vassals thus to dispose of their lands to the prejudice of the right of escheat enjoyed by the lord; forced the duke of Liegnitz to surrender his copy of the treaty; and exacted fresh declarations of fealty. The duchy of Jägerndorf received even more summary treatment. It had actually been acquired by the house of Brandenburg, and at the outbreak of the Thirty Years' War was in the hands of John George, a younger son of the elector Joachim Frederic. But John George, having embraced the cause of the opposition, was put under the ban of the Empire for rebellion, and Jägerndorf was reannexed to Bohemia. This proceeding was solemnly ratified in the treaty of Westphalia. In 1675 the duke of Liegnitz died without male heirs, and the elector Frederic William of Brandenburg then claimed the duchies of Liegnitz, Brieg, and Wohlau, under the treaty of 1537. But the emperor Leopold replied by seizing them as lapsed fiefs of the kingdom of Bohemia, with which they were practically incorporated. Eleven years later a slight apparent compensation was indeed made to the elector. Leopold ceded to him the circle of Schwiebus, as return for a renunciation of all claims upon the three duchies, and assured him the expectancy to East Friesland. But Schwiebus was soon afterwards restored by the elector Frederic III. in accordance with a pledge which he had given as crown prince, and for the surrender of the will which his father had made to his prejudice, while the expected vacancy in East Friesland obstinately delayed its arrival. For all its treaties and all its negotiations Prussia had, therefore, nothing to show.

The three duchies, with Schwiebus, Jägerndorf, and various other principalities, the history of which it is unnecessary to relate, made up the province of Silesia. In

1740 it seemed to be as firmly held as any of the dominions of the house of Hapsburg.

The province was well favored by nature. The numerous streams of the Giant Mountains fed the water-
wheels of the miller, and the Oder floated the products
of the loom and the mines out into the great channels of
commerce. The people were industrious, thrifty, and intelligent. Breslau, the capital, was a city of the first
rank; and many other towns, distributed throughout the
province, and throbbing with an active industry almost
rivalling that of Flanders, formed convenient local centres of wealth, enlightenment, and civic patriotism. The
Silesians had also preserved their local liberties in a much
purer form than they could be found anywhere in Prussia.
In doing homage to the crown of Bohemia they by no
means acknowledged an absolute king. They reserved
the rights which the code of feudalism secured to vassals;
and at least one solemn instrument, the charter *Its constitu-*
of king Wladislaus, in 1498, confirmed and *tion.*
even enlarged these rights.[1] It provided, among other
things, that the king's deputy, the governor-general,[2]
should always be a native-born Silesian prince, that the
representatives of the estates should meet twice a year as
a supreme court of justice, and that no tax should be
levied without the consent of the diet.[3] This charter was
confirmed in 1526 by Ferdinand; and in respect to the
right of taxation was fairly observed, both by him and
by his successors. Even in 1740 the budget of Charles
VI. was freely amended by the diet.[4] The executive

---

[1] The text is in Kries, *Historische Entwickelung der Steuerverfassung
in Schlesien*, Breslau, 1842, pp. 100–106.

[2] Oberhauptmann.

[3] Arts. I., II.–V., and XVIII.–XX. The eighteenth article
reads, "Promittimus etiam principibus, baronibus, vassalis, civitati-
bus, denique, omnibus incolis Silesiæ nos nullas exactiones institu-
taros, exceptis iis, quas de jure negare non possunt."

[4] Stenzel, iv. 80. Ranke, xxvii., xxviii., says: "die Stände be-

service had indeed become somewhat more centralized under Charles, for he had surrounded the governor with a group of crown councillors, who by a majority could overrule him. But the administration was easy, careless, conciliatory; the towns had liberal franchises; and the Austrian rule was not without strong elements of popularity.

Thus Silesia seemed to enjoy in many respects a favored and happy situation. Yet over the prosperity and happiness of the Protestants hung the sombre cloud of religious inequality, and the possible storm of religious persecution.

The freedom of the Protestant religion had indeed been established, though within narrow limits, by the treaty of Westphalia, and again extorted from the emperor Joseph I. by Charles XII. of Sweden, almost at the point of the sword.[1] But there were many ways in which, even within the bounds of legality, the Lutherans could be made to feel their inferiority. Strict orders were issued against the conversion of Catholics to Protestantism; and severe penalties, extending even to banishment with the loss of all their property, were imposed upon those who abandoned the church of Rome.[2] A Protestant father, who had a Catholic wife, was forced to see the education of his children put into the hands of priests. The number of Protestant clergy was limited. If an adherent of Lutheranism died in a Catholic parish, his body was denied Christian burial until the purse of his friends had silenced the scruples of the priests. Some of the worst of these regulations had

The Protestant population.

willigten der Regierung nicht was diese bedurfte, sondern was ihnen darzubieten gut schien."

[1] The text of the convention between Charles and Joseph is in Hensel's *Protestantische Kirchengeschichte der Gemeinen in Schlesien,* Leipsic, 1768, pp. 563–567.

[2] Ibid., pp. 632, 656.

been introduced by Charles VI., but under pressure from the Jesuits who surrounded him, and perhaps against his own sense of justice and humanity; for in 1737 he slightly relaxed the rigors of his policy, and authorized the officials to exercise mildness in cases of conspicuous hardship. Yet such was his fear of his confessor, that this order was kept strictly secret.[1] The decrees of intolerance could be proclaimed aloud in the market-place, but the counsels of charity were privately and anxiously whispered in the ears of the functionaries for whom they were intended.

This was the province which Frederic, in defiance of the pragmatic sanction, without any declaration of war, and in pursuit chiefly of territorial gain, was about to invade. On the sixteenth of December the Prussian army crossed the frontier. "I have passed the Rubicon," Prussians in wrote the king, "with flying banners and sound- Silesia. ing trumpets; my troops are in good spirit, my officers full of ambition, my generals thirst for glory; everything will go according to our wishes. Send Bülow to me; caress him, show him his master's own advantage; in short, let us use our knowledge of the human heart, and make self-interest, ambition, and all the springs of action which govern men, work for us."[2]

The province was in no condition to resist an invading army. Charles VI. had drained it of all its available troops for his unlucky campaigns against the Turks, and Maria Theresa, refusing to believe in the existence of danger, had taken no measures for restoring them. A field army existed not. Even the great fortresses, Glogau, Brieg, and Neisse, were feebly garrisoned, in bad repair, and not provisioned for a siege. The city of Breslau, the seat of government, refused, under the pro-

[1] Stenzel, iv. 81–85 ; M. Lehmann in the *Historische Zeitschrift*, 1883, No. 5 ; Hensel, p. 693.

[2] Frederic to Podewils, 16 December, 1740. Bülow was the newly appointed Saxon envoy.

visions of its charter, to admit Austrian troops; and
undertook to defend itself with the municipal train-bands.
Count Wallis, the military governor, shut himself up in
Glogau, while general Browne, a more active officer, had
barely time to distribute his few thousand men among
the several garrisons.[1] The Prussian march was therefore
unopposed in the field.

After a day's rest at Grünberg, the first Silesian town,
Frederic with the main army moved directly upon Glogau,
which was about forty miles distant, on the river Oder.
Wallis had only twelve hundred men; but he hastily laid
in a stock of flour, destroyed the suburbs, and made the
best possible preparations for defence. Botta's description of the roads proved to be not at all exaggerated.
Heavy rains continued during the march; the streams
Their steady
progress. were over their banks, and bridges had been
swept away. But the army toiled along through
the mud and water, and arrived on the twenty-second of
December at Herrndorf, five miles from Glogau, where
the king's headquarters were temporarily fixed.[2] At this
point a notification was received from Wallis that hostilities would be resisted to the utmost. This was not in
itself a formidable obstacle to the Prussian movements,
but the problem of a siege presented some practical difficulties. The army had no heavy guns, the capital was
not yet occupied, and time was extremely precious.

In the mean time Schwerin, with a second army, bore
off farther southward toward Liegnitz, a brisk manufac-
turing town on the Katzbach. It was easily surprised on
the early morning of the twenty-seventh; the garrison
was disarmed; and the sleepy burghers were roused from

[1] Arneth, i. 142; Grünhagen, i. 144. Browne had earnestly but
fruitlessly urged the wisdom of putting the province in a condition
for defence. (Cogniazo) *Geständnisse eines oesterreichischen Veterans,*
Breslau, 1789, ii. 35–37.

[2] Rödenbeck, *Tagebuch,* i. 30.

their slumbers by the beat of the Prussian drums in the market-place.

While these events were taking place Gotter arrived at Vienna, and in an audience with the grand-duke *Negotiations* on the eighteenth of the month renewed the *at Vienna.* propositions, which Borcke, the resident, had submitted the day before. They included the familiar offer of an alliance, and the support of the whole military power of Prussia for the queen, as well as the vote of Brandenburg for the grand-duke in the coming imperial election. An advance to the queen from the Prussian treasury of three million florins was also offered. But in return for all these favors the envoy was to demand as a distinct condition, what had before been only vaguely suggested, the cession of the whole province of Silesia.[1] Gotter's duty was to make a more solemn renewal of these demands, and to emphasize them with the reasons which were sketched in outline in his instructions.[2] Not the least cogent of these was probably, in Frederic's view, the liberal sums to be offered as bribes to the Austrian ministers. If count Sinzendorf would betray the honor of his mistress, and recommend the acceptance of the Prussian terms, he was to receive two hundred thousand thalers, while for a like service the private secretary of the grand-duke was to have one hundred thousand.

But the proposals which the envoy made aroused all the ancient pride of the Hapsburgs, and the *Firmness of* grand-duke answered for the queen with becom- *the queen.* ing spirit. Her majesty had other allies, he explained, who, instead of seeking new treaties, held themselves bound by those which already existed. The Bavarian protest caused no alarm ; France could be depended on to observe the plighted faith of the crown. The queen was

---

[1] Frederic to Borcke, 15 November, 7 December, 1740 ; Adelung, ii. 214, etc.

[2] Instructions, 8 December, 1740.

not averse to negotiation, but she could not negotiate with
a burglar who had broken into her house. The Prussian
troops must first evacuate Silesia.[1]

The emphasis of this refusal shook the faith even of
Gotter. He wrote to Podewils that in his opinion the
king ought to extricate himself from his situation in the
best manner possible, and Borcke had already made similar representations to Frederic himself.[2]

The report of Gotter's first audience reached Frederic
in the camp at Herrndorf, and led to a partial
modification of his demands. Orders were sent
back to accept a part of Silesia, but apparently
without much confidence in the result; the king added,
indeed, a postscript in his own hand to the effect that
the grand-duke was rushing to destruction.[3] The special
envoy had an audience on the first of January to present
the king's answer. He also threw out a suggestion that
the queen might save the appearance of things by surrendering Silesia as security for a loan of two million guldens
from Prussia, on the secret condition that the loan should
never be repaid, and the province, therefore, never demanded back.[4] The chancellor Sinzendorf affected to
favor this plan.[5] But after the Austrian negotiators had
succeeded, by the aid of one or two conferences, in taking
a formal protocol of the Prussian demands, which the
envoys in compliance with their orders had refused to communicate in writing, the case was
abruptly closed, a negative answer in the most
emphatic terms was handed to Gotter, and he was re-
quested to deliver it in person to his master. Three

Frederic lowers his demands.

Which are again re-jected.

[1] Grünhagen, i. 83–87; Arneth, i. 120, 121 ; Robinson's reports
apud Raumer, *Beiträge*, ii. 92.

[2] Droysen, V. i. 177, 180.

[3] *Œuvres de Frédéric*, ii. 63; Frederic to Gotter, 26 December, 1740.

[4] Gotter's report of his second interview. Grünhagen, i. 92–97.

[5] Arneth, i. 120, 131.

days later, on the eighth of January, Borcke was also notified that his presence in Vienna was no longer desired.

The Austrian answer was a masterpiece of caustic and subtle irony. The policy of adopting such a The queen's tone in the circumstances was perhaps doubtful, reply. and yet it is difficult not to sympathize with the indignation which so relentlessly laid bare the sophistry, the insolence, and the wickedness of Frederic's proposals. The offer to defend her against attack would, said the queen, have been welcome if she had been attacked, but in fact she was living at peace with all the world until the king of Prussia himself invaded her territories. As to the proffered loan, it had never before happened that war had been made upon a prince to compel the acceptance of money. With equal force she repelled Frederic's sinister hint that he could insure the election of the grand-duke as emperor ; the election, it was said, must be free, and the successful candidate ought to proceed from the unconstrained choice of the electors. And observing that she was not disposed to begin her reign with the dismemberment of her state, the queen insisted that the Prussians must at once withdraw from Silesia as the first condition of further friendship. In proof of her good faith she had given her answer in writing, although — a last touch of sarcasm — the king of Prussia had not seen fit to practise the same candor.[1] The protocol and other papers in the case were then published by the Austrian court for the information of Europe.

Frederic called this publication a gross breach of confidence.[2] But he had nevertheless foreseen a war of publicists, and had prepared to make the best use of his own arms and resources. The manifesto which he promulgated on crossing the frontier said nothing of his rights

[1] Olenschlager, i. 136, 137 ; Adelung, ii. 215, 216, etc.
[2] Droysen, V. i. 186 n.

to Silesia; he came, he said, as a friend and ally, occupying the province as a measure of precaution.[1] The rejoinder to the Austrian circular dispatch, or rather to the protest sent to the imperial diet, was defiant in tone and in at least one place trifled audaciously with facts. The queen had charged the Prussian envoys with holding for purposes of deception different language at different courts, and this Frederic's ministers denied.[2] Yet they knew that the king himself had expressly ordered such a policy to be adopted.[3] A paper of a different sort was prepared by Professor Ludewig, chancellor of the university of Halle, a paper which attempted to establish by historical and legal arguments the title of the house of Brandenburg to the province of Silesia.[4] The king himself, too, drew up in camp at Herrndorf a concise statement of the reasons which led to the invasion.[5] From these, from various diplomatic papers, and from the works of historians like Ranke and Droysen, those who are interested may learn all that is to be said in defence of the Prussian cause.

The historical facts which bear on the case are given correctly, I think, and without any prejudice, in the foregoing pages, and in an earlier work by the present writer.[6] They show beyond all doubt that the conduct of the court of Vienna in its relations with Prussia had been often ungenerous, and seldom straightforward. If urged

Prussian manifestoes.

[1] *Preuss. Staatsschriften*, i. 69–71 ; Olenschlager, i. 130, 131; *Heldengeschichte*, i. 455–457, etc.

[2] *Pr. Staatsschriften*, i. 84 et seq.; Adelung, ii. 223, in abstract.

[3] Supra, p. 56.

[4] Rechtsgegründetes Eigenthum des königlichen Kurhauses Preussen und Brandenburg auf die Herzogthümer und Fürstenthümer Jägerndorf, Liegnitz, Brieg, etc. It is reproduced in Olenschlager, i. 138–154 ; *Pr. Staatsschriften*, vol. i., and elsewhere.

[5] *Pr. Staatsschriften*, i. 75–78.

[6] Supra, pp. 61, 62, and Tuttle's *History of Prussia*, vol. i. pp. 255–259.

by a state whose own diplomacy had always been above
suspicion, and in an age when political measures
were determined by the test of morality alone, The claim to
Silesia ex-
this consideration would carry no little weight. amined.
But any wrong done by Austria to Prussia had been con-
doned by a long series of treaties between the two powers,
by alliances which more than once united their diplomatists in support of a common cause, and arrayed their soldiers against a common foe. Nor does the question of the
Jülich-Berg guaranty seem to have a very close connection
with that of Silesia. It is not even true that the guaranty was absolute, or that the apparent insincerity of the
Austrian court afforded any justification for the Silesian
enterprise. For the violation of the Jülich-Berg articles
of the treaty of 1728 relieved Prussia, at the most, only
from the obligation actively to maintain the pragmatic
sanction ; it by no means authorized direct attacks upon
that instrument. If Maria Theresa was not the legiti-
mate heir to the Hapsburg dominions, another was, and
to Silesia as well as to the rest. For Prussia was not a
party to the pragmatic sanction, she was only one of the
indorsers ; and the release of an indorser could not affect
the validity of rights which the queen derived from the
instrument itself.

To meet these difficulties, which are obvious, a different line of reasoning is taken up by Prussian apologists.
It is said that by the surrender of Schwiebus the house of
Brandenburg reëntered into possession of all the rights
which the great elector had exchanged for that district,
and that the elector Frederic III. expressly called attention to that principle of law. To the first of these considerations there is a double reply. In the first place, the
rights themselves were disputed, and in the second place,
it by no means follows, from the circumstances attending
the retrocession of Schwiebus, that it revived the earlier
rights, such as they were, of Brandenburg to the rest of

Silesia. And furthermore, there is no sufficient evidence that Frederic III. announced at the time, or afterwards, any such proposition.

If it be insisted that the wrong done to Prussia in these transactions, and the suspended claims to Silesia, continued to survive as traditions of the house of Hohenzollern, I am as little able as Stenzel to find any proof of the statement.[1] There is indeed in the Berlin archives a memoir, drawn up probably by the minister Ilgen, in which the duplicity of Austria is graphically and perhaps not untruthfully described.[2] But there is no evidence that the paper was ever laid before Frederic William I., or that the alleged claims of his house to Silesia were ever adopted by him. For it seems impossible to accept as a re-assertion of these claims, the fact that, at one point in the negotiations over the treaty of 1728, Frederic William suggested that Austria pledge herself, in case Prussia failed to acquire Jülich-Berg, to give an equivalent out of her own possessions.[3] It is, at best, a pure assumption to say that this referred to Silesia. But, if Silesia was meant, the form of the reference contains an implied recognition, not a denial, of the Austrian title.

With the voluminous statements and memoirs, and deductions, informations, and counter-informations, which the statesmen and publicists of the day hurled in the face of a patient world, the present generation has happily but little concern. They would perhaps deserve attention if they had sensibly influenced the course of events. But although the moralists weighed the arguments of the rival

[1] Stenzel, iv. 103 n.

[2] Given in full by Droysen, IV. iv. 310–317.

[3] Ex propriis. Cf. Droysen, V. i. 127. Walpole declared in parliament, 13 February, 1741, that if the late king, Frederic William, had lived until that time the claim to Silesia would not have been raised, for his guaranty of the pragmatic sanction contained no reservation in regard to that province. Coxe, *Memoirs of Sir R. Walpole*, London, 1816, vol. iv. p. 196 ; *Parliamentary History*, vol. xi. p. 1298.

parties, the policy of the cabinets was determined by considerations among which justice and honor had little place.

One of the first powers to guarantee the pragmatic sanction was Russia. Yet aside from feeble representations to Frederic, Russia took no steps toward the fulfilment of the obligation. She seemed even likely to accept engagements contrary to those of 1726 ; for when a palace revolution had overthrown the regent Biron, and substituted the regency of the grand-duchess Anne, mother of the infant tsar Ivan, Frederic found a favorable opportunity to make himself secure at St. Petersburg. The fall of Biron gave marshal Münnich a controlling voice in the councils of the empire. Münnich was step-father of major Winterfeld, an adjutant and a friend of Frederic's. Winterfeld was at once sent to the Russian capital with the king's portrait and thirty thousand thalers as presents for the new favorite.[1] An agreement was soon concluded which, if it received the approval of the regent, would secure Prussia against the armed opposition of her formidable neighbor.

Attitude of Russia.

The conduct of France was, however, far baser than that of Russia. The latter power had just cause for offence at the treacherous manner in which the emperor Charles VI. had made his separate peace with the Turks in 1739, but France had already received, in the assured succession to Lorraine, the price of its guaranty of the pragmatic sanction. In the royal councils the cold, calculating judgment of the cardinal still warned indeed against resolutions contrary to good faith, and enterprises which could lead only to disaster, though

Of France.

[1] From Münnich's own memoirs quoted in S. Sugenheim, *Russland's Einfluss auf Deutschland*, Frankfort, 1856, vol. i. p. 234, n. Münnich adds that he refused the money, which was then offered to and accepted by his son. Cf. Manstein, *Mémoires historiques sur la Russie*, Lyons, 1772, vol. ii. pp. 118, 119.

he took good care that no impulse of political virtue, no sudden outburst of manly generosity, should betray him into new pledges to the queen of Bohemia. Yet of all possible policies for France this of timidity, equivocation, and delay was the worst. It failed to conciliate the few who still cherished the honor of France; and it was wholly unsatisfactory to those ardent and buoyant spirits, who, turning away from the appeals which the danger of an innocent and beautiful queen made to their gallantry, saw in the crisis only a chance to carry the banner of France once more to the banks of the Danube, and to make the court of Versailles supreme arbiter in the politics of Germany.

The favorite member of this party was Charles Louis Fouquet, count of Belleisle, a man who repre-
Belleisle. sented in his own character all that was brilliant, enterprising, and unscrupulous in the nobility of France. Belleisle himself was no longer young, and he had been hardened by a long struggle against prejudice and jealousy. But he had the dangerous gift of throwing himself into the most reckless schemes with an ardor, an energy, and a fearlessness, which made him the natural leader of youth. His imagination was boundless; his intellectual resources, affluent; it was said of him that when he cast his eye on the map of Europe he saw old kingdoms disappear, and new ones arise, under the touch of his magic wand. In the feverish state of the public mind in France, this romantic adventurer threatened to cross and ruin all of Fleury's elaborate combinations. The cardinal was sensible of the danger, and, still trusting in his own astuteness, hit upon one of those ingenious devices for which he was so famous. It was to moderate Belleisle's impetuosity by taking it into his own service.

Early in December he summoned the count to Versailles; intimated to him that France would probably recognize Maria Theresa as queen of Bohemia and Hungary, but would support the elector of Bavaria for the imperial crown ; and announced that the king had selected him for a special mission to the German diet, where he was to represent the line of policy thus indicated. This of course fell far short of Belleisle's view of the situation. He retired to his apartments and spent the night in sketching a complete campaign, military as well as diplomatic, with the number of the forces, the division of the corps, the names of the generals, all complete. This he handed next morning to the amazed cardinal.[1]

During this time Frederic was flinging letter after letter into Fleury's face, each one only making his intentions more enigmatical. At one time the king seemed to expect the armed coöperation of France. At another he laid more stress upon the importance of his own measures ; it is for the young people, he said, first to join the dance. That is true, Fleury cautiously replied, but, as the ball is chiefly for the benefit of the young people, there ought to be some security that they will not in the end leave others to pay the piper.[2] It is indeed to the credit of the cardinal's penetration that he was profoundly suspicious of Frederic's good faith, and, though bewildered, was not deceived. He was ignorant, too, of the fact that, while the king was announcing his loyal devotion to France, he was at the same time writing in just the opposite sense to George the Second.[3]

The position of England was indeed a trying one. There could be no doubt that her interest, not less than her pledges, required her to support the imperilled cause of Maria Theresa. But under Walpole's cautious guidance, and in spite of the growing impatience

Frederic and Fleury.

England and Holland.

[1] Broglie, *Fr. II. et M. T.*, i. 177–184 ; Marquis d'Argenson, *Mémoires et journal inédits*, ed. 16mo, Paris, 1857, 1858, vol. ii. p. 382.

[2] Broglie, ubi supra, i. 187.

[3] See the new instructions to Truchsess, *Pol. Cor.*, i. 140, 141.

of the public, she seemed resolved to interpret those pledges in the narrowest sense, and to fulfil them by an officious diplomacy rather than by positive military measures.[1] She shrank from a policy which would give France a pretext for intervening. Yet she was required by prudence to take precautions, either political or military, or both, against such intervention whenever it should be threatened. This was the problem of English diplomacy at the present stage of affairs. Walpole hesitated to grapple with it, except indirectly through the aid of Holland. The States-General were invited to join in addressing a protest to Frederic against the invasion of Silesia, with the threat that the further prosecution of the enterprise would be opposed by force, as the pragmatic treaties required. But to support this protest only Dutch troops were suggested by the British envoy at the Hague. England herself offered none; and as it soon appeared that even the Dutch contingent was intended mainly for the defence of Hanover, the States-General, feeling perfectly safe on the side of Prussia, but fearful of compromising themselves with France, naturally hesitated to embrace such an unequal bargain.[2] Thus Walpole wasted precious time in negotiations with Holland, while the fact that if Silesia were to be saved it would have to be saved at once stared him relentlessly in the face. For every hour was tightening Frederic's grasp on his prey.

It was found impossible, on account of the want of heavy guns, to undertake the siege of Glogau, and prince

[1] Robinson's new credentials authorized him to offer England's aid to fight Prussia, or her good offices for an accommodation, but he was to express no preference for either course. Harrington to Robinson, 27 February, 1741. A little later, when the purposes of France became clear, the English government became more urgent for the scheme of pacifying Frederic by the cession of Austrian territory. H. to R., 5 March, 17 April, 1741. Hardwicke MSS., vol. 78.

[2] Cf. A. Beer, *Holland und der oesterreichische Erfolge-Krieg*, Vienna, 1871, pp. 6 et seq.

Leopold the younger, of Dessau, was hurried up with the reserves, which simply drew a blockade about the town. Frederic then set out for Breslau; on the last day of December he was at the gates of the city. This opportune arrival prevented the removal of the funds and archives, which were already packed and awaiting transportation when the Prussian cavalry appeared in the suburbs; and it enabled the king also to suppress the Austrian civil government at an early stage of his enterprise. The representatives of the queen had labored in vain against the jealousy or the disaffection of the city. The magistracy was timid, the guilds obstinate, the Protestant burghers positively hostile. Obstacles were thrown in the way of every project, whether of defence or of flight; and now it was too late for either the one or the other.

On arriving in the outskirts Frederic sent two officers into the town with reassuring explanations to the magistrates. He came, it was declared, as Breslau. a friend, willing to respect all the rights of the city, to occupy with his troops only the suburbs, and to make his entry without other escort than that of thirty gendarmes. Further negotiations on this basis led to the conclusion of a formal agreement, a treaty for the neutrality, as it were, of Breslau. The city pledged itself not to admit the armed forces of any other power within its walls, and to give no aid to the Austrians. The king on his part promised to commit no act of hostility; to leave in the suburbs only a single battalion to guard a dépôt of supplies; to suffer the ordinary traffic of the citizens to go on undisturbed; and in general to respect all of the rights and privileges which the city had enjoyed under Austrian rule.[1] While these negotiations were in progress, the so-called cathedral island, which belonged to the archbishop of Breslau, and was not within the jurisdiction of the city, was seized without opposition by a small force of

[1] Olenschlager, i. 288–290.

Prussians. The agreement was signed on the third of January. The king then took up his quarters in the city, where by frequent entertainments and a politic affability he made a favorable impression on the Protestant citizens, and even on some members of the Catholic nobility. But count Schaffgotsch, the civil governor of Silesia, and his colleagues in the executive board, were required to leave Breslau within twenty-four hours.

The rest of the month of January was spent by the Prussians in completing the occupation of the province. Detachments of troops shot out in all directions; one after another the smaller towns were taken; Schwerin pushed Browne through the passes of Upper Silesia into Moravia; and by the end of the month little except the fortresses of Glogau, Brieg, and Neisse remained in the hands of the Austrians. The army then went into winter quarters, under the command of Schwerin, and the king returned on the twenty-ninth of January to Berlin.

Podewils had become uneasy about the diplomatic situation. France had offered, if Frederic would give his vote, which he himself had lately said was in the market,[1] to the elector of Bavaria in the coming election of emperor, to recognize any just claims which he might assert to Silesia;[2] but there was no mention of armed assistance, and Podewils doubted whether it could be expected. This was clearly insufficient. But the minister also regarded the Russian treaty as a frail support, and saw no escape except in the joint mediation of Russia and England, which the king would have to facilitate by lowering his demands.[3]

---

[1] Valori, 12 December, 1740.

[2] Amelot, French minister of foreign affairs, to Valori, 5 January, 1741, in Broglie, *Fr. II. et M. T.*, i. 188, 189. Cf. Droysen, V. i. 208. The date, 14 January, given by Ranke, xxvii., xxviii. 575, must be incorrect.

[3] Droysen, V. i. 204.

The day after his arrival at Berlin, Frederic received Guy Dickens, and addressed him in the style More diplomacy. of a stage tragedian. He would perish, he declared, rather than give up his undertaking. The other powers need not imagine that he was to be shaken by threats. Whoever believed that, or even thought of measures against him, would learn that he was ready to give the first blow ; at the worst he would throw himself into the arms of France, fight and bite in all directions, and ruin everything about him.[1] All this was, however, intended only to give secondary emphasis to a letter which he wrote, in a much milder tone, to king George himself. The letter contained an offer of an alliance ; dwelt upon the tyranny of the Catholics in Silesia, and the community of interests which ought to unite the two great Protestant powers ; and professed an intention to retain only that part of the province, to which the house of Prussia had a legal title.[2] Valori, who had likewise his audience, received in the same manner blows with one hand and caresses with the other. The king spoke much of his rights in Silesia. The envoy invited him to indicate more clearly what those rights were ; and, receiving an evasive answer, inquired whether Prussia's best arguments were not thirty twenty-four pounders and fifteen mortars, just ready to leave the arsenal. "In truth," replied the king, "they will prove more cogent than all the others." [3]

In spite, however, of Podewil's aversion to a French alliance, and the king's own prevarication, the force of events drove Prussia rapidly in that direction, and France had gone too far to retreat. Frederic had early offered

[1] Raumer, *Beiträge*, ii. 107.

[2] Frederic to George II., 30 January, 1741. The most significant part was the postscript : "J'ai oublié de l'informer que j'ai conclu une alliance avec la Russie." Grünhagen, i. 325, takes this letter seriously. Cf. Raumer, *Beiträge*, ii. 110.

[3] Broglie, *Fr. II. et M. T.*, i. 202.

to waive his claim to Jülich-Berg, in order at once to satisfy France, and to secure the vote of the elector palatine for Charles Albert. In February the cardinal proposed to support the candidature of this prince otherwise than diplomatically, and to guarantee the king's claims to Lower Silesia.[1] At the same time he was replying to the appeals of Maria Theresa with vague compliments, which evaded the point at issue, and were offensive to her self-respect.[2]

On the nineteenth of February Frederic returned to the army in Silesia, where his presence was urgently needed. The occupation of the province had been easy; but its government, after the occupation, proved more difficult.

In Silesia, as in other territories where the attempt had been made to reconcile the process of central-ization with respect for the principles of local self-government, two parallel sets of functionaries ran through the whole scale of administration. One of these represented the estates; the other, the crown. The general diet voted the extraordinary taxes each year, and assigned its quota to every county or circle. The assessment and collection in the several counties was in the hands of local officials. A permanent committee of the estates, the "conventus publicus," sat at Breslau as an organ of communication between the province and the crown officials, who likewise formed a hierarchical scale, ending at the summit in the supreme governing board.[3] But when this board with its president was expelled from Breslau, it became necessary to substitute a new central organ, which should represent the Prussian, as the board

Administration of Silesia.

[1] Amelot to Valori, 20 February, 1741.

[2] Thus, when Maria Theresa urged that the grand-duke, in order to obtain the French guaranty of the pragmatic sanction, had sacrificed Lorraine, Fleury replied, "Il en est bien récompensé par le bonheur de posséder votre majesté."

[3] Oberamt.

had represented the Bohemian crown. The part was intrusted temporarily to the field-commissariat, at the head of which stood two energetic officials, Münchow and Rheinhardt. The rest of the system was left undisturbed, in the hope, apparently, that it would fall easily into the new order of things.

This hope proved, however, in part delusive. The public committee, which included delegates from all the counties of the province, and in which the Prussian methods. Catholic nobility had a controlling influence, was attached to the house of Austria, and, jealous of the local liberties, undertook for a time to guard the interests of both against the invader. Münchow and Rheinhardt called for a statement of the funds in the treasury, and gave notice that no further payments were to be made to the queen of Bohemia. The conventus replied that the funds belonged to the province, not to Bohemia, and put the seals on them. The Prussian officials next inquired what had been the average monthly receipts of the queen from the permanent revenues, and the annual subsidies. When an answer was refused, they made their own estimate, which was 191,000 thalers. An order was then issued by the king that all the existing taxes, direct and indirect, should continue to be levied, and paid into the treasury for the support of the Prussian army.[1] But the committee refused to coöperate, and its refusal threatened to paralyze the whole scheme. Constitutionally, its attitude was strictly correct. It urged that the special taxes voted for the previous year had already been collected ; that none had been voted for 1741 ; that even the administration of the excise, and other indirect tributes, was subject to the annual approval of the diet ; and that a diet could be lawfully summoned only by the lord of the land, the queen of Bohemia.

Schwerin tried to solve the problem in military fashion

1 Olenschlager, i. 296, 297 ; *Heldengeschichte*, i. 494.

by flinging Sala von Grossa, the leader of the opposition,
into jail. The king declared in a second order that the
191,000 thalers must be levied punctually, and warrants
for the collection of the arrears for January and February
be issued within twenty-four hours, or the field commissariat would levy military execution on the property of
delinquents. Still the members of the conventus insisted
on their helplessness. The king himself finally arrived,
and repeated these demands to a deputation which waited
upon him. Another Silesian official, count Proskau, was
banished the city. But the case was prolonged on one
pretext or another for several months; and revealed some
difficulties which Frederic had perhaps not foreseen. Attachment to the house of Austria he had expected to meet.
But the constitutional resistance of officials, who had the
liberties of their country to defend, and were accountable
to their fellow-citizens for the manner in which they fulfilled the trust, was a phenomenon with which his Prussian experience had not made him familiar. It is due,
however, to the king, to say not only that having occupied
the country he was undoubtedly entitled, pending the decision by arms, to its revenues, but also that he showed as
much forbearance as was compatible with the assertion of
this right. He was too wise needlessly to irritate, much
more by heavy exactions to impoverish, a province, which
he hoped to incorporate into the Prussian state.

The problem of settling the government of the invaded
province was no sooner solved than the king's at-
Schemes
against tention was called to a new and far more serious
Prussia.
one, which not only imperilled his recent conquests, but even threatened the safety and integrity of his
inherited possessions. This was the projected treaty of
partition between Austria, England, Holland, Saxony, and
Russia. The authors of the scheme proposed to apply to
Prussia the policy which Frederic had applied to Austria.
The project was communicated to Mardefeld by mar-

shal Münnich,[1] but evidently was not quite understood by
Frederic and Podewils. They regarded it as originating
with Saxony, and supposed that the adhesion of Russia
awaited only that of England.[2] But papers which were
submitted to parliament the following year showed that
the English ministers themselves were the authors,[3] and
that only Russia stood between Frederic and disaster. It
is now a question of no practical importance how great the
danger actually was ; it is enough that the king at least
took it seriously. The treason of Russia, he wrote to Podewils, was appalling. If later reports should agree with
those which had just been received, it would be necessary
to accept the French alliance at once. And then, let them
put on their armor with firmness, fight like heroes, conquer with prudence, and sustain adversity like stoics.
He had done what he could for the public tranquillity, and
it was his enemies who disturbed it. But whatever might
happen, he would at least have the satisfaction of overthrowing the house of Austria and ruining Saxony.[4] In
view of the crisis Frederic engaged the queen to write in
behalf of Prussia to her brother, Anthony Ulric, the husband of the regent Anna of Russia.[5] This was the moment,
he afterwards wrote, which the court of Vienna ought to
have seized for an accommodation with him. He would
then have been contented with the duchy of Glogau.[6]
It does not appear that any intimation to that effect was

[1] Podewils and Borcke to Frederic, 21 March, 1741.

[2] Frederic to Leopold of Dessau, 17 March ; to Podewils, 24
March, 1741.

[3] See the exhortations addressed by George II. to the Saxon envoy, in Grünhagen, i. 275, 276, and p. 309 n., the result of the same
writer's search for the author of the project. He attributes it to
Villiers, the English envoy at Dresden. The text, Ibid. pp. 310, 311,
or Adelung, ii. 273–277.

[4] Frederic to Podewils, 17 March, 1741 ; cf. same to same, 18 and
24 March.

[5] Frederic to Podewils, 18 March, 1741.

[6] Œuvres de Frédéric, ii. 66.

conveyed to Maria Theresa; but the observation of Frederic shows that he was blind to the real grandeur of the queen's position, since he refused to see that she was contending for a principle, and not for the possession of a paltry bailiwick more or less.

How far the English ministers were serious in this projected treaty of partition, or, more generally, in all their schemes for a forcible intervention against Prussia, will probably always remain one of the unsolved problems of history. I shall therefore make no attempt to solve it. But two considerations, which have the merit of reasonableness rather than of novelty, will, if accepted and kept in Policy of mind by the reader, afford a partial clue to the England. mysteries of English politics during this period, and serve to interpret the successive phases in the diplomatic campaign.

The first of these is that throughout the entire reign of George II. the interests of Hanover were a living and aggressive force in all the issues of cabinet strife at London. Ministers and ministries were distinguished by the degree to which they were willing that the policy of George's kingdom should be subservient to the policy of his electorate. The policy of his electorate, too, was his own. It was indeed influenced to some extent by privy councillors, who gained his confidence by flattering his vanity, or paying court to his female favorites; but it was not controlled by any parliament, or even by any effective public opinion. In respect to Prussia, it was undoubtedly hostile. The source of this hostility may be sought in the king's personal dislike of his Berlin relatives, or in the weak ambition of his Hanoverian counsellors, or in sincere distrust of an enterprising neighbor; the fact, I think, cannot be denied. This feeling would again be communicated necessarily to English statesmen, and would affect some of them more, some of them less. Walpole and Harrington, for instance, were not ac-

counted extravagant partisans of the king's Hanoverian
policy. But even they probably yielded their own convictions more than once to the wishes of their sovereign;
and the plan of the partition treaty may have been
adopted by them in this spirit, without any expectation
that it would succeed, or any intention to support it with
much vigor.

The other reflection is that the English ministers were
only observing the rules of common prudence when they
endeavored to provide alternative lines of escape from
the danger which confronted them. This danger was the
weakening of the house of Austria to such an extent
that the balance of power, and the independence of
Europe, would be destroyed. To meet this danger two
expedients offered themselves. The one was a combination between England, Austria, Russia, Hanover, and
Saxony, which should compel Frederic to withdraw from
Silesia, curb the rising ambition of Spain and Bavaria,
and thwart by anticipation any hostile purpose of France.
The other line of conduct was to urge an accommodation between Austria and Prussia, which would involve
indeed the loss of one of the queen's provinces. But it
would gain her a powerful ally, would make it possible to
oppose a strong front to all her other enemies, and probably to save the rest of her patrimony unimpaired. It
was therefore not inconsistent, or at least not contrary
to the practice of European diplomacy, for the English
statesmen to hold one of these policies in reserve, while
pushing at any time the other.[1] But it would be rash to
say positively which of these two plans the English ministers really preferred. Early in the year they invited
the queen herself to choose, and promised to coöperate
loyally in support of either.[2] Maria Theresa naturally
preferred the first method, which the projected treaty of

[1] See Harrington to Robinson, 3 April, 1741, in Adelung, ii. 296.
[2] Same to same, 27 February, 1741, Hardwicke MSS. vol. lxviii.

partition undertook to carry into effect. But the hesitation of Russia, the menacing attitude of France, and
orders of Frederic to the Old Dessauer, soon began to
incline the English cabinet more and more strongly
toward the second plan ; and in March their diplomatic
measures turned actively in that direction.[1]

The suspicious conduct of his neighbors had decided

Second
Prussian
army.

Frederic to draw together an army of observation at a point where it could act either upon
Saxony or upon Hanover, as circumstances
might require. Leopold of Dessau was ordered to hold
himself in readiness for this duty when the emergency
should arrive.[2]

Whatever might be the chances of the coalition, there
was no doubt in regard to the intentions of Austria.
The zealous efforts of the English diplomatists had not

Austrian
preparations.

succeeded in obtaining the slightest concession
from the queen ; and the combined resources of
herself, and the allies in whom she confidently trusted,
were thought to be sufficient to meet all danger. The
discrepancy between the real and the nominal strength of
her own army was indeed alarming. Instead of one
hundred and thirty-five thousand men left, according to
the official records, by her father, not more than half
the number were actually under arms, and these were
dispersed throughout the widely separated territories of
Austria.[3] The troops to be given by her allies were as

[1] Same to same, 5 March, 17 April, 1741.

[2] "Sollten die Sachsen in Böhmen marschiren um den Oesterreichern
gegen seine königliche Majestät zu assistiren, oder aber wenn sich
gewisse Apparence zeigt, dass die Sachsen mit den Hannöverischen
Truppen sich conjungiren wollen, so haben seine Liebden alsdann
allererst wider solche zu agiren, den schwächern Theil von Ihnen zu
attaquiren." — Instruction für den Fürsten von Anhalt, 12 February,
1741.

[3] A Wolf, *Oesterreich unter Maria Theresia*, Vienna, 1855, pp. 33,
55.

yet only the creations of a sanguine fancy. Hesse-Cassel was to furnish three thousand; Saxe-Coburg and the bishop of Würzburg were reckoned for their shares; George the Second would contribute the Danish and Hessian regiments which he had in the pay of England, and six thousand, besides, as elector of Hanover; Saxony would even exceed her stipulated quota; and, Russia being secured, even the Poles would take the field.[1] These were wild speculations, which could not fully have deceived even the queen herself. But she acted promptly, nevertheless, with such means as she could command. It early became known to Frederic that she was forming an army for the relief of the Silesian garrisons, and the expulsion of the invaders.

The command of this army was intrusted to count von Neipperg, one of the unfortunate generals of the Turkish war. He was no inexperienced soldier, for he had served since the year 1702, when he was a youth of eighteen years, in the Austrian army; and, like so many of his colleagues, boasted that he had learned the art of war under Eugene of Savoy. But he subsequently showed that the mantle of his master had not fallen upon him. His part in the disgraceful peace of Belgrade caused him to be included in the sweeping arrest of Austrian generals, by which the emperor Charles the Sixth hoped to divert attention from his own mistakes; but on the accession of Maria Theresa he was released from prison, and restored to active service. The favor of the grand-duke Francis secured him the command of the army of Silesia.[2] He was a soldier of the old school, formal, obstinate, pedantic; with a narrow mental range, and little control of circumstances; but brave, unselfish, and of undoubted devotion. If he entered upon his new

Marshal Neipperg.

---

[1] Austrian declaration at the Hague, winter of 1740–41. Beer, *Holland*, pp. 4, 5.

[2] Cogniazo, ii. 39.

duty with insufficient respect for his adversary, he had much to encourage him in the hope that he would be able, by rendering his mistress an opportune service, to efface the stigma upon his military reputation.

These preparations made it necessary for the Prussians, in order to be in a position to meet the danger, to secure the mountain passes, to capture Glogau, and to concentrate their forces.

There were a number of openings through the Giant Mountains, by which an army could make its way from Bohemia, Moravia, or Hungary into Silesia ; but one of these has now a peculiar interest as the scene of Frederic's narrow escape from capture by the Austrians. This was the Wartha pass, nearly due south from Breslau, and leading, by the fortress of Glatz, directly into Bohemia. The king, on a tour of inspection in the region, stopped for dinner, on the twenty-seventh of February, at the little hamlet of Wartha. He had only a small escort of one hundred and fifty dragoons, but the country was patrolled by active bands of Austrian cavalry, on the search for illustrious prey ; and during the royal repast a body of them suddenly appeared in the neighborhood. The king had barely time to mount and escape, while the dragoons, with the loss of several men, covered his hasty flight.[1]

Frederic in personal danger.

The Wartha pass was thus evidently in possession of the enemy ; the Austrian general Lentulus had in fact occupied it some time before, and now held it with a considerable force. It soon appeared, too, that the other passes were no better guarded by the Prussians, whose unpardonable negligence nearly ruined the whole enterprise.

That part of the king's programme which included the capture of Glogau was brilliantly executed. The military significance of this post lay in its proximity to the Prussian frontier, for, being thus in rear of Frederic's main force,

[1] Arneth, i. 151–155 ; Grünhagen, i. 166.

it might prove dangerous in case of any reverse in the field. It was still blockaded by five thousand men under the younger Leopold of Dessau.

This officer, whom, to distinguish from his father, the Old Dessauer, I shall call simply prince Leo- pold, was, under Frederic, the second in command Prince Leo- pold of in the army of invasion. Only Schwerin ranked Dessau. higher. But between Schwerin and Leopold no good feeling prevailed, and for this the latter must be held chiefly at fault. Schwerin was a bright, cheery, dashing soldier, without fear and without envy, chiefly anxious to be nearest the foe on the field of battle ; while Leopold was haughty, jealous, quarrelsome, not less stubborn than his father, and like him angry at the precedence given to one whom he regarded as a military adventurer. Nor was Schwerin the only, though he was the principal, comrade with whom Leopold had disputes and quarrels. His un- happy temper made him a constant source of discord in the army ; aroused much ill-feeling ; tried the patience of Frederic in many ways. But he was a soldier of un- doubted capacity, and had the fighting qualities which long distinguished the house of Anhalt-Dessau.

Early in March the king became impatient at the delay before Glogau, and sent somewhat vague orders Capture of to the prince for a prompt solution of the prob- Glogau. lem. The evening of the seventh brought a positive order to attempt the place by surprise, and carry it sword in hand. Leopold had demanded only one day for prep- aration. The eighth was, therefore, spent in fixing the details of the plan, which in the course of the day was re- duced to the most exact precision. Three simultaneous attacks were to be made by as many different detachments. One column was to advance along the banks of the Oder from below, another from above, while the third assault was to be between these two, and at right angles to the river. At eight o'clock in the evening the three detach-

ments formed in line ; at ten they marched quietly to their
rendezvous ; at twelve, as the strokes of the great clock in
Glogau pealed out through the silent night, the Prussians
swept in upon the works. The pioneers easily hewed
breaches in the palisades, and the grenadiers — prince
Leopold himself at the head of one party — then scaled
the icy glacis, overpowered the sentries, and stood before
the inner walls of the town itself. These offered but
little resistance. Axes and petards soon levelled the gates ;
and in spite of the force which Wallis hastily collected,
the Prussians fought their way through, and were soon
masters of the place. In an hour the work was done.
The garrison surrendered at discretion, and the Prussian
flag was hoisted on the ramparts.[1]

This brilliant achievement set free the blockading forces,
and Leopold, leaving only a battalion in Glogau, set out
promptly with the rest for Schweidnitz. At Schweidnitz
there was good company. Algarotti, Maupertuis, Jordan,
and others had run down from Berlin to get a taste of
military life in Silesia, and entertain the young monarch
with verses, metaphysics, and flattery. But Leopold's
arrival was the signal for the close of the festivities. All
of the literary friends except Maupertuis prudently fled to
Breslau. The diplomatic not less than the military outlook made it necessary now to take earnestly in hand the
work of concentration.

At St. Petersburg the aspect of affairs was daily growing more sombre, and gave rise to the liveliest
solicitude. The marquis Botta, on leaving
Berlin, had been sent to the Russian capital in
the interests of Maria Theresa ; and as he was known to
have strong social connections at that court, and to be
skilled in the art of intrigue, his efforts were watched by
Frederic with a degree of anxiety, which was not much

Affairs at
St. Peters-
burg.

[1] Orlich, i. 71–75, has the fullest account. But cf. Arneth, i. 157,
Droysen, V. i. 220, and Grünhagen, i. 168, 169.

lessened by the temporary success of Winterfeld's mission. Botta had the support of count Lynar, the envoy of August III. and a favored friend of the regent. Only the frail tenure of Münnich's influence seemed to stand between Frederic and the catastrophe which his enemies had prepared for him; and early in March the field-marshal, struggling to the last, was driven from office by his enemies.[1] Podewils gave a cry of anguish and despair. "Pandora's box is open," wrote he; "we are entering into the most fearful crisis that has ever confronted the house of Brandenburg." Nothing was left, in his judgment, except an alliance with France. Yet this was itself perilous, he thought, since the only object of France was to cut Germany up into small morsels, which she could swallow one after another, Prussia being reserved by Polyphemus for the last.[2]

Pandora and Polyphemus! When Podewils was excited, he became a pagan, and took refuge in mythology. Yet it appears that he greatly overestimated the importance of Münnich's fall. His enemies were apparently frightened by the construction put upon their triumph, while Ostermann, who now became chief minister and was a Prussian by birth, hastened to give friendly assurances, for which he had perhaps already been rewarded from the royal bounty.[3] The very event, besides, which seemed to make Russia's adhesion to the partition treaty possible, made it also harmless. Münnich was the only

[1] "His subservient attitude toward Prussia was incorrigible, although I often made known to him my fixed determination to support the queen, Maria Theresa." — The regent Anna to count Lynar, 24 March, 1741, in Herrmann, *Geschichte des russischen Staats*, Hamburg, 1849, iv. 666. Cf. Manstein, ii. 117.

[2] Droysen, V. i. 224, 225.

[3] See *Polit. Corresp.*, i. 223, 226, where Mardefeld is directly ordered to bribe Ostermann. Grünhagen, i. 288, quotes a statement that 100,000 thalers was placed at his disposition for this purpose.

Russian general who possessed the confidence of the army; and the discontent, the relaxed discipline, the enervation, which now set in, formed a useful though negative pledge of peace.

The lesson of the crisis seemed to teach both Podewils and the king the necessity of a prompt alliance with France. Valori was even invited to the camp in Silesia, and returned to Berlin with what he supposed was a definite pledge on the part of Frederic to accept a treaty substantially like the draft which he had submitted. But more favorable reports from London led to renewed overtures in that direction. Frederic wrote to his envoy urging him to use every effort to detach Great Britain from the cabal, and secure the mediation of George II. for Prussia. He was authorized to protest that up to that time the king's hands were free; he had concluded no alliance with France.[1] And, that greater emphasis might be given to these representations, the Old Dessauer was ordered to begin the task which had been assigned to him. On the second of April he led twenty-six thousand men into camp at Göttin.[2] His outposts were pushed close up to the Saxon frontier.

In Silesia the military movements were guided by an extraordinary infatuation. The policy of detached camps, distributed over a wide area, had been adopted on the advice of Schwerin, and against the protest of the Old Dessauer. It was contrary, Leopold urged, to all the rules of military science; if an Austrian army should break through into the province the feeble Prussian detachments would be swept up one after another, and the campaign be ended in a week. But Schwerin ridiculed these counsels as the fears of a pedant, and the isolated cantonments were kept up until the end of March. Then a concentration was ordered. But it was

The military situation.

---

[1] Frederic to Truchsess, 24 March, 1741.
[2] The figures of Grünhagen, q. v., i. 258.

finally made in a manner not foreseen in the king's plans, and far more suddenly than he had intended.

The immediate object was the siege of Neisse, the strongest of the Silesian fortresses. It was situated on the river of the same name, which a short distance above the town makes an abrupt bend, and thence flows nearly due north toward the Oder. The commandant was colonel Roth, a stout-hearted Protestant soldier. Up to this time the Prussians had only blockaded the place, but it was now determined to begin a regular siege. The conduct of the siege was entrusted to one of Frederic's old military tutors, general Kalkstein, who was at Grottkau with ten thousand men, while the heavy guns were at Ohlau, awaiting transportation. It was arranged that the investment should begin on the fourth of April. The duke of Holstein-Beck had five thousand men at Frankenstein, with which he was expected to cover the operations of the siege on that side. Schwerin himself was to be the main security against interference from the southeast, that is by Neipperg, if he should attempt to enter with his army through the passes of Upper Silesia. But Schwerin's forces were dispersed over the country, in Cosel, Troppau, Ratibor, and other towns. At last Frederic decided that they must be concentrated, and kept well in hand, at a single point. Jägerndorf was chosen for the rendezvous; and thither the king resolved to proceed in person in the course of a tour of inspection among the leading miltary posts.

On the thirtieth of March Frederic was at Neustadt, whither Schwerin went to meet him. Interrogated about Neipperg, the marshal confessed that he had no sure information, but believed *The Austrians enter Silesia.* that he was yet in camp at or near Olmütz;[1] a scout whom he had sent out would soon return with nearer intelligence. With a part of the force which he had

[1] Frederic to Leopold of Dessau, 11 April, 1741.

brought to Neustadt for the purpose of covering Schwerin's concentration, Frederic continued, in the company of the marshal, to Jägerndorf. Here on the second of April they received startling news. Deserters from an Austrian regiment of dragoons reported that they had left Neipperg's army in Freudenthal; that it consisted of over twenty thousand men; and that it was on the way to Neisse.[1] The sharp rattle of musketry, which at the same moment began to echo through the wild Jägerndorf valleys, confirmed the story, and even increased the alarm; an attack on Jägerndorf itself was feared, and the Prussians had there only some three thousand men. But Neipperg had merely sent out small detachments to feel the enemy, while he himself with the main force continued his march.

The Austrians were thus in Silesia. While Schwerin was lying at the mouth of the main pass, and sending out scouts who never returned, Neipperg had taken a parallel course, some ten miles farther toward the northwest; and by strenuous efforts had led his army over icy roads, and through narrow defiles, into the very heart of the province. By that act he also separated the two main sections of the Prussian army. One section was east of the river Neisse, one west; and Neipperg was swiftly driving himself like a wedge between them.

Orders were at once sent to the several Prussian commanders, to Kalkstein, to Marwitz at Schweidnitz, to the duke of Holstein at Frankenstein, to Kleist at Brieg, to Gessler at Ohlau, to join Schwerin's corps, which was hastily collected, and on the fourth of April put in motion, under the king's command, for Neisse. This nucleus consisted of some eight thousand men. The next day Kalkstein came in at Steinau,[2] and

Concentration of the Prussian forces.

[1] Orlich, i. 88.

[2] Droyson, V. i. 234, represents Kalkstein as being at Grottkau when the order to concentrate was sent. But could an order sent on the second have brought him and his army to Steinau on the fifth?

the united forces then struck across to Sorgau, where it was hoped to make the passage of the Neisse. But here, to their dismay, the Prussians found a heavy force of hostile cavalry, and learned that general Lentulus, marching in from Bohemia by way of Königgrätz and Glatz, had effected a junction with Neipperg. Baffled at Sorgau, the Prussians hastened down the river. At Löwen the king with the main army crossed without difficulty, while prince Leopold with a smaller division had to build a pontoon bridge at Michelau. The two wings were then reunited on the west bank, where Kleist and Marwitz also joined; and the next day, the ninth, a furious snow-storm, and the exhaustion of the troops after their trying marches, made a short rest indispensable. Quarters were found in the line of villages from Michelau to Pogrell.

The Prussian movements, which were resumed on the tenth, had to be made with the greatest circumspection. It was known that Grottkau had fallen, and that the enemy thus cut off the duke of Holstein, established direct connection with the garrison of Brieg, threatened Ohlau, where the siege artillery and a large supply of provisions were stored, and barred the way to Breslau and Berlin. The strategy of the Austrians was admirable, and if their movements had been more rapid they would effectually have prevented the concentration of the Prussian forces. But they were too late for that, and could now only force Frederic to accept battle in circumstances which seemed to be not unfavorable to themselves.

On the tenth, then, the Prussians cautiously continued their retreat. The detachment of horse, which The enemy was pushed out in advance under command of overtaken. colonel Rothenburg to clear the way, had frequent skirmishes with the pandours and other irregular cavalry in the Austrian service; but the movements of Neipperg's main force were wrapped in mystery, and his strength was only vaguely known. Toward noon, however, Rothenburg struck a considerable body of hostile hussars, and learned from the prisoners, who were captured in the smart fight which ensued, that Neipperg with his whole army was at and about the village of Mollwitz, a short distance ahead. But Rothenburg's orders were not to precipitate a general engagement, and he returned with his news to the Prussian headquarters, which he found near the little hamlet of Pampitz.

On receipt of this report the army was again put in

Prussian
order
of battle. motion, and directly toward Mollwitz. About one thousand yards from the village it began to form in order of battle. The first line was to consist of twenty battalions of infantry in the centre, and ten squadrons of cavalry on either wing, and the second to have in all eleven battalions and ten squadrons. The king took position on the right, Schwerin on the left, while prince Leopold had the second line. It was proposed to have the front extend from the village of Hermsdorf to the Laugwitz brook. Each Prussian regiment of foot had two field-pieces; and the king, imitating a device of Gustavus Adolphus, stationed some companies of grenadiers between the squadrons of cavalry. The whole force numbered about twenty-two thousand men. In cavalry it was greatly inferior to the enemy, but in infantry and artillery far superior; and the advantage of aggregate numbers was slightly on the side of the Prussians.[1]

The army of Neipperg had halted for its noonday rest

The Austrian
formation. and dinner. It was on the way to Ohlau, and, in total ignorance of the approach of the Prussians, was formed, of course, with its front toward the northwest. The tardy report of the scouts that the enemy was in the immediate neighborhood made necesary, there-

[1] Grünhagen, i. 180, gives the total strength of the Prussians at 22,440, and that of the Austrians at 22,160.

fore, a sudden and total change of formation. But the
marshal was a good though somewhat pedantic tactician,
and an order of battle was adopted on the usual plan,
infantry in the centre and cavalry on each wing of the
first line, and a second, shorter line at the proper distance
in the rear. General Römer had the cavalry on the left,
and count Berlichingen on the right.

While the Austrians were thus forming for defence,
the Prussians advanced steadily, firmly, with
music playing and flags flying, to the attack.
As soon as they came within range, the artillery
opened the battle. Its effective fire interfered with the
Austrian formation, and inflicted heavy losses; but the
regiments continued to fall into place one after another
with admirable order, and Römer's squadrons defiantly
faced the Prussian right. This part of Frederic's line
was in an unsatisfactory condition. General Schulenburg, whose extreme right ought to have touched the
village of Hermsdorf, had miscalculated the distance, and
now, in the face of the enemy, attempted to correct his
error and redress his line. This caused, of course, a
momentary confusion, and Römer, whose men were besides impatient under the galling fire of the Prussian
artillery, hastened to take advantage of it. He gave the
order to charge. In an instant his magnificent cavalry
fell like a torrent upon Schulenburg, doubled his dragoons
up, and swept them in complete disorder from the field.
The intercalated grenadiers alone held their ground as
the storm swept over them, and in good order rejoined
their colleagues of the foot. At the other end of the line
Berlichingen had charged with equal effect, and there
also the Prussian cavalry was thrown into disorder. But
in both parts of the field the infantry arrested the victorious onset. Against this solid wall the Austrian horse
charged over and over again without making any serious
impression. Römer himself was killed, then his second

Battle of Mollwitz, 10 April, 1741.

in command; some of his squadrons captured the Prussian guns, which were far in advance of the first line; others fought their way between the first and second lines, and actually rejoined their own army at the opposite end to that from which they had set out.

The Austrians had thus far failed to break the Prussian infantry line. But they had ruined the Prussian cavalry, and their own infantry, which had not as yet been seriously engaged, was now preparing to advance. Among the Prussian officers there were many who regarded the day as lost, and awaited orders for a retreat. One circumstance disturbed even Schwerin himself. As detachments of Römer's dragoons dashed between the two Prussian lines, the infantry of the second line had fired without orders, and of course through the hostile horse into the rear of their own comrades of the first line. This was a symptom of demoralization which Schwerin had not expected from the well-trained Prussian foot; and it led him to expect the worst consequences from the next onslaught of the enemy. As a precaution, therefore, against disaster, and in order to have his own hands free, he urged the king to leave the field, and put himself beyond the reach of danger. Fortunately for Prussia this wholesome advice was followed.

Relieved of all care for the king's person, Schwerin at once made his dispositions to win the battle. He sent notice to Leopold that the king had left him in command, and that he would be obliged if the prince would prevent his troops of the second line from firing into those of the front, to which caustic message Leopold returned a somewhat defiant reply, but promised at the same time to do his duty.[1] The field-marshal then rode along the line, and addressed spirited exhortations to his infantry, on whom the fortunes

Final charge of the Prussians.

[1] Grünhagen, i. 187, 188 ; Varnhagen v. Ense, *Ausgewählte Schriften,* xii. 188, 189.

of the day in the last supreme trial now depended. For
Neipperg had finally formed his foot, and prepared to
follow up the advantage which his cavalry had gained,
by a final and decisive advance along the whole line.
But in an infantry fight the Prussians had all the advantage of discipline, weapons, and rapid firing. The murderous volleys which met the Austrians threw them into
confusion; they wavered; and at this critical moment
Schwerin ordered a counter advance of the whole Prussian force, which, in magnificent order, with the steadiness and precision of the parade-ground, pressed forward
against the foe. The Austrian officers were lost in admiration of this impressive charge. But their regiments,
not attracted by such an ominous military spectacle, refused even to look it in the face, and Neipperg saw himself forced to order a retreat while it could be effected in
good order. By eight o'clock the Prussians were masters
of the ground. But the darkness of the night, the demoralization of their cavalry, and the opposition of prince
Leopold made a pursuit impossible. The Austrians retired undisturbed to Grottkau, and thence to Neisse, where
they found shelter under the guns of the fortress.

The losses in this desperate battle were nearly equal,
or about four thousand five hundred killed,
wounded, and prisoners on each side. The Aus-   The losses.
trians lost two generals, Römer and Goldy; Neipperg
himself was wounded. Among the Prussian killed were
the margrave Frederic of Schwedt, the king's cousin,
count Finkenstein, son of his old tutor, and general Schulenburg, the dragoon commander, who by a soldier's death
expiated the unfortunate error of formation which had so
nearly lost the day. Schwerin himself was wounded, like
Neipperg, and in the hour of victory had to turn over
the command to prince Leopold.[1]

[1] The success of the Prussians is generally ascribed in part to
their iron ramrods, which enabled them to load and thus to fire more

An illustrious prisoner whom the Austrians took was
Maupertuis. He had rashly accompanied Frederic to Upper Silesia instead of returning like
his more prudent literary colleagues to Breslau;
and was drawn by curiosity to the field of battle. In the
panic which followed Römer's first charge he was picked
up by a party of Austrian horse, robbed of his watch
and other valuables, and sent as a prisoner of war to
Vienna. There, after identifying himself, he was treated
with consideration, and soon exchanged for cardinal Sinzendorf, primate of Silesia, whom Frederic had ordered
under arrest.[1]

Capture of Maupertuis.

The king's own adventures were scarcely less exciting.
It had been his object, on leaving the field, to
cross to the right bank of the Oder, along
which in case of defeat he could make his escape to Berlin.[2] He had with him only a small party of friends and
attendants, for the cavalry escort, sent after him by Leopold, failed to overtake him, a circumstance which shows
a wonderful rapidity of flight on the king's part, and
probably supports the statement of Prussian historians,
that he had an unusually fine mount even for a king.
The first stopping-place was Löwen on the Neisse, about
fifteen miles from the battle-field; thence Frederic pushed
on to Oppeln, some twenty miles farther, on the Oder,
where he proposed to cross. But here the fugitives found

Frederic's adventures.

rapidly. But Cogniazo, *Geständnisse*, ii. 47, justly observes that,
since the losses were nearly equal, the troops of Neipperg must have
aimed better, though they fired less often. Does this illustration support the thesis supported by some military critics that even the modern breech-loaders have not made battles any more destructive, since
rapidity of firing has been gained at the cost of accuracy?

[1] La Beaumelle, *Vie de Maupertuis*, Paris, 1856, pp. 68–70.

[2] According to Orlich, i. 103, Frederic even dispatched a lieutenant
to Leopold of Dessau with verbal orders to remove the archives from
Berlin, and take such other measures of precaution as he might think
wise.

the gates closed, and, on announcing themselves as Prussians, were greeted with a volley, which showed the town to be in possession of the enemy. Frederic plunged the spurs into his horse, and turned back at once in the direction of Löwen, leaving such of his company as were not killed, or wounded, or captured to follow as best they could. Löwen was finally once more reached, and there, in an old mill where he had taken refuge, the king received the next morning news of the victory. The announcement was received with feelings of joy, not unmixed perhaps with feelings of personal chagrin. When he visited the battle-field he was less ready to compliment Schwerin on his victory than to reproach him for the advice, which made it indeed possible to gain the victory, but placed the king himself in such a humiliating position before the army and the world.[1] Of all this there is, however, nothing in his own account of the battle. He freely admits the faults of his generals and himself; but neither in his history, nor in the elaborate report which he sent the next day to the old prince of Dessau, is there any reference to his own flight and nocturnal adventures on the rough Silesian roads.[2]

[1] See Varnhagen v. Ense, ubi supra, xii. 193, 194 ; Grünhagen, i. 193.

[2] See *Œuvres de Frédéric*, ii. 76, 77. The report to Leopold is in Orlich, i. 324–327.

CHAPTER IV.

THE DIPLOMATIC INTERLUDE.

THE importance of the victory of Mollwitz was not lessened by the inglorious part played by the Prussian commander-in-chief. Its echoes were heard in every part of Europe. If at a few capitals they aroused some faint exultation, they caused the profoundest dismay at many more; and there was no exception to the universal amazement with which the world learned that the untried troops of Prussia had defeated, on the soil of an Austrian province, the chosen veterans of the house of Hapsburg.

Significance of Moll-witz.

For one thing, the defeat of Maria Theresa's only army swept away all the doubts and scruples of France. The fiery Belleisle had already set out upon his mission to the various German courts, armed with powers which were reluctantly granted by the cardinal, and were promptly enlarged by the ambassador to suit his own more ambitious views of the situation. He travelled in Oriental state. His extensive suite was made up of men of fashion, of noble blood, of easy and elegant manners, and of that peculiar combination of reckless morals with a fastidious deportment, which could be found nowhere else in such perfection as among the gallant aristocracy of France. The appointments of the embassy were all sumptuous and magnificent. Even the liveries of the valets aroused admiration in the minds of reigning princes of the German Empire, and added to the cogency of the marshal's appeals.[1]

Belleisle's mission.

[1] Luynes, iii. 308, 435, 436.

The use of such extrinsic aids was agreeable to Belleisle's taste, and was part of his diplomatic art. But they
were kept strictly subordinate to his principal aim, which
was an aim long since clearly defined, and never suffered
to escape from view. For the almost royal pomp with
which he strode into the presence of princes of the blood,
the copious eloquence with which he pleaded his cause,
the audacious combinations which his exuberant fancy
held up to view, the versatility, the invention, the enthusiasm which the marshal displayed at all the courts
that he visited, and in all the interviews he held, were
only the outward decorations of one of the most iniquitous schemes ever devised by an unscrupulous diplomacy.
The scheme, when stripped of all its details, did not indeed at first appear absolutely revolting. It proposed
simply to secure the election of Charles Albert of Bavaria as emperor, an honor to which he had a perfect
right to aspire. But it was difficult to obtain the votes
of certain electors without offering them the prospect of
territorial gains, and impossible for Charles Albert to
support the imperial dignity without greater revenues
than those of Bavaria. It was proposed, therefore, that
provinces should be taken from Maria Theresa herself,
first to purchase votes against her own husband, and then
to swell the income of the successful rival candidate.

The three episcopal electors were first visited, and sub-
jected to various forms of persuasion, — bribes,
flattery, threats, — until the effects of the treat- The electors
of the Em-
ment began to appear; the count palatine was pire.
devoted to France; and these four with Bavaria made
a majority of one. But that was too small a margin for
Belleisle's aspirations, or even for the safety of his project. The four remaining votes belonged to the most
powerful of the German states, Prussia, Hanover, Saxony,
and Bohemia ; and the union of these could easily detach
one or more of the ecclesiastical electors from Belleisle's

coalition. Each of these states presented, too, peculiar difficulties of its own. Bohemia, if it voted at all, would of course vote for the grand-duke Francis. Saxony and Hanover were already negotiating with Maria Theresa; and it was well understood that Austria could have Frederic's support by paying his price.

The case of Bohemia was met by a plausible legal technicality. It was urged that Maria Theresa was either a usurper in Bohemia, or the lawful heir; that on the first supposition the vote of that kingdom could be cast only by the true heir, whether the elector of Bavaria or some other prince; but that on the second hypothesis the Bohemian vote would have to be rejected, because a woman could not be a member of the electoral college, or delegate that membership to her husband. The court of Saxony was not yet ready, however, to adopt this syllogism, and a few days after the battle of Mollwitz the order of Belleisle's movements brought him to Dresden.

Should Bohemia have a vote?

In the mean time Valori had not ceased to press Frederic for the conclusion of the treaty with France. But he had met only evasion and dissimulation. New demands had been presented, in part seriously, in part only as pretexts for delay; the desire to have France promise a Swedish diversion, in order to prevent the interference of Russia,[1] was serious and wise. But nothing could show more clearly the audacious range which the diplomatic intrigues of the time were accustomed to take.

The truth is that Frederic wished to prolong the negotiation with France, avoiding an engagement on the one hand, and a rupture on the other, until the arrival of lord Hyndford, the newly appointed ambassador of England.[2] Valori appealed, therefore, to Belleisle, and the marshal came to swell the

Belleisle in the Prussian camp.

---

[1] Frederic to Podewils, 18 March, 1741.

[2] Frederic to Leopold of Dessau, 12 April, 1741.

ranks of the foreign envoys who were paying court to the
victor in his camp. Frederic himself, writing four or
five years later, made light of this visit. He ridiculed
the vanity and presumption of Belleisle, and perhaps with
some justice ; but he made one statement which even his
most intrepid apologist is not willing to accept. He relates that, finding the marshal one day in an unusually
dreamy mood, he inquired if he had received bad news.
"None whatever," is the alleged reply, "but I am embarrassed to know what to do with Moravia." Frederic says
he suggested that it be given to Saxony as her share of
the plunder, a plan which the marshal found admirable.[1]
Belleisle's own account represents him as confronting the
king with heroic mien, and sharply rebuking him for his
long-sustained duplicity. And the very meekness with
which the king took this reproof confirmed him in the
belief that further dissimulation was intended.[2]

On the seventh of May finally lord Hyndford arrived.
He was a Scotch peer; described as enjoying Lord Hynd-
the special confidence of the English cabinet; ford.
and gradually discovered to be blunt and outspoken,
little skilled in intrigue, yet not without a certain dry
sagacity, which enabled him early to master Frederic's
character, and penetrate his motives of action. In his
first audience he was rudely called upon to explain the
language held by the English envoy at St. Petersburg,
and in the king's speech to parliament. Then the terms

---

[1] Œuvres de Frédéric, ii. 79. To this explicit statement Droysen,
V. i. 257, opposes the consideration that it "entspricht der Sachlage
nicht;" while the duke de Broglie, writing from a different standpoint, says of the presumption which the story ascribes to Belleisle,
"on voit combien peu il s'accorde avec l'état d'inquiétude ou l'avait
jeté la déloyale irrésolution du roi." Fr. II. et M. T. i. 334. But the
story agrees so well with the known character of the two chief actors
that one would hesitate to reject it, even if it were less piquant.

[2] Belleisle's report, 30 April, 1741, in Ranke, xxvii., xxviii. 579–
586.

of a possible peace between Prussia and Austria were discussed. Hyndford inquired whether the king would abide by the offer formerly made through Gotter, — Lower Silesia with Breslau to be ceded to Prussia, in return for three million florins and military assistance. Frederic gave an affirmative answer, and added that the queen would never receive more favorable terms. This was the Prussian ultimatum. But Hyndford, instead of presenting these as the king's terms, invited sir Thomas Robinson, his colleague at Vienna, to urge Maria Theresa to make propositions of her own.[1]

By an unfortunate coincidence Hyndford was just at this time called on to take a step which cast

Protest of England and Holland.

some suspicion on the sincerity of his attempted mediation, and gave a certain support to the charge of duplicity made by the king. This was to present the joint protest of England and the United Provinces against the invasion of Silesia. The form of the paper, as originally proposed by Robert Trevor at the Hague, had been modified by the caution, and its presentation delayed by the timidity of Holland. Now, at the eleventh hour, after the English ministers had nominally adopted a different line of policy, the concurrence of the republic was announced.[2] Hyndford took the responsibility of withholding the document for a few days, but its arrival and doubtless its nature was made known to Podewils, and by him to the king. It drew forth a fine outburst of indignation. They had to deal, he wrote, on the one side with the most obstinate people in the world, and on the other, with the most ambitious. To preserve the charac-

---

[1] Arneth, i. 217 ; Podewils' notes of the interview in *Polit. Corresp.*, i. 239–241 ; Ibid., p. 259 ; Coxe, *House of Austria*, iii. 254; Carlyle, *History of Friedrich II.*, iii. 324, 325, gives, though in his own jargon, Hyndford's report ; Raumer, *Beiträge*, ii. 131. These authorities differ somewhat as to details, but agree in substance.

[2] *Preuss. Staatsschriften*, i. 304, 305.

ter of an honest man among tricksters was difficult; what then should be done? " War and negotiation; that is exactly what is being done by me and my minister. If there is anything to be gained by being honest, let us be honest; if it is necessary to deceive, let us deceive." [1]

The answer which finally arrived from Vienna to Hyndford's report proved to be, as the king had predicted, evasive and unsatisfactory.[2]

The intricate and ambitious policy of Frederic had thus finally brought him back to the very situation which, in regard to his diplomatic efforts, he held on crossing the frontier of Silesia. He had tried the policy of negotiation before fighting, and had been met with contempt. He had fought and defeated an Austrian army, and Maria Theresa was as resolute as before to defend her lawful possessions. No resource was therefore left except the French alliance. Podewils, who dreaded war, and desired that the king should seek a reasonable accommodation with Austria, made a last effort to arrest this momentous decision.[3] But he was overruled by the force of events, and the king's own resolution. On the thirtieth of May the order to sign the French treaty was dispatched. Its contents were to be kept strictly secret, and Podewils was to make the Prussian copy with his own hands, not using even the services of a clerk.[4] It was signed at Breslau on the fourth of June, though it bears the date of the fifth.

Alliance of Prussia and France.

---

[1] Frederic to Podewils, 12 May, 1741.

[2] Raumer, *Beiträge*, ii. 137, 138.

[3] See his exchange of views with the king in *Polit. Corresp.*, i. 246–248.

[4] Frederic to Podewils, 30 May, 1741; *Mémoires des Négociations du Marquis de Valori*, Paris, 1820, i. 106–109. Valori asserts that he finally brought Frederic to terms by threatening to advise his court to seek a more favorable alliance elsewhere. It is a curious fact that after this long delay some slight trouble about the ratifications brought forth, 16 June, 1742, a furious letter of rebuke to

This treaty long remained unpublished, but its leading stipulations are now well known. The essence of it was contained in four secret articles. In these the king of Prussia renounced his claim to Jülich-Berg in behalf of the house of Sulzbach, and agreed to give his vote to the elector of Bavaria for emperor. The king of France engaged to guarantee Prussia in the possession of Lower Silesia, to send within two months an army to the support of Bavaria, and to provoke an immediate rupture between Sweden and Russia.[1]

Immediately after ordering Podewils to sign the treaty Frederic wrote to Bellisle and to Fleury in the most endearing and enthusiastic terms. To the cardinal he said that his fidelity to the engagement would cause all delays to be forgotten. There would never be any cause to complain of him, or to regret the alliance, and thenceforth he would dispute with Louis' minister the title of the best Frenchman.[2] The letter to Belleisle was longer, but not less effusive. In this the king was a better Frenchman than the marshal, and a more faithful ally than France had ever had. "I expect," he continued, "to see, this day two months, your flags unfurled on this side of the Rhine; I admire in advance the manœuvres which you will make, and which, being lessons for every soldier, will give me support and encouragement. . . . Count in everything upon Prussia as upon France. Let no distinction be made between them, and let the king of France be convinced that though I have required time to decide, the delay will only make my good

The best of Frenchmen.

Podewils, who was accused of selling himself to England, and was warned that there were fortresses in Prussia for ministers who disobeyed the orders of their master. This cruel letter Podewils showed to Valori.

[1] Broglie, *Fr. II. et M. T.* i. 342, 343 ; Flassan, *Histoire de la diplomatie française*, v. 142, 143. But Flassan dates the treaty a month too late.

[2] Frederic to Fleury, 30 May, 1741.

faith the more inviolable." [1] The rest of the letter is in the same style.

Belleisle, though not completely deceived, was at least flattered by the royal caresses. But the cardinal was not thrown off his guard for an instant. *Fleury on Frederic.* He must avow, he wrote, that the king of Prussia caused him great anxiety; he listened to no counsel, and formed his resolutions lightly, without taking measures to insure their success. Good faith and sincerity were not his leading virtues; he was false in everything, even in his caresses; it was doubtful if he was safe in alliances, for he had no principles except self-interest. Frederic would like to regulate everything in his own way, without consultation with others; he was detested by all Europe. [2] If Fleury had heard the first dialogue between the king of Prussia and Hyndford, he could not have touched more accurately one side of the royal character. For when Hyndford made an appeal to his magnanimity, the critic of Machiavelli replied that he would hear nothing of magnanimity; a prince ought first to be guided by his interests. [3]

After the adoption of the treaty between Prussia and France, the presentation of the dual protest, which Hyndford and Ginkel, the envoy of Holland, made on the eighth of June, became an empty form. Frederic treated it with contempt; and ordered Podewils to return a conventional answer, which should intensify Hyndford's delusion. [4]

[1] Frederic to Belleisle, 30 May, 1741.

[2] Fleury to Belleise, 7 June, 1741, in Broglie, *Fr. II. et M. T.*, i. 351–353. Cf. Fleury to the elector of Bavaria, March, 1741, in Schlosser, *Geschichte des XVIII. Jahrhunderts*, 3d ed., ii. 16 n. This passage occurs : "Ce prince [Frederic] se vendra à celui qui l'achète le plus cher."

[3] Coxe, *H. of A.*, iii. 254.

[4] Frederic to Podewils, 8 June, 1741; the Prussian reply, *Staatsschriften*, i. 304–306 ; both, in German, Adelung, ii. 384–387.

The alliance which Frederic concluded with France necessarily brings the history of Prussia into somewhat closer relation to that of the other enemies of the house of Austria. The treaty was one thread in the web which Belleisle was weaving about the young queen of Hungary.

On leaving Silesia the marshal had returned to Saxony, where he again met the elector and resumed his negotiations. August III. was one of the weakest, and yet not one of the worst princes of his age. His instincts were pacific and honorable; he was decorous in his morals, which had a somewhat morbid religious basis; he was a patron of the arts. He might perhaps have enjoyed a happy and popular reign, if his relations in Poland had not made him dependent on Russia; if his political weakness had not made him the victim of an intriguing and ambitious minister, the count Brühl; and if his superstition had not given his confessor, Guarini, an unfortunate ascendency over all the processes of his mind. The confessor was a Catholic and the minister a Protestant, yet they coöperated efficiently in controlling the elector; and their policy was one of cowardly and treacherous hostility to Prussia. August was elector of Saxony and king of Poland, and thus bound the electorate and the republic together in a personal union. To add to this a geographical union, by acquiring a strip of intervening territory in Silesia, was a leading object of Saxon politics. Various schemes leading to this result had been proposed, — one by Frederic in his interview with Belleisle, one by England in the project of an alliance against Frederic, and others which perhaps had no other basis than the active imagination of Brühl himself.[1] The mission of Belleisle was to encourage these hopes, or as an alternative to hold out the prospect of acquiring Moravia, and, most important of all, to submit to August, in his capacity as vicar of the Empire, the question of the

The court and politics of Saxony.

[1] See Arneth, i. 202, 203, 206–209.

legality of Bohemia's vote in the electoral college. Leaving the Saxon court to ponder these problems, — for it was no part of his programme in these preliminary visits to exact specific pledges from the doubtful princes, — the marshal next proceeded to Bavaria.

Charles Albert could not be called a doubtful prince. He had early announced his claim to the Austrian succession; and the policy of France in putting him forward as a candidate for the imperial crown was not likely to encounter any obstacles on his part. It is true that there were not wanting veteran counsellors who tried to warn him against the French alliance by citing the calamities which that alliance had brought upon his house in the war of the Spanish succession. But these unwelcome advisers received no hearing. An envoy from Spain was already in negotiation with the elector for a common assault upon the Austrian dominions, and Bellisle's judicious mediation quickly brought about an agreement. This is commonly known as the treaty of Nymphenburg. It is indeed somewhat doubtful whether such a treaty ever existed in written form ; no authentic copy has been discovered.[1] But it is known that France secured the promise of the elector to take the field in support of his claims, and agreed to strengthen his small force with a French army corps. This military force the elector was to maintain from his own treasury, in order to carry out the fiction that France was not a belligerent. At the same time, however, France promised regular subsidies in aid of that treasury, and she was to concentrate an army of forty thousand men along the Rhine in order to coerce the action of the episcopal electors, and hold Hanover in check.[2]

Alliance of France and Bavaria, May, 1741.

---

[1] Cf. Ranke, xxvii., xxviii. 443 n. ; Flassan, v. 129 ; Droysen, V. i. 288 n. ; Schlosser, ii. 24, 25. But Droysen denies the genuineness of the instrument which Schlosser found and copied in the French archives.

[2] Olenschlager, iii. 39, 40.

Everything being thus ripe for the initial military steps of France, Belleisle returned to Paris to hasten their preparation. There can be no doubt that he at least intended faithfully to keep the pledges given to Frederic. But he did not find the same alacrity in the French ministers, for Fleury, who was still controlled by his conscience or his timidity or his scepticism, and Amelot, who was opposed to the war, and had not been treated with sufficient consideration by the impetuous marshal, threw many obstacles in the way of a prompt and decided action, and gave Frederic a pretext for sharp remonstrances about the delay. But Belleisle finally vanquished all difficulties. On the fifteenth of August the French corps, destined to serve as an auxiliary force to the elector of Bavaria, crossed the Rhine at Strasburg, forty thousand strong. Belleisle himself was nominally its commander-in-chief.[1] But as his diplomatic services were for the time more important, it was agreed that he should not join the army in person until after the imperial election ; and general de Leuville was therefore chosen as temporary substitute. Charles Albert had already begun offensive operations by seizing the city of Passau, in Upper Austria, where he awaited the French reënforcement. In due time the junction was effected ; and on the tenth of September the allied forces occupied without resistance the city of Linz, capital of Upper Austria, which the elector entered in state, as an heir receiving a lawful possession. The opening of the enterprise was thus not inauspicious.

The French cross the Rhine.

In the mean time Frederic had been gradually strengthening his position in Silesia, and preparing for a renewal of the campaign when it should become necessary. The regular siege of Brieg was begun while Belleisle was at his headquarters, under the direc-

Fall of Brieg.

[1] That is to say, under Charles Albert. See Louis' order of the twentieth of July in Olenschlager, iii. 19, 20.

tion of Walrave, a skilful Dutch engineer in the Prussian service. After the first line of trenches had been opened, and the bombardment begun, the place capitulated.

A still more important, though less justifiable measure, was the military occupation of Breslau, and the overthrow of its local independence. The charge, probably not quite unfounded, that the city had not strictly observed the terms of the agreement of the third of January, but had kept up regular communication with the Austrian court and commanders, was the pretext for this measure.[1] It was easily consummated on the tenth of August. A Prussian force appeared at the gates of the city, and solicited the privilege of marching through, which, under the terms of the agreement, could only be done in detachments, escorted by the municipal militia. But, by a prearranged accident, a baggage wagon, which followed the first battalion, broke down at the proper moment, so that the gate could not be closed; and, additional Prussian troops then rushing in, the city was won. Schwerin summoned the municipal officers, disarmed the militia, and the next day exacted an oath of allegiance from the authorities. Three weeks later a proclamation summoned all citizens of Lower Silesia serving in the Austrian armies to return to their homes, on pain of being treated as deserters and traitors.[2]

The political not less than the military importance of this step appears at once. But from another point of view it may also be regarded as a significant answer to a fresh attempt at mediation on the part of the indefatigable English diplomatists.

The ambassador of George the Second at Vienna, sir Thomas Robinson, was an old and not a very wise man. His manner was brusque, arrogant,

Occupation of Breslau.

Sir Thomas Robinson.

[1] See *Polit Corresp.*, i. 290–293, Frederic to Schwerin; Grünhagen, i. 233–235.

[2] Mylius, *Corp. Const. March. Cont.* ii. 27–30.

and offensive even beyond that of his race, which was more than once a fatal obstacle to success in the diplomacy of the time. But it was specially unfortunate at the capital of Austria in the reign of Maria Theresa. The inborn and high-bred dignity of one of the most ancient courts of Europe was roused rather than restrained by a rudeness of language which seemed to mock its own misfortunes, and was not softened even by the youth and sex of the queen herself. To her, indeed, the manner of the envoy was doubly offensive. It angered her alike as a ruler and a woman, — as a ruler whose pride was exposed to the hard and cruel reproaches of a nominal friend; as a woman whose distress excited, not tact and forbearance, not a courteous, respectful, and decorous sympathy, but only the patronizing and intolerant frankness of an aged tutor. If his blunt exhortations moved her to tears, he saw them flow unmoved. If they roused her anger, and she replied with proper spirit, he bore the rebuke with callous unconcern. But with all his vehemence and rudeness of manner he was faithful to his sense of duty; and, while serving the most selfish court of Europe, was for his own person unselfishly devoted to the interests, so far as an Englishman could understand them, of the house of Austria. In this spirit he sought and received from his own government the permission to accept from the queen a mission to Frederic's headquarters in Silesia.[1] The consent of Maria Theresa was more difficult to obtain; and she only yielded to the envoy's persistent appeals after many stormy interviews, with great reluctance, and probably only in order to convince him and his government of the folly of a mediation in which she herself had little confidence. The terms which he was empowered to offer can be explained by no other theory.

Robinson, accompanied by lord Hyndford and Pode-

[1] Lord Harrington to Robinson, Hanover, 21 June, 1741. Hardwicke MSS. vol. 78.

wils, arrived in camp, and had an interview with Frederic, on the seventh of August. His first offer was Attempts mediation. to pay Frederic the sum of two million thalers if he would at once withdraw from Silesia; to which the king replied that the offer was an insult, for he was not a beggar. Robinson next suggested the cession of Austrian Guelders and the duchy of Limburg. This making no impression, Hyndford suggested that, as a last concession, the duchy of Glogau might be ceded. This only increased the king's real or affected indignation; and he finally announced that he would be satisfied with nothing less than the whole of Lower Silesia, including Breslau. Robinson declared that the queen would never accept such terms. The conversation then passed to the general European situation, from which Robinson sought to draw support for his mediation. But the king met him point by point, now with practical considerations, now with inhospitable rudeness; and finally abruptly closed the interview by retiring behind the inner curtain of his tent.[1] Lord Hyndford, who had passed through similar ordeals himself, and thought he understood better than his colleague the king's manner, explained his abrupt departure by the charitable theory that he felt the anger rising, and hastened to retire before it should become uncontrollable. The probability is, however, that in this instance Frederic's outburst of temper was simply a part, and not a very agreeable part, of his tactics.

The officious mediator had therefore to report the complete failure of his mission. Yet he was so far from discouraged that he returned three weeks His failure. later with fresh propositions. He offered this time a part of Lower Silesia, on condition that the king enter into al-

---

[1] *Polit. Corresp.*, i. 297–301, Podewils' minutes of the interview; Raumer, *Beiträge*, ii. 139–145; Arneth, i. 239; Grünhagen, i. 429–433. The English instructions for Robinson, dated 21 June, 1741, in Hardwicke MSS. vol. 78.

liance with Maria Theresa, and support her with ten thousand men. But as he brought no credentials, either from the king of England or the queen of Hungary, Frederic refused to discuss his propositions, or even to receive him in audience. His only reply was an order for Robinson to leave Breslau within twenty-four hours.[1]

A week later, on the eighth of September, the queen again made overtures, more liberal and more direct, and reflecting beyond doubt the impression caused by the combined French and Bavarian invasion. The grand-duke authorized lord Hyndford to offer all of Lower Silesia, with the Neisse as the boundary on the west of the Oder, and the Brünitz on the east, the conditions being a right of free passage for Saxony by way of Grüneberg to Poland, the support of the queen and of the pragmatic sanction by Frederic with ten thousand men, and his vote for the grand-duke in the imperial election. These propositions met with no better success. Frederic refused to violate the treaty, which pledged his vote to the elector of Bavaria, and English diplomacy registered another failure.[2]

Hyndford has no better success.

During these anxious summer months Maria Theresa and the Austrian court had resided mainly at Presburg, in Hungary. Here she had been occupied in the solution of domestic as well as international problems.

[1] Droysen, V. i. 313–315 ; Arneth, i. 242 ; Frederic to Podewils, 1 September, 1741. The postscript to this letter, in the king's own hand, has some choice expressions. " Faites-moi partir ce coquin de négociateur. . . . Chassez-moi ce coquin de Robinson . . . s'il reste plus de 24 heures à Breslau, je prends l'apoplexie . . . sa . . . reine de Hongrie et son fol de roi d'Angleterre n'ont qu'à être la dupe, l'une de son orgueil, et l'autre de sa sottise."

[2] Frederic to Hyndford, 14 September, 1741. The last sentence of the letter will interest the reader at a later stage of events : " Je vous prie," concludes Frederic, ". . . de me croire assez honnête homme pour ne pas violer mes engagements." Grünhagen, i. 146, justly assumes that this answer was intended for the eye of Valori, who was in the Prussian camp.

The Magyars, as a manly and chivalrous race, had been touched by the perilous situation of the young queen; but, while ardently protesting their loyalty, insisted not the less on the recognition of their own inalienable rights. These had been inadequately observed in recent years, and in consequence no little disaffection prevailed in Hungary. The magnates resolved, therefore, as they had resolved at the beginning of previous reigns, to demand the restoration of all their rights and privileges. But it does not appear that they wished to take any ungenerous advantage of the sex or the necessities of Maria Theresa. They were argumentative and stubborn, yet not in a bargaining, mercenary spirit. They accepted in June a qualified compliance with their demands; and when on the twenty-fifth of that month the queen appeared before the diet to receive the crown of St. Stephen, and, according to custom, waved the great sword of the kingdom toward the four points of the compass, toward the north and the south, the east and the west, challenging all enemies to dispute her right, the assembly was carried away by enthusiasm, and it seemed as if an end had forever been put to constitutional technicalities. Such was, however, not the case. After the excitement caused by the dramatic coronation had in a measure subsided, the old contentions revived, as bitter and vexatious as before. These concerned especially the manner in which the administration of Hungary should be adjusted to meet the new state of things. Should the chief political offices be filled by native Hungarians, as the diet demanded? Could the co-regency of the grand-duke, which was ardently desired by the queen, be accepted by the Magyars?

For two months the dispute over these problems raged at Presburg, until finally Maria Theresa herself found a bold, ingenious, and patriotic solution. The news of the Franco-Bavarian alliance and the fall of Passau deter-

Maria Theresa and the Hungarians.

mined her to throw herself completely upon the gallantry and devotion of the Magyars.

It had long been the policy of the court of Vienna not to entrust the Hungarians with arms. Even in this crisis the older counsellors of the queen, men who remembered how the plots and armed uprisings in Hungary had lamed the energies of Austria in the wars of Louis the Fourteenth, labored to dissuade the queen from a step which, instead of bringing relief, would only add one more of the enemies of the house of Hapsburg. But Maria Theresa had not been robbed, in spite of her experience with France and Prussia, of all her faith in human nature. She took the responsibility of her decision, and the result proved that her insight was correct.

She calls them to arms.

On the eleventh of September she summoned the members of the diet before her, and, seated on the throne, explained to them the perilous situation of her dominions. The danger, she said, threatened herself, and all that was dear to her. Abandoned by all her allies, she took refuge in the fidelity and the ancient valor of the Hungarians, to whom she entrusted herself, her children, and her empire. Here she broke into tears, and covered her face with her handkerchief. The diet responded to this appeal by proclaiming the " insurrection " or the equipment of a large popular force for the defence of the queen.[1] So great was the enthusiasm that it nearly

The insurrection.

[1] " è questa l'esposizione dello stato infelice della Monarchia, la ricerca e la fiducia insieme negl' ajuti degl' Ungaresi. V. V. E. E. osserveranno essersi poscia espressa la regina come da ogn' altro abbandonata, che ricorreva alla fede, all' armi et all' antico valore dell' Ungaria, implorando diffesa all' imminente pericolo del regno, della Real persona, et de' Reali Figlioli. Proruppero in lagrime, indi con una sol voce tutti offersero e sangue e vita. Commossi' da gloria, da amore, et da sdegno tutti entrarono nella gran Sala, e stabilirono questo il caso dell' insurrezione." Relation of Capello, the Venetian envoy, Arneth, i. 405 ; n. 18.

swept away even the original aversion of the Hungarians to the grand - duke Francis, who to the queen's delight was finally, though not without some murmurs, accepted as co-regent. On the twenty-first of September she presented him to the assembled estates. After taking the oath in the most solemn form, the prince addressed to the delegates a short speech, ingeniously fitted to the temper of the nation, full of manly and patriotic sentiments, and fortunate in the respectful though not enthusiastic reception which it met. More applause was awakened when the queen caused her infant son, the archduke Joseph, to be held up in view of the assembled multitude. Two weeks later she formally granted most of the demands of the diet in regard to the details of the government, filled the high offices of state, conferred honors and titles upon the most deserving of the patriots, and thus, by a statesmanship far wiser than that of her advisers, secured Hungary for her cause at a time when that cause needed the aid of every one of her subjects. The knights then returned to their estates, where they communicated their own fire and enthusiasm to their retainers, and swiftly organized regiment after regiment of the boldest horsemen in Europe.[1]

This uprising was organized not an hour too early, for dangers were pressing upon the queen from every side. Linz had already fallen; the way to Vienna seemed open to the Franco-Bavarian army. A second French corps under marshal Maillebois, crossing the Rhine toward the middle of September, took quarters in the very heart of Westphalia, where it held Hanover in check on the one side and Holland on the other, and

Her difficulties thicken.

---

[1] Coxe, *H. of A.*, iii. 269–271 ; Arneth, i. 253 et seq.; Adelung, ii. 274, etc. A great body of picturesque myths has formed about these transactions. I have tried to describe them according to the most authentic evidence, and in a spirit equally removed from the license of the enthusiast and the cynicism of the sceptic.

was also in a position to coöperate with the Prussian army
of observation at Göttin.   The secret treaty of June between George II. and Maria Theresa, by which the former
had renewed the guaranty of the pragmatic sanction,
and under which he had assembled a force of Danish
and Hessian mercenaries, was thus rendered practically
inoperative.   The Swedes had already, in consequence
of French pressure, declared war against Russia, so that
no hope remained of help from St. Petersburg.   And on
the approach of Maillebois' army George II. had even
made overtures to France for a treaty which should
secure the neutrality of Hanover.

The military movements in Silesia were in the mean
time conducted apparently without fixed plan on
either side, and led to no positive results.   Neipperg did not venture beyond the shelter of Neisse ; and
Frederic hesitated to give battle with such a disadvantage
of position.   But he was gradually strengthening and improving his army, especially the cavalry.   In a skirmish
at Rothschloss, on the seventh of May, a superior force of
Austrian horse under Baranyi was dispersed by Prussian
hussars ; and a certain major Zieten, who was to make a
great name in the future, won there his first laurels.[1]   But
this was the only description of fighting which took place,
and the summer was passed mainly in fruitless manœuvres.[2]   Both commanders seemed reluctant to try the issue of another battle.

If the soldiers rested, the diplomatists were not, however, idle.   In the west, marshal Maillebois had
been anxious to march directly upon Hanover,
but gave up the plan in deference to the advice of Frederic.   Still the mere presence of a French army in West-

Operations in Silesia.

Diplomatic movements.

[1] Valori, who assisted at a review, 28 July, 1741, wrote to Fleury
that " cette cavalerie est la chose la plus surprenante qui se voie dans
ce genre."

[2] Orlich, i. 119–145, gives painfully minute details.

phalia filed George II. with alarm for the safety of his German possessions; supported by Frederic, he pressed his efforts for an accommodation in respect to them.[1] On the twenty-seventh of September Louis XV. agreed to a provisional recognition of Hanover's neutrality. This agreement, ratified a month later,[2] to the great indignation of the English parliament, released France from one possible enemy, and left the army of Maillebois free to operate elsewhere. Frederic had been not less uneasy about Saxony, which had played an ambiguous part, and whose army of twenty thousand men was no insignificant factor in the military problem. But the indefatigable Belleisle also solved this problem. Austria herself had refused to ratify a treaty of alliance with Saxony, offered, though at an exorbitant price, by August III.;[3] and finally, by the treaty of the nineteenth of September, Belleisle brought Saxony completely over into his own camp. In this compact the marshal's plan for constructing Europe first appears in all its au- *Saxony joins the queen's enemies.* dacious proportions. The elector of Saxony was promised, in return for his vote and his military assistance, Upper Silesia and Moravia, with the royal title;[4] the elector of Bavaria was to have Bohemia, Upper Austria, Tyrol, and the Breisgau; Lombardy was assigned to Spain; and Maria Theresa was to retain only the rest of the possessions which she had inherited. The adroit

[1] "Je l'assure que je ferai mon possible pour faire accepter ce plan par le roi de France." Frederic to George II., 16 September; also to Podewils, 7, 20, and 21 September, 1741, etc. It appears that while Frederic's real reason was a reluctance to see a French army in such close proximity to his own dominions, he represented his course to George in such a light as to make it a real concession, deserving of pecuniary and other rewards.

[2] Flassan, v. 133–140.

[3] Arneth, i. 206–210.

[4] That is, for Saxony and the territories to be annexed. Olenschlager, iii. section 3, has the documentary history of the Saxon intervention.

diplomacy of Belleisle thus secured Frederic against attack from either of his suspected neighbors, while the allied armies at once marched upon Bohemia and Prague.[1]

Yet it appears from the apologists for Frederic that his desire to have Saxony and Hanover eliminated from the list of Maria Theresa's supporters rested upon a profound error, which he only discovered after the desire had been gratified. The two treaties, it is said, opened up an alarming view of the rising influence of France in German politics, which it was necessary at any price to check. But of all this there is not a word in Frederic's own narration, and the reader will take the speculations of modern writers with a proper degree of hesitation.[2] The transaction which is now to be described needs no subtle hypothesis to make it clear.

The king of Prussia had been foiled in all his designs upon Neisse, for Neipperg lay like a watch-dog before its gates, and resisted every effort to draw him into an open engagement. Yet the possession of the fortress was indispensable to Frederic's plans. A new policy was therefore adopted, to which the situation of the queen, menaced as she was by the diplomacy of Belleisle and the army of Charles Albert, seemed to promise better success. Lord Hyndford was then in Breslau, in a state of deep dejection. He was, therefore, not a little surprised to receive an intimation through a Prussian officer of staff, colonel Goltz, that Frederic was ready once more to open negotiations. On the thirteenth of September he announced the king's terms.[3] What was accomplished by them will appear in the sequel; the essential thing at first was to have them accepted as a basis

Secret overtures by Frederic.

[1] Orders were at once sent to Leopold of Dessau to give up the camp at Göttin, and send his troops into winter quarters.

[2] On the contrary the king wrote in 1746: "Quoiqu'il eût quelque sujet de se plaindre de la France, ces mécontentements n'étaient pas assez forts pour rompre avec elle." *Œuvres de Frédéric,* ii. 91.

[3] *Polit. Corresp.,* i. 359.

for negotiations, and for this only twelve days were offered. Hyndford reported the affair at once to the queen, and was informed by return courier that authority had been sent to Neipperg to make an exchange of views. In the mean time Frederic moved his army across the Neisse, and posted it in a way to threaten Neipperg's communications; on the second of October he was at Friedland. This delay had been caused by the remoteness of Neisse from the Austrian court, and the time which was consumed in the exchange of letters between them. And as the queen was not sufficiently prompt in the matter, Frederic wrote to the cardinal that she had offered him terms of peace, and intimated that he would accept them unless his allies showed more energy;[1] in other words, unless they pressed operations in a way to enforce upon Maria Theresa the necessity of accepting the terms which he himself had offered to her.

The negotiations at length reached a point at which a personal interview could be arranged between the king and Neipperg, at the castle of Klein-Schnellendorf, midway between the two armies. Every precaution was taken to deceive the watchful Valori, who was still in the Prussian camp.[2] Frederic was accompanied only by Goltz; Neipperg, by general Lentulus; lord Hynford acted as mediator, or rather as clerk and witness. And here after some discussion an agreement was concluded on the ninth of October.[3]

Preliminaries of Klein-Schnellendorf.

The agreement or convention contained eighteen articles. The first four provided for a sham siege of Neisse, to last fifteen days, when the commandant was to surrender the place, and retire into Moravia. In the fifth

[1] Frederic to Fleury, 2 October, 1741.
[2] Valori, *Mémoires*, i. 127.
[3] These are the essential steps in the negotiation. Further details, which do not however change the character of the transaction, may be found in Arneth, Droysen, Grünhagen, and Raumer.

article the king of Prussia promised to take no further hostile measures against the queen of Hungary or her allies, and, in the sixth, to demand only Lower Silesia with the city of Neisse. The seventh article declared that the parties would endeavor to conclude a final treaty of peace by the end of December. Article eight contained the formal cession of Lower Silesia by Neipperg, in the name of the queen; article nine, the promise of the marshal to retire on the sixteenth of October with his army into Moravia; articles ten to sixteen, arrangements by which the Prussian army might take winter quarters in Upper or Austrian Silesia; and article seventeen, a stipulation for occasional skirmishes, which should aid to carry out the deception, together with an agreement to make arrangements for the line of conduct to be observed the coming spring in case the final treaty of peace should not be concluded during the winter. The last article contained the pledge of Hyndford, Neipperg, and Lentulus to regard the provisions of the agreement as an inviolable secret. The protocol was signed by Hyndford alone, and attested by his official seal.[1]

In pursuance of this novel convention Neipperg at once began his homeward march, and, followed a day or two by the Prussian army, finally retired behind the mountains into Moravia. The siege of Neisse was conducted in the same bloodless manner. Shots were idly exchanged until the first of November, when the garrison capitulated, and the Prussians occupied the city. Thus diplomacy, more effective and less costly than battles, put Frederic in possession of Upper as well

The Austrians evacuate Silesia.

[1] These articles have been often published; they are given in full in Garden, *Histoire des traités de paix*, iii. 262–264, Adelung, ii. 488–490, and *Polit. Corresp.*, i. 371, 372. The 17th article deserves to be read carefully. It is often said that the convention became void when the specified time elapsed within which the definitive treaty of peace was to be concluded, whereas the possibility of such a failure was expressly foreseen, and arrangements were made for it.

as Lower Silesia, together with the last fortress which remained in Austrian hands.

The indignant reader, who is now ready to cry out against Frederic's betrayal of his allies, France and Bavaria, must await patiently the sequel of the affair. It is evident that the scheme implied treachery to somebody; was it France or Austria, or both? The king himself answers this question, though inconsequentially, in the account which he himself gives of the transaction. He was reluctant, he asserts, to admit the complete preponderance of France in German politics, and was, therefore, not unwilling to restore a temporary equilibrium between the houses of Hapsburg and Bourbon, by allowing the army of Neipperg to march to the defence of Vienna. But he had no intention of relieving the queen of all her embarrassments, and he insisted accordingly on the strictest secrecy in regard to the agreement of Klein-Schnellendorf, a condition which he was perfectly sure would not be observed. It was the interest of the court of Vienna to divulge the nature of the convention, and this inevitable imprudence would give the king a pretext for breaking it at his own convenience.[1]

Thus Frederic himself on his own motives in this strange transaction. But was his version, with all its cynical frankness, and the support which it finds in circumstances themselves, the true one? The only reply to this question, if it may be called a reply, is that the inquirer who follows the course of the affair, and is not too anxious to defend Frederic against the consequences of his own candor, will reach either the same solution of the problem, or one even less favorable to him. The very ease and abundance of the king's treachery bewilder the efforts of the interpreter. At the very time, for in-

Frederic's purposes.

---

[1] *Œuvres de Frédéric*, ii. 91–94. But how could it be for the interest of the queen to divulge the secret if such an indiscretion was to be followed by the repudiation of the agreement?

stance, that Frederic was thus setting free an Austrian army for the defence of Vienna, he was strenuously urging the Franco-Bavarian commanders to march promptly upon that capital.[1]

The pretext arrived, as Frederic had foreseen, at an early day. It was in the nature of things that the easy capture of so strong a fortress as Neisse, and the unopposed retreat of Neipperg in the face of a superior army, would arouse suspicion, and render it impossible, even with the best disposition on the part of both courts, to keep the transaction long concealed.[2] There is no doubt that it was made known to the elector of Saxony by the Austrian resident at Dresden, but it is also maintained, and with some support from the dates, that the only source of his information was common rumor.[3] The queen's envoy at Frankfort was the object of a similar charge, and a similar defence. This controversy still occupies the publicists of Prussia and Austria; but for the neutral historian it is enough that before the end of October the suspension of hostilities in Silesia was known to every diplomatist in Europe.

The convention becomes known.

Frederic was prompt to seize his opportunity. Prince Leopold penetrated into the county of Glatz, which did not belong to Silesia at all, and quartered his troops on the innocent inhabitants. It is stated indeed that the occupation of Glatz was conceded by Neipperg in a special article, not included in the protocol.[4] But the statement requires qualification. It ap-

And is repudiated by Frederic.

[1] Frederic to the elector of Bavaria, 7 October, 1741.

[2] Valori, who witnessed the so-called siege, describes, *Mémoires*, i. 128, his suspicions.

[3] That a similar rumor prevailed at Breslau appears from a report of Podewils, who was not in the secret, dated the 18th of October. *Polit. Corresp.*, i. 382. Cf. Goltz to Hyndford, 21 October, 1741; Arneth. i. 336. But Luynes, iv. 17, says Austria circulated at Paris reports of the treaty with Frederic.

[4] Droysen, V. i. 349, 350.

pears to be true that in the course of the interview at Klein-Schnellendorf Frederic threw out a vague remark to the effect that, if necessary to protect Bohemia against the Saxons, he would send a force over the frontier ; and in a supplementary conference, held on the eleventh of October between Hyndford, Neipperg, and Goltz, the latter explained that an advance of the king's forces into Bohemia would be likely to provoke a quarrel with Saxony, and thus give Prussia an excuse for withdrawing from the anti-Austrian coalition.[1] But no article to this effect was adopted, and Neipperg himself pronounced the movement unauthorized by any stipulation.

On the first of November, finally, the same day on which by the capitulation of Neisse he reaped the principal fruit of the agreement with the queen, Frederic gave his adhesion to the Saxo-Bavarian treaty for the partition of Austria. Negotiations on this subject had been in progress for several weeks, running of course parallel to those which led to the protocol of Klein-Schnellendorf. But it does not seem necessary now to trace out the course of discussions, which Frederic, knowing the depravity of diplomatists and foreseeing the changing conditions of his own policy, can hardly have treated as serious. The elaborate trifling about the cession of Glatz was afterwards fitly ridiculed in his history. The county itself was a fief of the crown of Bohemia, and according to the solemn theory of the allies the elector of Bavaria was the lawful owner of that crown. He was therefore sovereign lord of Glatz. Hence, to carry out the fiction, an agreement was made by which Charles Albert was to cede the county to Prussia, and accept four hundred thousand thalers in payment ; or, as the royal historian says, the Bavarian sold a principality which he had

Adhesion of Prussia to the Saxo-Bavarian treaty.

[1] Grünhagen, ii. 34, 54, 55. Orlich, i. 148, 149, also mentions the plan.

never possessed. This was not the least of the triumphs of the ingenious marshal Belleisle.[1]

After concluding this honest piece of business Frederic

Homage in Breslau.

made a visit to Breslau, in order to receive in person the homage which, on the seizure of the city by Schwerin, had only been rendered to his deputies. This ceremony took place on the seventh of November, and for reasons of policy was made as imposing as possible ;[2] there was significance in the notification that a new prince reigned in Silesia. A new system of government had already begun to supplant the old institutions. In October a royal decree had swept away the committee of the estates, the local boards of finance, and the other agents of provincial self-government, which, though awkward and clumsy, like most organic restraints upon arbitrary power, were precious to a people in whom the traditions of liberty had so long survived. The municipalities were reorganized in the same spirit. And the day after the ceremony of homage, the king, evading a specific request to promise fidelity to the ancient rights and liberties of the province,[3] made known to the assembled dignitaries the principles on which the further administrative reorganization would be conducted. The rule of absolute religious equality would thenceforth be enforced. The supervision of justice was to be entrusted to two boards of jurists, one

[1] *Œuvres de Frédéric*, ii. 85 ; Flassan, v. 147, 148 ; Schlosser, iii. 350 ; Droysen, V. i. 363.

[2] Rödenbeck, *Tagebuch*, i. 57; Grünhagen, ii. 50–53. The latter makes the safe remark that the poetical inscriptions so freely displayed do not give the reader a high opinion of the talent of the Breslau bards. This couplet, for example, was officially illuminated on the city hall :

> Hier brenen, grosser Prinz, nicht schlechte Lampen-Kertzen,
> Nein, nein ! Es brennen selbst der Unterthanen Herzen.

[3] He would respect them, he declared, "in so weit selbige ihnen selbst und der allgemeinen Wohlfahrt auch wahrem Interesse und Aufnahme zuträglich, und damit compatibil werden möchten," which of course left everything to his discretion.

at Breslau, one at Glogau, and in each of them native Silesians, as most familiar with the law of the province, were to form a majority. The revenues were likewise to be administered by two boards ; but in these, Silesians, as ignorant of Prussian methods, were to have no place until they had qualified themselves by an apprenticeship in older provinces of the kingdom. Taxes were to be impartially assessed, after a careful appraisal of all real and personal property. In place of the irregular and forcible impressment of the Silesians into the Prussian army, which apparently had followed the military occupation, a regular system of annual levies was promised and not long afterwards introduced.[1] The Prussian system of direct contributions from the peasants, and an excise in the towns, was extended over the whole province, the estimated receipts being fixed at a little less than two million thalers. The Silesians found this exorbitant, but there was no appeal.[2]

The reorganization of ecclesiastical affairs followed the same territorial divisions. At each of the seats of government, Glogau and Breslau, a superior consistory, with Protestant and Catholic members, formed the chief executive and judicial organs for church causes within the corresponding districts ; and from these as well as from the higher officials of the Catholic hierarchy, appeals could be taken to the central ecclesiastical authorities of Berlin. Count Sinzendorf, cardinal-bishop of Breslau, was early restored to his functions. He had at first fallen under some suspicion on account of his Austrian birth and connections, but by the prudence of his conduct soon regained the confidence of Frederic, and continued thenceforth to enjoy it. Mutual

Ecclesiastical reorganization.

---

[1] Edict of 25 December, 1741. R. de l'homme de Courbière, *Geschichte der Brandenburg-Preussischen Heeres-Verfassung*, Berlin, 1852, p. 102.

[2] Stenzel, iv. 162–165 ; Grünhagen, ii. 43–53.

good sense and mutual forbearance thus made it possible to maintain relations of the utmost value to the church and the province.[1]

In one year from the time when Schwerin first crossed the frontier, Lower Silesia was thus conquered, administratively reconstructed, and brought into harmony with the entire Prussian system, by a king, who had nevertheless found time to entertain ambassadors, make treaties, write bad poems, and keep up an active correspondence with many friends on the most varied topics of literary interest.

In the mean time the Franco-Bavarian army, having practically completed the conquest of Upper Austria, early in September pushed its scouting parties up to the very suburbs of Vienna. Frederic expressed keen disappointment that it had not undertaken the capture of the imperial city.[2] But this delay had permitted count Khevenhüller, one of the most active of the Austrian generals, to organize a force for the defence of the capital; and the district of which Vienna was the centre was not claimed by the elector, or conceded to him in the treaties of partition. Upper Austria, which he demanded, was already in his possession; and Bohemia, to which he aspired, was not unnaturally the next object of his military movements. Count Ségur, with ten thousand men, was left at Linz, but the rest of the army took up its march early in October for Prague.

Franco-Bavarian campaign.

[1] Adelung, iii. 4, 5 ; Stenzel, iv. 327 ; *Fragmente aus der Geschichte der Klöster und Stiftungen Schlesiens,* Breslau, 1812, pp. 439–441.

[2] See, *Œuvres de Fréderic,* ii. 104, the cogent memoir which the royal historian says he addressed to the elector on this subject on the twenty-ninth of June. This paper does not appear in the *Polit. Corresp.,* which, however, contains a communication differently worded, though to the same effect, dated the thirtieth. Cf. Frederic to the elector of Bavaria, 26 July, 1741. Baron Schmettau was sent to the camp of Charles Albert to press these counsels; his instructions, undated, *Polit. Corresp.,* i. 286.

The garrison of the city was small, numbering scarcely three thousand men, under general Ogilvie. But the defensive posts were strong. The grand-duke Francis, with a considerable force, made up of Neipperg's returning army,[1] a corps under prince Lobkowitz, part of the garrison of Vienna, and numerous irregular Hungarian levies, was hastening to its relief. The place, if taken at all, must therefore be taken at once, and fortunately for Charles Albert he had one officer who rose to the level of the emergency. Maurice of Saxony was an illegitimate son of August the Strong by the beautiful Aurora von Königsmark. A soldier of fortune, and a man of morals not less dissolute than those of his father, he was nevertheless endowed with great strength of mind, and had especially a native genius for military command. After strange vicissitudes he had finally accepted service in the army of France, and was one of the generals in the corps which Louis XV. sent to the aid of the elector of Bavaria. The besieging force comprised, besides the Franco-Bavarian army, a Saxon corps of some twenty thousand men under count Rutowski, another bastard of August II., and was numerically not inferior to the Austrians under the grand-duke. But Belleisle, who, having completed his diplomatic labors, had expected to take the command, was detained at Dresden by illness; timidity and irresolution reigned in the councils of the allies. The problem was finally solved by the sagacity, ardor, and fine tactics of Maurice of Saxony. The plan as agreed on by the several commanders assigned to Maurice with the French troops only a feigned attack upon the Neustadt, while the principal assault on the

----

[1] According to a despatch of Hyndford, quoted by Raumer, ii. 150, Frederic had himself given suggestions to Neipperg, at Klein-Schnellendorf, about the method of effecting a junction with the other Austrian forces. The reader will compare this with Schmettau's mission.

opposite side was confided to the Saxons. The night of the twenty-sixth of November was chosen for the attempt. But in the progress of the scheme Maurice saw an opportunity to convert his feigned attack into a real one, and his column was the first to force the gates of the city. The Saxons fought with equal valor; and, profiting by Maurice's unexpected success, soon afterwards carried their part of the town. Thus the grand-duke learned, just as he was expecting to give battle, that he was twenty-four hours too late.[1]

The next day the elector made his triumphal entry into the city. On the seventh of December he received homage as titular king of Bohemia, established a council of government, and on the nineteenth returned to Munich. Belleisle arrived in Prague a few days after the capitulation and took the command. Various detachments of French, Bavarians, and Saxons occupied the leading towns in the vicinity; and the grand-duke returned to the neighborhood of Budeweis, whence he could threaten either Bohemia or Bavaria, as occasion might arise.

The relations of the northern powers began at this time again to attract attention. Sweden had duly begun hostilities against Russia, which were feebly conducted, and wholly inadequate as a check upon any purpose which the regent might have to assist Maria Theresa. The purpose undoubtedly existed; but the event proved that France had other means of thwarting it. This was a new revolution at St. Petersburg.

War between Russia and Sweden.

The princess Elizabeth, daughter of Peter the Great, was the natural head of the pure Russian party, which looked with hatred on the German fa-

Elizabeth of Russia.

[1] St. René-Taillandier, *Maurice de Saxe*, Paris, 1870, pp. 212–215; Rutowski's report, Prague, 27 November, 1741, apud Vitzthum d'Eckstaedt, *Maurice comte de Saxe*, etc., Leipsic, 1867, pp. 415, 416; Luynes, iv. 47.

vorites of the regent. Her descent from the great tsar made her almost sacred in the eyes of the populace. Her person was fair, her figure noble, her manner gracious and winning. But the violence of her passions, which scandalized even the corrupt society of the Russian capital, gave such a direction to her life that she was thought to be reconciled to her exclusion from the throne, and to have no more dangerous ambition than to enjoy the company of her lovers. The turn of events made her, however, a useful instrument of French policy. This policy was represented officially by the marquis de la Chétardie, the ambassador of Louis XV. at St. Petersburg, and unofficially by one Lestocq, the physician and confidant of Elizabeth. The gold of the one bribed a sufficient number of the guards. The wily tongue of the other overcame the scruples of the princess, and she consented to be the beneficiary of a new revolution. In the night of the fifth of December the plot was easily carried out. The troops seized the gates of the palace, tore the reigning family from their beds, and hoisted the standard of Elizabeth, who the next morning was proclaimed empress without opposition.[1] The young tsar was sent to a remote prison in the interior. Münnich and Ostermann were banished to Silesia, and the foreign element was gradually eliminated from all branches of the public service. Frederic himself made, in consequence of this policy, one noteworthy acquisition in Euler, the great mathematician. Lascy, also an eminent foreigner in the Russian service, entered the army of Austria; while still another, Löwendahl, a Swede, accepted and honored the uniform of France.

Among the native Russians who were selected to fill these vacant places, count Alexis Bestuschef soon acquired the most influence in political affairs. Bestuschef.

[1] Manstein, ii. 168 ; report of Finch, the English envoy, apud Raumer, *Beiträge*, ii. 171.

He was born in 1693, and during thirty years had followed a public career with many varieties of fortune. In 1713 he was attached to the embassy sent by Peter the Great to the congress of Utrecht, but left it to enter the service of Hanover. Four years later he again became a Russian official. During the reign of the empress Anna he was a follower of Biron, and enjoyed high favor; but on the overthrow of his patron he was flung into prison by the regent. The accession of Elizabeth restored him again to public life. Titles, offices, pensions were lavished upon him; and for a dozen years, as chancellor of the realm, he was the most powerful person in the councils of the empress. His character reveals little indeed to explain this singular prosperity. Beyond a certain low cunning, and some knowledge of human nature, he had few qualities even of a mediocre mind; and his grasping selfishness was notorious. He was greedy of everything which could satisfy his desires — of rank, office, power, money, liquor, even of ease. In the perilous vicissitudes of Russian politics he aimed always to be on the winning side. He accepted bribes, and then betrayed those who had bribed him. He was fond of strong drink, of rich food, of every kind of riotous living, and every form of personal extravagance. His indolence was almost constitutional, and foreign envoys often had to await his pleasure for days or weeks at a time. But he was not bloodthirsty or vindictive, and put down his enemies by intrigue and address rather than by the gendarmes and the scaffold. His vices, too, were not of a kind which Elizabeth could fairly condemn. In his love of the bottle and the table, of flattery, of showy profusion, of easy and idle luxury, he dutifully followed the example of his sovereign; and as he seemed always ready to approve the crudest impulses of her political unwisdom, she early recognized him as her ideal minister and servant. Once installed in such a position of favor, he began, without much system yet without any scruples, to use it for his own advantage.

In his history of this period Frederic expressly disclaims all responsibility for the Russian revolution. But in the end he practically approved the French schemes by intimating, when approached on the subject, that he had no objections to offer on account of the tie of relationship which bound him to his brother-in-law, Anthony Ulric of Brunswick, husband of the regent, and generalissimo of the Russian forces. He replied, he says, that he recognized no relations among European princes except those who were his friends.[1] In view of the schemes which the regent was known to have in preparation, even her weak and timid husband became almost an enemy of Prussia, and Frederic saw the unhappy pair pass into exile without a protest.

The first reports from the scene of this characteristic coup d'état were highly favorable to those powers which gave it their support or sympathy. Mardefeld reported that the new empress cordially hated Austria and England; and she herself gave assurances that her policy would be that of a close alliance with Prussia.[2] No sooner, however, was the revolution at St. Petersburg effected than Frederic began to be apprehensive about its possible results. He scented danger alike in what France did, and in what she neglected to do; in the energy with which she carried out the plans of the alliance in Russia, and the lassitude with which she supported them in Germany. He keenly deplored the recall of Belleisle, and the appointment of marshal Broglie to the command at Prague.[3] Yet three days later, in a letter to his minister, he expressed equal alarm at the

Frederic's inconsistencies.

[1] Œuvres de Frédéric, ii. 100–102. Cf. Droysen, V. i. 382; Frederic to Fleury, 20 December, to Mardefeld, 23 December, 1741.

[2] Droysen, V. i. 383.

[3] Frederic to Fleury, 20 December, 1741.

growing influence of France at St. Petersburg.[1] Valori acutely remarks that Frederic's distrust of France steadily increased from the time of Klein-Schnellendorf, because he felt that he had forfeited any right to good faith on the part of his ally.[2] But it is charitable to assume that the loss of energy which was expected to follow the change of command in Bohemia touched him most closely, for he was already taking measures to throw some of his own energy again into the scale against Maria Theresa.

It was undoubtedly a misfortune for France, and a
Weakness of Fleury. stain upon his own reputation, that cardinal Fleury, who heartily disapproved the war, still remained in power, exercising a vast influence upon both diplomatic and military operations. For that influence was not likely to be in favor of loyalty and vigor in either the one or the other. It is true that he had no confidence in Frederic. It is also true that marshal Broglie, though a general of the old school, slow, pedantic, obstinate, was of unquestioned personal courage, and had claims to recognition which could not fairly be overlooked ; it is even alleged that Belleisle had himself asked to be relieved on account of the state of his health, and because he desired to be at Frankfort-on-the-Main during the imperial election.[3] But Fleury's heart was never in the war, and being constantly on the watch for occasions to end it diplomatically, he was reluctant to create, by earnest military measures, too great a gulf between his own court and that of Austria.[4] This policy seemed to be astute, but proved to be disastrous. It gave a pretext for duplicity to the allies of France,

[1] Frederic to Podewils, 23 December, 1741.

[2] *Mémoires*, i. 129.

[3] But it is also denied. It appears that in a fit of ill-humor Belleisle once asked to be relieved, but perhaps with the hope and the expectation that the request would be refused; cf. Broglie, *Fr. II. et M. T.*, ii. 152, 153.

[4] See in Adelung, ii. 546, the cardinal's statement to the Austrian envoy.

while it exposed her arms to humiliating reverses in the field.

The capture of Prague was, however, an advantage which Frederic hastened to seize before it should be lost by new blunders of the French ministers or the French generals.[1] Prince Leopold was ordered to collect his forces for the siege of the capital of Glatz. He had treated the country with a rigor which would have been cruel on the part of an enemy, and was inexplicable on the part of a friend. The youth were forced into the Prussian service; exorbitant contributions were collected; the Protestants were encouraged to emigrate to Silesia;[2] it seemed to be his policy to impoverish and depopulate the country. The elector of Bavaria, as king of Bohemia, protested against such severity; and even the compassion of Leopold's intendant, colonel Goltz, whose department the plunder enriched, was excited. Frederic's reply was a hint to the prince to be more prudent in his violence. He ought to pluck the chicken without making it cry.[3] It was now proposed to abandon these pleasantries, and undertake the capture of the chief fortified place in the county. Early in December a corps under Schwerin had also been put in motion, had passed from Upper Silesia into Moravia, and on the twenty-seventh day of the month occupied almost without opposition the important city of Olmütz.

The question now arises, What was the object of measures taken in such clear violation of the truce with Austria? Did they, or did they not, aim at something beyond the concession which the queen had made in the convention of Klein-Schnellendorf? It is

The Prussians in Glatz.

Frederic's motives.

---

[1] See Frederic to the king of Bohemia, i. e., the elector of Bavaria, 9 December, 1741.

[2] Frederic to prince Leopold, 9 December, 1741.

[3] See a letter of Goltz in Varnhagen von Ense, *Ausgewählte Schriften*, xii. 202–204; Stenzel, iv. 171, 172 ; Orlich, i. 159.

from the nature of things impossible to give any answer raised above all doubt by specific evidence ; but the theory which seems to have the strongest support in the facts and probabilities is that the king's object in breaking the truce was to enlarge, not simply to secure, the acquisitions already made. That those acquisitions were sufficiently secured, both in a diplomatic and in a military sense, is not denied except by the most fanatical of Frederic's champions. They were guarded by the good faith of the court of Vienna, by the word of an Austrian marshal who prized his military honor, and by the signature of an English envoy, whose own reputation and the interests of his government were pledged to the sacred observance of the compact. In virtue of this engagement the king obtained far more than he had originally demanded. If it be urged that Austria failed to comply with the impossible condition that the truce should remain a secret, the answer is that Frederic himself, writing four years later, ridiculed the grand-duke for taking the truce seriously.[1] Every material advantage which the agreement promised to the king was fully secured by the first of November. The formal treaty of cession, which the agreement held out in prospect, still indeed awaited its conclusion ; but the time fixed for that act had not expired when Schwerin was let loose upon Moravia. And in view of the general situation Frederic was stronger in December than in October. In October the French and Bavarians were lying inactive at Linz, and the queen had a strong fortress, with a formidable army, in Silesia. Frederic may, therefore, have accepted the convention of

---

[1] "Le duc de Lorraine . . . se flattant que le roi prendrait des pourparlers pour des traités de paix," etc. *Œuvres de Frédéric*, ii. 92. To Hyndford, who suggested that the Austrians might embarrass him by publishing the terms of the preliminaries of Klein-Schnellendorf, Frederic replied that by so doing they would only expose their own stupidity and folly. Hyndford, 12 November, 1741, apud Raumer, *Beiträge*, ii. 156.

Klein-Schnellendorf without any very strong belief in the queen's disposition to keep it, if fortune should prove favorable to her. But he resumed hostilities just after the capture of Prague had added to her perils, and when there was accordingly every reason why she should wish to retain the neutrality of Prussia by the religious fulfilment of the conditions on which it had been promised. That he regarded these measures as a renewal of the war is made clear by the whole tenor of his correspondence during the second half of December. The alleged betrayal of the secret by Austria was only a pretext, not a cause.[1]

The treaty with Bavaria, the occupation of Glatz, and the invasion of Moravia failed to frighten the court of Vienna into further sacrifices. They had rather the contrary effect of confirming the queen's belief in Frederic's perfect dishonesty; of releasing her from her own engagements; and of firing her soul with fresh indignation. Soon afterwards, too, her own fortunes began so far to improve that she became again really formidable, and compelled Frederic to think of more serious measures. When this necessity seemed clear, he acted with his usual promptness.

About the middle of January Frederic proceeded to Dresden as the first step in the execution of his new plan of action. The object of the visit was to concert measures with the court of Saxony for a joint campaign in Moravia; and the king has left an amusing account, from his own hand, of the council of war in which he labored to secure the approval of August for his energetic programme. The conference was attended, besides the two kings, by count Brühl, Valori, Maurice of Saxony, Rutowski, and Des Alleurs, the French envoy at Dresden. Frederic argued the case map in hand. He showed that the problem was easy, and that

Frederic in Dresden, January, 1742.

[1] See Grünhagen, ii. 65, 72, 73.

the campaign would be short; while the promise of Moravia as a new acquisition for the house of Saxony tempted the cupidity and silenced the scruples even of Brühl himself. But, according to Frederic, the end was not reached until an orderly announced that the hour for the opera had arrived. August hastily gave his assent, and rushed off to hear his favorite singers.[1]

The general plan provided that a corps of Saxon troops and the French division of general Polastron should join the Prussian army, and during the campaign be under the orders of Frederic; a king of Prussia could not serve as a subordinate.[2] The question of supplies being raised, Frederic undertook to obtain the services of Séchelles, a skilful French commissary officer. Valori supported these plans, and Belleisle wrote letters of encouragement. But marshal Broglie, who had not been taken into council, was not a little puzzled by this easy manner of appropriating his officers and men without his consent.[3]

Military convention with Saxony.

The movements of Frederic were quickened at this time by the urgent danger of Bavaria, and the appeals for help which went up from the elector. Field-marshal Khevenhüller finally completed his preparations for an offensive movement against Ségur at Linz. On the last day of December he set out from Vienna. He had about twenty thousand regular troops; while a large force of half-organized cavalry, pandours, croats, hussars, was kept under a fair degree of military restraint, and most audaciously handled by partisans like

Khevenhüller.

---

[1] *Œuvres de Frédéric*, ii. 107–109.

[2] Frederic to Belleisle, 15 January, 1742.

[3] Cf. Valori, ii. 250 ; Schmettau to the "king of Bohemia," in *Polit. Corresp.*, ii. 14–19 ; *Œuvres de Frédéric*, ii. 106. Frederic says, "le roi s'y détermina," i. e., to resume hostilities, "en même temps bien résolu pourtant de n'y employer que le moins de ses troupes qu'il pourrait, et le plus de celles que ses alliés voudraient lui donner." Cf. Luynes, iv. 94, 95.

Bernklau, Trenk, and Menzel. The army of Neipperg at Budeweis covered his advance from the side of Bohemia. In one week after opening the campaign Khevenhüller had Ségur blockaded in Linz; Schärding, near Passau, was seized by a coup-de-main ; and Menzel's wild horsemen began to scour the frontier districts of Bavaria itself. On the twenty-fourth of January Ségur surrendered Linz, obtaining indeed the privilege of free withdrawal for his troops, but on the condition that they should not again serve against the queen for twelve months.[1] Bavaria was thus thrown open to the Austrians on the very day when, at Frankfort-on-the-Main, Charles Albert was receiving the vain compliment of an election as emperor of Germany.

For the restless labors of Belleisle were finally crowned with this supreme triumph. The vote of Bohemia was excluded, but all the others, eight in number, were duly cast for Charles Albert ; the election was thus unanimous. The coronation of the new emperor, who took the title of Charles the Seventh, was fixed for the twelfth of February.

The elector of Bavaria chosen emperor.

[1] The wits of Paris circulated a satire on this transaction, in which the writer, affecting to refute the charge that Ségur had surrendered at discretion, said : —

> Á discrétion, c'est mal dit.
> De Linz il a lui-même écrit,
> Qu'à la tête de son armée
> Tambours battans, mèche allumée,
> Seulement pour un an il va
> Se réposer, car il est las.

CHAPTER V.

FREDERIC'S SECOND CAMPAIGN.

THE elation which Belleisle would naturally feel over
the successful completion of his diplomatic campaign was tempered by the perilous outlook of
the military situation. In Bavaria the road to Munich
stood open to Khevenhüller. In Bohemia marshal Broglie
had formed an intrenched camp at Pisek, between Prague
and Budeweis; but he had only sixteen or eighteen thousand men, and was held in check by a superior force of
Austrians. The new demonstration by Frederic came,
therefore, as a most opportune measure of relief.

The military outlook.

The form or direction which this relief should take had
been, however, one of the burning problems of
the Dresden conference, and had been solved in
a manner which implied a victory of Frederic's vehemence,
supported by Belleisle and Valori, over Saxon hesitation,
encouraged by the professional advice of Broglie. The
problem was really a simple one. There were two Austrian armies in the field, one confronting Broglie, and one
penetrating swiftly into Bavaria. It was therefore necessary for the allies to adopt a plan of action which would,
at once, save Broglie from attack by superior numbers,
and arrest the victorious march of Khevenhüller. About
this, too, all parties were agreed; the only question was
what plan of action was best suited to the end in view.
August and his military counsellors proposed a junction
of the Prussians and Saxons with Broglie, and a direct
advance upon the Austrian army in Bohemia, which it

Frederic's plan.

was thought would thus be forced either to retreat before
superior numbers, or to call Khevenhüller to its support.
In either case the advantage would rest with the allies.
The rival plan of Frederic was not to reënforce the
French marshal, but to make a diversion in his behalf.
By invading Moravia, and threatening Vienna, he hoped
to draw the army of Bohemia, now under Charles of
Lorraine, brother of the grand-duke, out of its position in
front of Broglie, rescue the latter from a dangerous situation, and enable him to reopen communications with Bavaria. The only enemy in the way was a force of a few
thousand men under general Lobkowitz at Iglau. At this
place there was also a large dépôt of supplies ; and these
it was thought would be abandoned, and fall into the
hands of the allies, as soon as they appeared before the
city. But beyond Iglau the Saxons refused to go. They
accepted Frederic's plan only in part, and, while willing
to coöperate in the first stage of his campaign, still kept
up a certain connection with Broglie by stipulating that
they should be at liberty to go into winter quarters after
the fall of Iglau.

From Dresden Frederic made a hurried visit to Prague,
where he conferred with the French and Ba-
varian generals, though not with Broglie. The Frederic
joins the
army.
marshal was at Pisek, and either because he was
lacking in courtesy as Prussian writers say, or awaited an
invitation as his own apologists allege, he failed to pay
his respects, and the king next proceeded to Glatz. The
town itself had already surrendered to prince Leopold.
But the garrison retired into the citadel, where it continued to battle manfully against hunger and disease, and
in fact did not yield until April, and then on highly
honorable terms. Frederic took, however, such comfort as
there was in the situation, and then hastened to Olmütz,
where he arrived on the twenty-eighth of January. He
had invaded Moravia in violation of the agreement of

Klein-Schnellendorf, which left the frontier defenceless. He now joined his army at Olmütz in pursuance of a new plan of hostilities against Maria Theresa, arranged by himself with his allies, and secured by new pledges of fidelity.

Yet his first act after reaching the army was not to fight, but to negotiate. Podewils was ordered on the thirtieth of January to make representations to Hyndford which, without positively committing Prussia, would leave the door open for an exchange of views.[1] Five days later Frederic received a secret envoy, baron Pfütschner, who brought overtures from the queen. Schwerin and Eichels favored their acceptance. Even Frederic did not wholly reject them, but simply offered some rather evasive suggestions of his own, proposed a channel through which further negotiations could be conducted without the knowledge of his allies, and thus gained time for further military preparations.[2]

In the mean time another set of negotiations between Frederic and the Saxon officers aimed to arrange the details of the coming campaign. They were long, stubborn, and vexatious; and it is difficult to say whether Frederic's impatience with the timid plans and lukewarm zeal of the Saxons, or their own reluctance to follow him far beyond their base of supplies and lines of communication into the depths of Moravia, was, in the

Secret negotiations at Olmütz.

Dissensions of the allies.

[1] *Polit. Corresp.*, ii. 23.

[2] Droysen, V. i. 398, 399 ; *Œuvres de Frédéric*, ii. 109, 110 ; Frederic to Valori, 4 February, 1742 ; Pfütschner's report of his mission in Arneth, ii. 35–38 and 469–475. It appears that this was the grand-duke's diplomacy in which the queen had no confidence, for she said, "Schreiben Sie dem Könige, wenn Sie es so wollen, aber er ist dessen nicht würdig, und wird einen üblen Gebrauch davon machen." I pass the incident rapidly over, since it led to nothing, and had no apparent influence on subsequent negotiations. That it was known to the allies appears from a letter of Maurice to Broglie, 10 February, 1742, in Vitzthum, *Maurice de Saxe*, pp. 436–440.

circumstances, the more justifiable. Marshal Broglie, who of course looked on the project with aversion, only reluctantly allowed the division of Polastron to take part in the first stage of the campaign. The Saxons, whom Rutowski commanded, insisted on the military convention of Dresden; they would proceed as far as Iglau, and no farther.[1] This may have been a timid, ungenerous, and unwise policy, but it was at least intelligible and straightforward. No charge of duplicity could up to this point be made against the Saxons.

The town of Iglau was occupied by the allied troops under prince Dietrich of Anhalt-Dessau, third son of Leopold, on the fifteenth of February. *Occupation of Iglau.* The intended surprise failed; and Lobkowitz not only drew his troops safely away, but even destroyed the entire store of supplies which Frederic had planned to capture. Here, too, Polastron and the French division departed, in obedience to orders previously received from Broglie, for the camp at Pisek. With him went, too, Maurice of Saxony, who, having predicted the failure of the expedition, accompanied it to see the fulfilment of his prediction.

Frederic showed a strange irritation over this not unexpected order, and wrote the marshal an extremely piquant letter. " I make no comment," *Frederic to Broglie.* he said, " on the bad grace of recalling troops which are marching with their allies against the enemy. Such a proceeding enriches the history of noble actions, and cannot fail to animate marvellously my zeal for the common cause. I doubt not that, as soon as you are reënforced by the corps of general Polastron, we shall hear of the brilliant success of your enterprises." [2] No friend of

[1] The chevalier de Saxe to August III., 30 January, 1742, being a report of a council of war at Landskron three days before. Vitzthum, *Maurice de Saxe*, pp. 423–427.

[2] Frederic to marshal Broglie, 11 February, 1742.

Frederic can read this letter with pleasure. Even if military reasons justified his displeasure in some degree, it was highly ungenerous to address an old French soldier in a tone which the difference in rank made it impossible for him to adopt in reply.

Maurice was another object of the king's resentment. He had played, so Frederic wrote, a bad part in the whole affair. He had run on errands from Pisek to Dresden, from Dresden to Prague, from Prague into Moravia, and from Moravia back to Dresden. He had made himself officious everywhere, and given offence in the highest degree.[1] The two men who were subsequently to be known as the foremost soldiers of the age were thus alienated in their first intercourse by serious differences of opinion, and even more serious misunderstandings. But they learned later to know each other better; and when Maurice visited Berlin, covered with the renown of great victories in the Netherlands, he was welcomed with the most flattering hospitality.

Frederic and Maurice de Saxe.

After leaving Iglau the Saxons continued as far as the limits of the county of the same name, and there they halted. The military agreement of Dresden gave them this right. But it was also stipulated that in case they should be unwilling to advance farther, they should go into winter quarters there, and thus be within supporting distance of the king, who proposed to push on to the river Taya; whereas Rutowski's orders were now to detach his force entirely, and conduct it to marshal Broglie in Bohemia. With great difficulty Frederic persuaded him to await the reply to a letter which he himself had sent to Dresden, once more imploring August to allow the Saxons to complete the campaign. He pointed out the ingratitude of an ally who would desert him at such a crisis. For that ally he had already conquered Upper Silesia, and nearly com-

Progress of the campaign.

[1] Frederic to August III., 14 February, 1742.

pleted the conquest of Moravia. He pledged his honor
that the campaign would end successfully if he were properly supported by those who had a far greater interest in
its issue than he himself. But should he be deserted, he
would at least feel relieved of all responsibility. He
would choose his own course of action, uninfluenced by
any further care for his allies.[1] These entreaties and
threats proved effective, and August, abandoning his
earlier purpose, sent Rutowski orders to keep his force
at Frederic's disposition. The reunited army then advanced to the line of the Taya, where it distributed itself
in camp for the rest of the winter. Frederic's headquarters were at Znaym. As soon as the weather in the
spring permitted, it was proposed to resume operations
with the siege of Brünn, the capital of Moravia.

One of the most distinguished of military critics, writing indeed long after the event but in no spirit
of hostility to Frederic, flatly condemns the   Spirit
Moravian campaign, which he calls an eccentric   of the
Saxons.
operation, and gives his preference to the plan of Broglie
for a union of all the allied armies in an offensive movement against prince Charles.[2] The Saxons, it is evident,
never wholly abandoned this, and gave the rival project, to which they nominally adhered, only a lukewarm
support. Their solicitude about the safety of Broglie
was of course mainly inspired by fears for their own
safety. The defeat of the marshal would open up to the
Austrians the way to Dresden. A diversion into Moravia
and upon Vienna might, as Frederic argued, draw the
principal army of the queen to the defence of her capital,
and thus release Broglie from danger ; and if such a result were likely to follow, it was undoubtedly better to
make the Moravian army so strong that it could meet the

[1] Frederic to August III., 15 February, 1742.

[2] Jomini, *Traité des grandes opérations militaires*, 4th ed., Paris,
1851, vol. i. p. 48.

enemy in battle. But there was still the other chance that prince Charles would seize the opportunity to crush Broglie, and march directly upon Prague and Dresden. As Frederic's army advanced, and the prince showed no disposition to move against it, the doubts of the Saxons increased. By the time Iglau was reached, they were ready to violate their promise to the king by transferring their own troops to what seemed the point of greatest danger. If at the eleventh hour they renewed their connection with the Prussians, they did so in a spirit of doubt which was not favorable to unity of action.

The anxiety of Frederic to have the Saxon troops in his control was, however, due in part to political considerations, which have not been sufficiently noticed. They are not revealed in his letters to August, the emperor, Broglie and Fleury, not even in those to Belleisle or Valori. But they clearly appear in his confidential communications to Podewils. He regarded the stipulations of Dresden as of the greatest value, because they gave him control of sixty thousand men, put him in possession of the larger part of the territory claimed by the Saxons, and, with the army of the Old Dessauer ready for action in the rear, made him arbiter of the war. " To tell you the truth," he added, in a letter more than usually frank and full of significance, " I cannot say when I shall be able to return to Berlin, for my great object now is not to let the Saxons escape from my hands. " [1] In other words, he had, or pretended to have, so little faith in his allies that he feared to trust them together. They had no more confidence in him; and the Moravian campaign, originally perhaps unwise, was thus doomed to failure by the jealousies, suspicions, and antagonisms of those who undertook to carry it out. Maria Theresa was not ignorant of these dissensions, which,

Political motives of Frederic.

[1] To Podewils, Olmütz, 30 January, 1742.

however, only lessened, not removed, the danger to which she was exposed.

In the face of this danger, this "second murderous attack," as she called it, the queen again appealed to the Hungarians, and proclaimed another levy en masse. The response was prompt and emphatic. The nobles armed their peasants with such weapons as were at hand, mounted them on the swift horses of the country, and in a short time were hanging on the flanks of Frederic's army, cutting off and picking up isolated detachments, interrupting his supply trains, destroying bridges, and threatening his communications in every direction. The Moravian peasants drove their cattle into the woods, concealed their provisions, and, where the occasion offered, organized into armed bands, in imitation of their Hungarian brethren. Such enemies were not dangerous in the open field, where the Prussian infantry easily dispersed them; but in all those minor exploits which embarrass an invading army they were consummately ingenious and successful. Frederic was greatly embittered by this mode of warfare. He threatened to treat all such irregular warriors who might fall into his hands as bandits and assassins; sweeping reprisals were made, and enormous contributions levied, upon the unfortunate country. Podewils and Schwerin deprecated such severity. Valori wrote that since the time of the Goths nobody had conducted war in that style. Even the Saxons complained that the country was so systematically devastated that no food was left for their troops, and the natives themselves were only enraged by the policy which was intended to subdue them.[1]

In March the Prussian outposts were gradually pushed forward in the direction of Brünn, and the investment of the city began. Zieten, with a regi-

New Hungarian levies.

Investment of Brünn.

[1] Droysen, V. i. 406 n., 414; Arneth, ii. 45; Grünhagen, ii. 156, 157; Valori, i. 149.

ment of Prussian hussars, made a daring raid into the
very suburbs of Vienna. Prince Dietrich scoured the
frontiers of Hungary of the rising bands of insurgents,
and secured the communications of the army. Broglie was
to prevent any movement on the part of prince Charles.
But the city of Brünn presented obstacles which had not
been wholly foreseen, and here the grand invasion of
Moravia came to an end. The garrison consisted of only
five thousand regular troops. The commandant, colonel
Roth, was, however, a man whose nerve Frederic had
learned to respect the year before at Neisse ; and he had,
besides the garrison, some three thousand Hungarian hussars, whom he knew how to use to the best advantage.
Holding these reckless riders in hand as a huntsman his
hounds, he sent out squadrons hither and thither, wherever there was a bridge to be destroyed, a convoy to be
intercepted, a line to be pierced, and made the life of
the besiegers indescribably anxious and miserable. The
levies, which had been dispersed by Dietrich, reassembled
as soon as he withdrew, renewed their forays, approached
the suburbs of Olmütz, and even caused anxiety for the
safety of the stores in Upper Silesia. A solemn council
of war, held at Vienna on the twenty-fifth of February,
had decided that Austria should try her fortunes in another battle before accepting Frederic's terms. An army
for the relief of Brünn was already forming.

It was, however, not in the field alone that the queen
was strong and confident. The turn which political affairs had lately taken was also highly
favorable to her interests, and gave her an advantage which Frederic was not slow to perceive. In
England sir Robert Walpole, after a ministry of twenty
years, and fighting to the last, went down under the blows
of his implacable enemies. The new cabinet, which was
whig like its predecessor, contained many adherents of the
fallen premier, and these were nearly all mediocrities;

Fall of sir
Robert
Walpole.

but it had one man of first-rate ability. Lord Carteret became one of the secretaries of state for foreign affairs, the department in which Walpole's policy had been the most unpopular.

To nearly all of the other members of the government Carteret was an unwelcome colleague. As men trained in the methods of the great peace minister, they looked with distrust upon his audacious schemes, and were not without some solid reasons for opposing them, but their principal objection to his presence in the cabinet was probably the immense superiority of his talents. Carteret is indeed one of those men whose extraordinary reputation posterity finds it difficult to understand. No great speech of his survives; no great act of legislation, or other triumph of statesmanship, has made his name immortal. He was dissolute, indolent, reckless, cynical. His political views, or at least his diplomatic measures, are now almost universally condemned as violent, aggressive, and dangerous. He was intolerant of the opinions of his colleagues. But the testimony of his own age makes him one of the finest scholars, one of the most brilliant orators, one of the keenest wits, and one of the ablest politicians, then in public life; nay, even commends his homely and robust common-sense, the last quality to expect in a member of that group of fierce parliamentary insurgents who harried the life of Robert Walpole. Like Pitt, a dozen years later, he was the real leader in a cabinet of which he was not the nominal head. With him a new era seemed to begin in English foreign politics.

His system differed from that of Walpole both in its tone or temper and in the ends at which it aimed. It was in the first place positive not negative, active not passive, aggressive and not merely defensive; the minister had his objects clearly before his eyes, and pursued them with an inflexible though reckless

determination.   His objects, too, had a look of novelty to
a generation which had grown up since the days of Marlborough, and had been enervated by Walpole's cautious
and conservative statesmanship.   Walpole had cultivated
friendly relations with France, had drawn a thrifty distinction between Hanoverian and English interests, and
had given the queen of Hungary only diplomatic aid, of
doubtful value, with a view to facilitating the least costly
escape from her difficulties.   But Carteret revived the
spirit of the war of the Spanish succession in a programme which included, besides the rescue of the queen,
the humiliation of France, and the reassertion of England's influence in continental affairs.   His views were
well known while he was still in opposition, and his accession to office was therefore hailed at Vienna with delight.   Against France at least he could be expected to
act with energy.[1]

The change of ministry in England, though the greatest,
was not the only piece of good fortune which
now raised the spirits of the Austrian party.

Continued good fortune of the queen.

About the same time a large instalment of the
promised English subsidy arrived to relieve the extreme
necessities of the queen's purse, and news was received of
the successful opening of negotiations for peace with the
king of Sardinia.   The landing of a Spanish army in
Italy made even the neutrality of Charles Emmanuel a
great military advantage.   But the outlook was favorable
for an offensive alliance by which his not insignificant
force should coöperate against the invaders.   A little
later this auspicious arrangement was actually made in a
treaty between the two courts.[2]

Frederic gave orders that Carteret should be caressed,
and even affected to be indifferent about the defection of
Sardinia.[3]   But he neglected no opportunity to secure his

[1] Cf. Arneth, ii. 62.   [2] Wenck, i. 162–676.
[3] Frederic to Fleury, 23 February ; to Podewils, 18 March,

own ends, and escape from his difficulties, by a separate
peace with the queen. All the resources of his diplomacy
were called in play, and all in vain. The court of Vienna
was now in little humor for concessions.

The military outlook grew daily more unfavorable to
Frederic. Valori announced by a courier that prince
Charles of Lorraine was moving from Budeweis upon
the French under Broglie ; the marshal, it was added,
threatened to retire behind the fortifications of Prague.
The rumor was false, for the movement was only a feint.
The prince had on the contrary received positive orders,
which ended a long exchange of views and an angry discussion of plans, to march against Frederic, and give him
battle if he should make a stand.[1] For this pur- Broglie calls
pose he had been reënforced by some ten thou- for help.
sand men detached from Khevenhüller. An equal force
was making ready at Vienna. The prince was therefore
strong enough to leave several regiments to watch Broglie,
while with a formidable army he marched to the deliver-
ance of Moravia. In the mean time the supplies of the
invaders were running short. The country was stripped
of food, and no stores had been left behind on which to
draw for support. With or without reason, Frederic had
expected Schwerin to form a magazine of supplies at
Olmütz ; and when he learned of the neglect to make
such provision, he held the marshal responsible, and sent
him a sharp letter of rebuke. But the high-spirited soldier at once demanded a leave of absence, which was un-
graciously granted. In the rest of the campaign the Ney
of the Prussian army took no part.[2]

1742. The middle of March Frederic's headquarters were transferred from Znaym to Selowitz.

[1] The military advisers of the queen were divided upon the question whether to attack the French or the Prussians. Cf. Arneth, ii.
41–44.

[2] Œuvres de Frédéric, ii. 109, 114. Cf. Varnhagen von Ense, xii.
204–209, and Grünhagen, ii. 163–165.

As soon as Frederic received the news, which seemed to be confirmed by another report a few days later, that the enemy were marching toward Prague, he at once saw that his own expedition would have to be abandoned. Failing to relieve Broglie by a diversion, he was obliged to support him with reënforcements. The Saxons were the nearest to Prague, and were of course alarmed for the safety of their own country ; so that, as the chevalier de Saxe, who had succeeded Rutowski in command, showed an order from Broglie to come to his support, Frederic promptly gave them permission to go.[1] In his own history he furnishes a different account of this proceeding. He intimates that he only feigned to believe the reports of Broglie because they gave him a convenient pretext for dismissing his useless allies, without whose presence he could make his own retreat more rapidly and more safely ; and Valori says that the king told him afterwards that he had never received a more agreeable letter than that of the French marshal.[2] But the correspondence of Frederic as now published gives little support to this cynical version. It shows very little doubt on his part about the truth of the story, and no irritation whatever with Broglie or the Saxons. The hurried dispatch of the chevalier de Saxe toward Prague implied indeed the abandonment of his own plan, and the failure of that plan he charged in part to the lukewarm support given by the allies ; but the complaints and recriminations, which had filled the first three months of the year, now belonged to the past. The growing difficulties of his position, which he bitterly described in many letters, led him some time before to consider the wisdom of a retreat. Valori's cry of alarm turned the scale.[3]

The departure of the Saxons made it impossible for the

[1] Frederic to the chevalier de Saxe, 1, 2 April, 1742.

[2] *Œuvres de Frédéric*, ii. 113, 114 ; Valori, i. 151, 152.

[3] Vide " Précis des raisons qui ont déterminé le roi de Prusse de

rest of the army to remain longer in Moravia. If prince Charles should move in the direction of Brünn, the Prussians alone would be too weak to give him battle; while, if Broglie's report should prove true, and Prague be really threatened, they would need to be in a position whence they could reach out a helping hand to the allies. In either case a retreat from Moravia into Bohemia seemed the best policy, and the direction which was chosen had in view either alternative that the enemy might adopt. The bulk of the Prussian army was to rendezvous about Chrudim, near Pardubitz. From there it could march easily to the defence of Prague or thwart an invasion of Silesia, as need might require; and to insure the presence of an adequate force for this duty Frederic ordered large reënforcements from the Old Dessauer, together with the available reserves of prince Leopold at Glatz.[1]

And decides on a general retreat.

If Frederic really intended by his abrupt dismissal of the Saxons to punish them for their bad conduct, his plan was highly successful. Their homeward march proved a trying problem. They were harassed by pandours along the whole line of their retreat, and after losing many men in skirmishes, from exposure and exhaustion, finally escaped with a mere remnant of the force which had originally taken the field. In spite of Frederic's appeals they refused to go to Prague, and did not rest until they crossed the frontier of Saxony.[2]

The flight from Moravia; the Saxons.

The retreat of the Prussians themselves, begun on the fifth of April, was scarcely less difficult, though effected with smaller loss. Frederic's force numbered after the departure of the Saxons about twenty-six thousand men.

marcher avec ses troupes de la Moravie en Bohême," enclosed to Chambrier for Fleury, 6 April, 1742, and accounts to other correspondents during the first half of April.

[1] Frederic to Valori, 11 April, to Belleisle, 12 April, 1742.

[2] *Œuvres de Frédéric*, ii. 114.

Of these the larger part, or some nine thousand foot and seven thousand horse, was placed under command of prince Dietrich, with orders to return to Olmütz, and hold it if humanly possible; if not, to retire into the nearest town in Upper Silesia, where supplies and reënforcements would be found. The object of this movement was to secure that part of the frontier against the roving bands of Hungarian insurgents. The presence of any more formidable enemy was not foreseen.

With the rest of the army, not more than ten thousand in number, the king set out by way of Wischau, Prostnitz, Müglitz, Trübau, and Leutomischl for Chrudim. The ubiquitous pandours opposed the march with all their dash and energy. The most constant vigilance could not wholly thwart the tactics of enemies whose lightness of movement enabled them to appear and disappear with equal rapidity; small detachments of Frederic's force often had to fight against immense odds; and general Möllendorf's repulse of two thousand Austrian horse, with only eight hundred dragoons of his own regiment, was justly accounted a brilliant, if not a very important, feat of arms. Finally, however, the end was reached. When the royal army, after leaving Müglitz, turned westward into Bohemia, the pandours no longer molested it, and about the middle of April it went into camp at the appointed place. Prince Leopold was already there with reënforcements, and his father was on the way with twenty thousand more. The total force was expected to reach forty-five thousand men.[1] The larger part of these, too, were fresh troops.

The trials of the Saxons, and of the Prussians under Frederic, were, however, light in comparison with those which prince Dietrich had to endure. His column had the right in the plan of retreat. He had to cover and protect the rear of Frederic's force, and

The Prussians under Frederic.

Prince Dietrich.

---

[1] Frederic to Valori, 11 April, 1742.

thus enable it to march with the utmost possible rapidity. But he also had to defend himself against an enemy far more formidable than bands of predatory horsemen, — against the army of prince Charles of Lorraine, thirty thousand strong.

The Austrian general had in fact broken camp at Budeweis the first day of April, and marched directly into Moravia. On the eighth he arrived at Znaym, which the Saxons had left only three days before. Thence he pushed on to Austerlitz, where he took up the reënforcements that awaited him, and then followed rapidly in pursuit of Dietrich. The Austrian light horse and irregulars, aided even by the Moravian peasants, who armed themselves as best they could, had so harassed the Prussians on the march that their progress was difficult, painful, and slow. A day's march from Olmütz they learned what enemy was behind them. Dietrich at once formed for battle in a strong position, and the next day, the twenty-second, awaited the attack. But as the enemy did not appear he called a council of war. The unanimous opinion of the officers was that in view of the superior strength of the Austrians, their own want of supplies, the exhaustion of their troops, and the danger to their communications, it would be folly to attempt to hold Olmütz, and that nothing remained except to seek safety, while it was yet possible, in Upper Silesia.

Even this proved difficult. The industrious pandours were already ahead of them ; had seized every village ; occupied every pass. Messengers were sent out only to fall into the hands of the enemy. The wagons had to be used as movable breastworks, behind which the weary but undaunted Prussians received the assaults of swarms of exultant horsemen, now in their rear, now in their front, now on their flanks. But these skirmishes were seldom bloody, and whenever the Prussians had a chance to use their rifles the enemy suffered the greatest loss. Three days after leaving Olmütz the advance of the army reached Troppau. The actual loss of men was not great, and even the disabled were nearly all saved. The principal sacrifice was that of some sixty field-pieces and a considerable quantity of ammunition, which had to be left at Olmütz. But the troops were worn out by fatigue, hunger, and privations of every sort, and even after reaching Silesia they long suffered from inadequate supplies.[1]

The failure of the Moravian campaign gave rise to endless recriminations between the Prussians and the French, the echoes of which have not yet subsided. Until recent times the view which prevailed, even in France, was, up to a certain point, favorable to Frederic; the retreat from Brünn was attributed to the refusal of marshal Broglie to support the king. The arguments of Droysen defend this view with great ingenuity and ability, while those of an eminent descendant of the marshal, to whose researches I confess my obligations, will carry an opposite conviction to many minds. And it may be the fate of a neutral, who attempts to pronounce a judicial opinion between the parties, to be rejected and condemned by both.

A concise statement of the case would probably say that military indecision lamed the efforts of one party, and political insincerity governed the conduct of the other. The strategy of the French, from the time of the capture of Linz, was thoroughly bad; their movements lacked energy; their general was old, infirm, irresolute, nerveless. They were not even harmonious among themselves, for, while Valori, Belleisle, and all of the younger, more enterprising officers supported the Prussian alliance, Fleury and Broglie, who had grown gray amid the depravity of courts, placed little confidence

Reflections on the failure in Moravia.

---

[1] I have followed principally Grünhagen, ii. 179 et seq. Of Dietrich's heroic conduct Frederic makes no acknowledgment in his history.

in the permanence of military leagues between powers of
such diverse interests, and were jealous of any triumphs
which would not add first of all to the glory, or at least
the advantage, of France. An intermediate obstacle to
success was the mutual antipathy, the blame for which it
is difficult to apportion, of Frederic and Broglie.[1] But
that the plan of the Moravian campaign was adapted to
the interests of all the allies, or that Frederic aimed at
anything except the attainment of his own ends, seem
to me propositions which the evidence fails to support. It
is true that Frederic speaks in one of his letters of the
policy of giving a mortal blow to the house of Austria.[2]
But elsewhere he expressly disclaims such a purpose; and
even Ranke throws doubt upon the sincerity of the movement against Brünn.[3] The secret negotiations with Austria, which followed step for step the march of the army,
are fatal evidence against the king. The most that could
be urged in his behalf is his profound distrust of France,
and the conviction, inspired by that feeling, that it was
necessary to win his own game at once, lest it be ruined
by a sudden treaty between Austria and France. That
such a treaty had not yet been concluded was not the
fault of Maria Theresa. It is now known that she had
repeatedly made advantageous offers of peace to France,
as she had to Prussia; and these overtures were no secret
even to Frederic himself. They had indeed been uni-
formly rejected by the cardinal, and with almost unneces-

[1] The common theory traces it back to the Strasburg incident.
See supra, p. 22; in the *Historische Zeitschrift*, No. 1, 1884, the article
"Friedrich der Grosse und die Familie Broglie," by R. Koser; and
Beauvau to Fleury, Munich, 15 December, 1741, in Broglie, *Fr. II.
et M. T.*, ii. 371.

[2] Frederic to Jordan, 25 February, 1742.

[3] Frederic to Pfütschner, in Arneth, ii. 36, 37; Ranke, *Sämmtliche
Werke*, xxvii., xxviii. 502. See in Flassan, v. 149–151, Amelot to
Belleisle, 19 April, 1742, a letter in which the French suspicions
about Frederic's retreat find pungent expression.

sary emphasis.[1] In its outward aspects the fidelity of
France, even if its motives were not the noblest, presents
a striking contrast to the preliminaries of Klein-Schnellendorf and the negotiations at Olmütz. But Frederic's
low standard of political integrity naturally led him to
fear that French virtue would not long withstand the
pressure which Maria Theresa was daily putting upon
it, and he hastened accordingly to strike a blow which,
under the name of a joint military action, was really intended only to serve his own ends.[2]

And this pretentious blow had missed its aim. An ill-
conceived and hastily prepared campaign, undertaken
without due reflection by its commander, and feebly supported or secretly opposed by his allies, failed to strike
terror, as had been expected, into the heart of the queen
of Hungary, and came to an ignoble end before the walls
of Brünn. The confidence of Frederic had again outrun
his discretion. He was now, as in Silesia a year before,
straining every nerve to correct his mistake, concentrate
his forces, and put himself in fighting order before the
enemy should spring at his throat.

In the other fields of military and political action the
Ill success
of the allies.
outlook for Austria was scarcely less bright.
While the king of Sardinia was changing from
an enemy into a neutral, and the English parliament was
voting fresh subsidies to the queen, Khevenhüller occupied Munich, and levied contributions throughout Bavaria, as in a conquered country. The unfortunate elector, an exile at Frankfort, was piteously begging for men
and money, with which to support the vain dignity of

[1] Broglie, *Fr. II. et M. T.*, ii. 341, mentions overtures by the queen
31 January, 17 February, and 16 March, 1742, all alike repelled by
the cardinal.

[2] "La supercherie, la mauvaise foi, et la duplicité sont malheureu-
sement le caractère dominant de la plupart des hommes qui sont à
la tête des nations, et qui en devraient être l'exemple." Frederic to
Voltaire, 3 February, 1742.

holy Roman emperor.[1] The French in Prague and the French at Pisek were helpless or inactive; their only recent achievement was the capture of Eger, — a very creditable piece of work in itself, but one which seemed to prepare a retreat instead of an advance.[2] The Saxons had returned utterly demoralized to their own country. Even the king of Prussia, the most formidable enemy in the field, had made an ignominious retreat, after a campaign in which not a battle had been fought. The queen's own army in Moravia was flushed with a bloodless triumph, and its superiority in numbers ensured her no little advantage even in diplomacy. This was the moment at which, according to many historians, she ought to have listened to the voice of reason, and accepted the moderate terms that were offered.

The advice, familiar in the copy-books, to be moderate in prosperity, is never perhaps very welcome to the prosperous. But it is peculiarly offensive when addressed by an aggressor to an intended victim, who has suddenly arrested him in his ambitious career; and a just resentment then readily magnifies the importance of what may be only a temporary success. It is easy enough to say now, after the event, that this was the error of Maria Theresa; that she mistook moral for material strength. The old feeling of indignation at the unprovoked invasion of Silesia, and the exultation caused by the enemy's retreat from Brünn, may indeed have tempted her to weigh the chances of another battle with less nicety than would have been prudent. But it is rash to say that her military resources did not at this time

Firmness of Maria Theresa.

[1] A satirical medal which circulated at the time represented on the obverse Charles Albert as elector, with the inscription "Aut Cæsar aut Nihil," and on the reverse the same prince as emperor, with the words " Et Cæsar et Nihil."

[2] Maurice of Saxony was the commander of the victorious force, which however, being drawn from Broglie, weakened the marshal to that extent.

justify her in making one more attempt to save her patrimony unimpaired.

Even lord Hyndford was not disposed at this juncture Hyndford at to advise an abject submission. He had been Breslau. invited by the king as early as the eighteenth of March to meet Podewils at Breslau for a conference on the subject of peace.[1] But either because he was not anxious to be again the dupe of Prussian diplomacy, or because the new English ministers had given him instructions to take a bolder tone, or because, as Frederic and Podewils thought, he was striving to gain time for the military operations of prince Charles, he showed little alacrity in his movements, made the journey by way of Dresden, and arrived in the Silesian capital only on the seventeenth of April. Even after his arrival he maintained an air of reserve and indifference, which caused no little distress to Podewils.

The minister communicated Frederic's demands in the Frederic's form of an ultimatum. They required the cession ultimatum. of Lower Silesia, of Glatz, and of two Bohemian counties, Königgrätz and Pardubitz ; furthermore, in vague terms, a reasonable satisfaction for the allies of Prussia.[2] But Hyndford flatly refused to transmit these propositions as an ultimatum to Vienna, or to do more than report them as his impression of the basis on which the king was willing to treat. In later interviews he intimated that the demand for satisfaction to the allies would arouse suspicion, and that the queen would require the support, not simply the neutrality, of Prussia.[3] Nothing could move the stubborn envoy, not even the offer of ten thousand thalers, which Podewils was charged

[1] *Pol. Cor.*, ii. 83.

[2] Conditions sur lesquelles j'ai ordonné à mon ministre d'état, comte de Podewils, d'entrer en négociation avec milord Hyndford, etc. Selowitz, 22 March, 1742 ; *Pol. Cor.*, ii. 84, 85.

[3] Grünhagen, ii. 216, 217.

as a last resort to make. "The king does not know me," haughtily replied Hyndford, "nor the peers of England." "But," urged Podewils, "a minister, who has happily conducted a negotiation according to his conscience, can properly accept proofs of the gratitude of a great prince." "Let us be satisfied to bring about a peace," was the reply. "The future will arrange itself."[1]

The objection which Hyndford raised to the stipulation in favor of the other allies was wholly superfluous, and, like the article itself, probably a mere matter of form. The exact value of the demand, or rather of his obligation to insist on it, had already been fixed by Frederic himself, either just before or just after presenting it. The process of the computation is shown in two papers, prepared by the king's own hands, and included in the published volumes of his political correspondence.[2] One of these is a statement of the reasons which supported the alliance with France; the other, of the reasons for the opposite policy of a separate peace with the queen. It was perfectly proper that the first should open with a reason drawn from the obligations of good faith.[3] But the motives for a breach of faith, as presented in the second paper, are scarcely less cogent; and although no opinion between the two is given, the overtures to Hyndford, and various letters to Podewils, show that Frederic was not only willing, but even eager, to desert his allies, and make his own terms with the queen. This would be more advantageous to him, he said, than a general pacification.

Frederic moralizes.

For this reason, instead of breaking off the negotiation, when Podewils reported how Hyndford had received the

---

[1] Grünhagen, ii. 221. Droysen omits to mention this scandalous attempt at bribery. Raumer, *Beiträge*, ii. 158, says 100,000 thalers.

[2] Vol. ii. pp. 98–100.

[3] "Il est mal de violer sa parole sans raison ; jusqu'au présent je n'ai pas rien de me plaindre de la France ni de mes alliés."

ultimatum of the twenty-second of March, he began at
His anxiety for peace. once to find pretexts for modifying it. With
his resources this was not difficult. The more
active intervention of England in behalf of the queen,
the suspicious tone of Valori,[1] the cost of the war,
the danger that a reverse in the field would imperil the
conquests already made, the want of energy on the part
of the allies, — such were some of the reasons which, often
before expressed, were now repeated in categorical form.[2]
If they were reasons for peace, they were also reasons for
modifying demands which Hyndford had clearly shown
would, if insisted on, make peace impossible. Hence the
daily letters to Podewils began to show a more conciliatory disposition. The king offered to enter into a defensive alliance with the maritime powers, and, after the
general peace, even with the queen herself. He suggested
various methods by which the cession of the two Bohemian
circles could be made more agreeable to Austria. And as
a last concession he was willing to waive them entirely,
and accept Upper Silesia as an equivalent. The progress
of Frederic's mind along this course, the multitude of
plans which he daily put forward, some contradicting
others, or thrown out in one letter only to be recalled in
the next, and the mass of sophistical deductions with
which he tried the patience of Podewils, may be seen in
the correspondence for the last two weeks of April. His
own belief in the acuteness of his logic and the strength
of his position was, however, so great that he awaited with
confidence the return of the courier whom Hyndford had
sent with the ultimatum to Vienna.

The courier reached Breslau with the queen's answer on
The famous case of madame Abbé. the fourth of May. But in the mean time a new
obstacle had arisen. In Berlin the envoy had a
woman named Abbé, the wife of a publican, as

[1] In an audience the 19th of April, *Pol. Cor.*, ii. 118, 119.
[2] To Podewils, 20 April, 1742.

housekeeper, — though rumor whispered that she was something more than that, — and this excellent matron had been arrested some time before on the complaint of her creditors. The judges before whom she was brought refused to entertain the case. The plaintiffs then appealed to Frederic ; and on their representation he ordered the commandant to arrest her by military process, and hold her in confinement until the debt was paid. It pleased Hyndford, who perhaps was not unwilling to find pretexts for delay, to call this a breach of diplomatic privilege ; the instant release of the woman was demanded. Podewils reported the case in this new aspect, and by the order of Frederic, who wrote that more important affairs than those of a wretched bankrupt were at stake, the housekeeper was set at liberty. But the king took occasion to write Hyndford a sharp letter on the subject. After reminding him that the rights which belonged to the envoys of foreign powers were not unknown at Berlin, he inquired whether he had not made a mistake in associating the affairs of a woman of doubtful repute with the august name of the king of England. The house of a diplomatist ought not to become an asylum for prostitutes. Similar abuses introduced licentiousness in Rome, whence followed thievery, violence, and murder, until order and good morals were entirely destroyed. The government of Berlin having erred in respect to form, he had ordered due reparation to be made. But he could not avoid the reflection that if England adopted such an imperious tone now, when she was by no means the first power in Europe, she might in the future, if fortune should favor her, adopt the style and language of Louis the Fourteenth. France would then become the chief protector of the liberties of Europe.[1]

[1] Frederic to Podewils and to Hyndford, 6 and 7 May, 1742 ; Grünhagen, ii. 229–231. To complete the story, and as an instructive illustration of the evils of paternal government, it must be

For four days after their arrival, and until the receipt of Frederic's letter, Hyndford carried the Austrian counter-propositions in his pocket, refusing to present them. Finally, on the eighth of May, his mind being duly calmed by the perusal of the royal communication, he laid them before Podewils. The queen offered to cede Lower Silesia as far as the river Neisse, and with it either Glatz or Upper Silesia, as Frederic might prefer, but only on condition that Prussia guarantee the remaining Austrian territories, and furnish military aid for their defence. The two Bohemian counties she refused absolutely to surrender. She might even have pointed out that it was somewhat inconsistent for Frederic to ask her to cede to him a part of Bohemia, when, by a treaty lately concluded, he had recognized the title of the elector of Bavaria to the whole of it. But this would have been a useless retort, and the answer which Hyndford submitted was a simple statement of her own terms. " Have you nothing more to offer," inquired Podewils, amazed and incredulous. " Nothing," replied the envoy. " Then we are both to be pitied, for we have labored in vain." [1] The discussion was thus abruptly closed.

The queen's proposals.

Hyndford's rage over Frederic's refusal to make war on his own allies found vigorous expression in his reports to his government. Curiously enough, he seemed to treat it as evidence of a perfidious nature. " What trust can be placed in a prince," he wrote, " who has neither truthfulness, nor honor, nor religion ; who regards treaties as meant only to deceive fools ; who makes the most sacred things objects of ridicule ; who has no plan and asks no counsel, but seeks to make everything bend to his own

added that it subsequently transpired that the creditors had made false representations to Frederic, whereupon they in turn were imprisoned.

[1] Grünhagen, ii. 231, from Podewils' report ; Arneth, ii. 67, 68 ; Droysen, V. i. 438.

caprice; and who prefers the slightest success of the moment to the solid and durable advantages of the future?"[1] These are hard words, and the dupe of Klein-Schnellendorf had some personal excuse for using them. But Hyndford was not exactly fitted for a teacher of political ethics. Although he had found Frederic's demands exorbitant, and refused to give them his approval, he actually regretted that the queen had declined to accept them, and boldly gave the reason for his regret. He was of the opinion that the cessions ought to have been made, for they would have been only temporary. They would have been extorted by force, and a double breach of faith; and nobody could have complained if the house of Austria, using the law of retaliation, had seized the first opportunity to recover them.[2] Such was Hyndford's theory of the negotiations. If this view had prevailed at Vienna, there would have been of course little discussion of the nature of Frederic's demands, for the intention to repudiate any agreement at the first suitable moment would have made it relatively of small importance what extent of territory was nominally ceded. But it is evident that no such cynical line of reasoning was adopted in the councils of Maria Theresa.

When Podewils' report of the queen's proposals reached Frederic he treated them as a direct challenge. "Since the Austrians are blind," he wrote, "we must complete their ruin; it seems to be the will of Providence." And he added, as if an agent chosen to execute that will, "on the thirteenth we take the field; such is the result of these negotiations."[3] The king's zeal for the allies and the common cause at once revived. Valori had been at Chrudim for several days, but had effected nothing; for, although his suspicions were aroused

Rupture of the negotiations.

[1] Raumer, ii. 158.   Translated back from the German.
[2] Ibid. pp. 159, 160.   From Hyndford's report, 23 May, 1742.
[3] Frederic to Podewils, 11 May, 1742.

by the signs of a mysterious correspondence with Breslau, Frederic explained that it concerned only private matters, and entertained him with a lively account of the misfortunes of Hyndford's housekeeper.[1] Now the envoy was taken into confidence. The Austrian propositions were shown to him, and it was explained that they had been at once rejected as incompatible with the king's duty to his allies.[2] Two days later Frederic wrote to the cardinal that with Belleisle, who would be in his camp on the twenty-second, he looked forward to a cordial coöperation. But for audacity a letter of the same date to Chambrier surpasses everything that Frederic's diplomacy had yet yielded. Chambrier was his own envoy at Paris ; and whether the communication was intended for his private guidance, or was to be submitted to the cardinal, does not absolutely appear. But it is equally remarkable whether the one theory or the other be adopted.

That part of the letter which is of the most interest
A candid letter.
begins with the statement that the queen's propositions had been laid before Valori as a mark of the writer's sincerity and his attachment to the king of France. The court of Vienna, Frederic then explains, "offered me the cession of Upper Silesia, the guaranty of Jülich and Berg, and other advantages, if I would furnish troops to expel the French from Germany. But I at once rejected such propositions as unworthy of my glory, and contrary to my rules of action. They threatened to make a separate peace with the emperor, and I replied that I was so sure of the good faith of my allies that I was not to be moved by such menaces. Upon this they offered, as a proof of their sincerity, to show that France had sent a secret emissary, named Fargis, to negotiate at Vienna. I answered that if the

[1] Frederic to Podewils, 6 May, 1742.
[2] Broglie, *Fr. II. et M. T.*, ii. 270–272, quoting from Valori's report of 11 May. Cf. Frederic to Chambrier, 14 May, 1742.

cardinal had sent an agent to Vienna, which I was far from believing, I was certain that he had nothing in view prejudicial to the allies of his master; and when they began to give the full details of this pretended negotiation I cut them short abruptly, for I connected the device with previous schemes of the court of Vienna, and saw no utility in further discussion. In the division of the allies that court hopes to find its own safety. . . . Thanks to the cardinal for the confidence which he has in us. He will always have reason to be contented with the king of Prussia, who prefers the friendship and alliance of France to all the advantages that can be offered by the queen of Hungary and her allies." [1]

Now the audacity of this lay not in the mere perversion of facts, for the age allowed much license to diplomacy, or even in the assurances of unshaken fidelity to the common cause, for a prince who meditates treachery cannot be expected to avow his intention to his allies. These parts of the letter required indeed some boldness, and therefore deserve admiration. The French government was not ignorant, and Frederic knew that it was not ignorant, of the general course of the negotiations at Breslau; [2] and he was too sagacious to suppose that his own version of them would be implicitly accepted. His general and special assurances of good faith were likewise lost upon a court, which had learned from experience to have no confidence in the word of the king of Prussia. No little courage was thus required to challenge the information and the scepticism of cardinal Fleury. But a higher order of daring is revealed in the almost passionate repudiation of any distrust, or any reason for distrust, of the court of Versailles; for Frederic had actually given orders to use the pretended mission of Fargis, the French emissary at Vienna, as an

Toujours de l'audace.

---

[1] Frederic to Chambrier, 14 May, 1742.

[2] Vide Frederic to Podewils, 6 May, 1742.

excuse for his own separate peace, as soon as it should be concluded.[1] And the king's information, such as it was, about this personage, came not from the queen of Hungary, but from Klinggraeffen, the Prussian envoy at the allied court of Munich.[2] In view of these facts, is it strange that Eichel was appalled by the extraordinary letter to Chambrier? His only prayer was, he wrote to the equally mystified and equally anxious secretary of state at Breslau, that they might not be overwhelmed by the waves into which they were recklessly plunging. Miscemus ima profundis; may God grant us ne pereamus in undis![3]

And now Belleisle, the one Frenchman who still had faith in Frederic, was expected in the Prussian camp. With his usual versatility he had once more laid aside the uniform of the diplomatist for that of the soldier. An arrangement had been made by which he was to relieve Broglie in Bohemia, while the latter was to take command of the new French army, forming under count Harcourt for the relief of Bavaria. But before these transfers could be carried into effect, the movements of Frederic changed the whole face of the military situation.

Belleisle and Broglie.

It is worthy of note that Frederic, on retiring into Bohemia, had not taken up a defensive position behind the Elbe, but rather an offensive one in front of it, with a line stretching from Chrudim as a centre toward Kuttenberg on the right and Leutomischl on the left. The corps of Leopold of Dessau reached the camp on the twenty-sixth of April. This was two or three days later than the appointed time; and as the delay was charged to the act of the prince in departing somewhat from his prescribed route, though he followed the advice of those who were familiar with the

The Prussians reën-forced.

---

[1] Frederic to Podewils, 9 May, 1742.

[2] Same to same, 29 April, 1742.

[3] 16 May, 1742. *Pol. Cor.*, ii. 163 n.

country, Frederic sent him a short letter of reprimand.
" I am surprised," he wrote, in his peculiar German,
" that as an old officer you do not carry out my orders
more accurately. If you were more skilful than Cæsar,
and did not strictly follow your instructions, the rest would
do no good. I hope that this warning will suffice, and that
you will give me no further cause for complaint."[1] Then,
as a species of punishment, he sent the offender to Upper
Silesia, to command the force which had the not very
stirring duty of guarding the passes and the magazines.
The old warrior kept silence until after the close of the
campaign. Then, after writing a pathetic defence of his
conduct, he sent in his resignation, and proposed to leave
the service ; it was with no little difficulty that he was
finally pacified. Thus at a critical moment Frederic de-
prived himself of the aid of his two leading generals.
First Schwerin and then the Old Dessauer was sent to
the rear; and prince Leopold was left the highest officer
under the king. The Prussian army now comprised some
thirty battalions of foot and sixty squadrons of horse, together about thirty thousand men.[2] A further reënforcement of eight or ten thousand, under general Derschau,
was expected on the twentieth of May.

Early in the month the army of prince Charles crossed,
near Iglau, from Moravia into Bohemia. It was
at first supposed by Frederic that the inten- Movements
tion was to reënforce Khevenhüller, whom the Charles.
French advance under Harcourt had compelled to evacuate Munich and retire upon Passau ; and he sent warning
accordingly to marshal Broglie.[3] But the sincerity of
this belief on the king's part may perhaps be questioned.
There is no evidence for the current story, told to the
marshal's prejudice, that he refused Frederic's invitation

[1] Orlich, i. 221, 222 ; Grünhagen, ii. 236.
[2] Grünhagen, ii. 236.
[3] Frederic to Broglie, 5 May, 1742.

to join his army to the Prussian, or that such an invitation was ever given,[1] while it is known that Belleisle's plan, ardently supported by Valori, for a combined movement toward the Danube, found no favor at Chrudim; that the king himself desired to meet the Austrians and try the issue alone with them.[2] In any event it soon became apparent that the prince was shaping his course, not toward Passau or Pisek, but toward Prague.[3] It is now known that his instructions were to recapture the city, which had only a small French garrison; to separate by this stroke the French from the Prussians; and in case the latter interrupted his march, to give them battle.[4] But since a battle was what Frederic desired, he prepared to throw his army across the prince's path.

The outlying camps were broken up on the eleventh, and, strictly according to programme, the whole army was drawn up two days later about Chrudim. Here an inspection was held. Everything was in faultless order; officers and men alike eager; and Frederic surveyed his brave battalions with feelings of natural exultation. But there was little time for military pageants. It was known that the enemy was in the neighborhood, marching rapidly northwestward, on the main road to Prague. To thwart this movement Frederic with six thousand men hastily departed on the fifteenth for Kuttenberg; prince Leopold was to follow with the main body of the army the next day.

The king, marching swiftly all day, arrived toward evening at the little village of Podhorzan, where he ordered a bivouac for the night. On the opposite hills, only three or four miles away,

Movements of the Prussians.

---

[1] Droysen, V. i. 441 n.

[2] Broglie, *Fr. II. et M. T.*, ii. 271, 273, from Valori's report, 12 May, 1742.

[3] Frederic to Jordan, 11 May; same to Broglie, 10 May, 1742.

[4] Arneth, ii. 48.

could be seen a considerable force of the enemy. It was at first taken for the column of Lobkowitz, and gave rise to anxious inquiries whether prince Charles was about to be reënforced.[1] But at daybreak the next morning it was no longer to be seen, and the Prussian vanguard pushed on unopposed to Kuttenberg. The task assigned to prince Leopold proved to be far more difficult. He had the artillery to escort, and there was only a single bridge, that of Sbislau, by which it could cross the river Dobrawa. Fortunately the light horse of the Austrians, though ranging all day in the neighborhood, had neglected to destroy the bridge, and the Prussians passed over in safety. But the way was full of natural obstacles; communication with the king was difficult; and there was no bread for the troops. It was found impossible to reach Czaslau that night, for the army had been in motion twenty hours, and it was hazardous to venture far in the darkness with an active enemy following every step. A halt was therefore made for the night at the hamlet of Chotusitz. After several messengers had tried to reach the king and failed, a fourth finally brought him the report of Leopold's progress, and the announcement that a battle was probable the next day. About midnight an answer was received. The king promised to join his lieutenant early the next morning.[2]

The Prussian troops lay on their arms all night. The situation was extremely critical, for it was in the power of the Austrians to attack the two divi- *The Austrian advance.* sions of the enemy before they could reunite, and crush them one after the other. It is believed that by energetic movements this might have been done on the sixteenth, while the tired and hungry troops of Leopold were winding their way through narrow defiles, climbing rugged hills, and fording streams. But the opportunity was lost through the procrastination of prince Charles, and his professional adviser, marshal Königsegg. The night attack which Leopold feared was, however, planned, and nearly executed. The Austrians set out from their camp at Ronow about nine o'clock in the evening, and in three columns with a reserve, leaving their baggage and heavy guns behind, marched silently toward Czaslau. The surprise of the Prussians would have been complete, and the result for them disastrous, if the distance had been less and the roads better. Leopold's scouts brought no report of the movement; no sound revealed the approach of an enemy. But it was four o'clock in the morning when the Austrians reached Czaslau, and seven o'clock before they were fully formed for attack. Before that time they had been discovered, and the Prussians were likewise arranged in order of battle.[1]

Leopold chose the village of Chotusitz as his centre, and extended his line thence loosely to the pond of Cirkwitz on the right; and still more loosely to the park of Sehnsitsch on the left, with infantry in the middle, and cavalry at each wing, according to the recognized tactics of the time. Just as these dispositions were completed the king arrived with his battalions, which were ranged in the second line, or reserve. The battle was at once opened, the Prussians attacking from their right, and receiving an attack on their left.

The charge of the Prussian cavalry under general Büddenbrock at the extreme right was an imitation of that of Römer at Mollwitz. It succeeded in the same manner in breaking the first line of the enemy's horse, but was arrested and hurled back by the second. General Rothenburg with his dragoons galloped to the rescue; and the second, more powerful shock car-

Battle of Chotusitz.

---

[1] Cogniazo, ii. 80, attributes the prince's delay in part to the difficulty of dragging the field guns over the heavy roads.

ried the Prussians entirely through the Austrian cavalry, and even doubled up the nearest infantry battalions. At this point, however, their progress ceased. The Austrian hussars recovered from their disorder, reformed, and fell upon the flank of the enemy so fiercely that after making desperate efforts, and suffering heavy losses, Rothenburg and Büddenbrock had to withdraw their shattered squadrons for rest and reorganization. On their left the Prussians were even less successful. The assault of the hostile cavalry was impetuous and overwhelming. It broke through the first line of horse, then the second,[1] and next turned at an angle upon the infantry. At this crisis, too, prince Charles sent his foot forward to coöperate with the horse; and their combined efforts carried the village of Chotusitz, which, though the key to the Prussian position, had been left with an inadequate force to defend it. But the contest was desperate and bloody. The Prussian battalions reformed for defence as often as they were driven back; every inch of the ground was disputed; a chaplain named Seegebart rushed about in the thickest fire, animating the defenders by his stirring exhortations;[2] the unlucky village itself burst into flames, which intensified the ghastly terrors of the scene. But it is maintained by the Austrians that the day was lost through the misconduct of their own cavalry, which, instead of pursuing their advantage and rendering the victory complete, stopped to plunder the Prussian camp. The fatal delay caused by this disorderly proceeding turned the fortunes of the battle. Upon a slight though command-

[1] Frederic charged this temporary disaster to Leopold, who "ayant trop tardé a mettre les troupes en bataille, n'avait pas eu le temps de la former sur le terrain le plus avantageux." *Œuvres de Frédéric*, ii. 122. The prince in turn laid the blame on general Jeetze, who commanded on the left.

[2] On Seegebart see the editor's note to *Œuvres de Frédéric*, xvii. 212. The anecdote seems to be well authenticated notwithstanding Frederic's own incredulity. Cf. Frederic to Jordan, 5 June, 1742.

ing eminence the king drew a number of three-pounders, a gun recently introduced for field service, and poured a murderous fire upon the over-confident enemy, before which their regiments could not be held together; a fierce infantry charge completed the work. Slowly, sullenly, in good order the Austrians abandoned the field. In three hours all was over.[1]

For so short an engagement the battle of Chotusitz was extremely sanguinary. The Prussians lost in killed and wounded four thousand men, besides one thousand prisoners; the Austrians about three thousand killed and wounded, and over three thousand prisoners.[2] Prince Charles carried away as trophies fourteen standards and two battle-flags, but the Prussians captured eighteen pieces of artillery, and remained as victors on the field of battle. The force of the enemy was so weakened by desertion that three days afterwards the officers could muster only fifteen thousand regular troops, out of thirty thousand who went into battle.[3]

The losses.

Only a nominal pursuit was made. Prince Charles retreated, gently pressed by Büddenbrock, to Willimow, the next day to Chotiborg, and thence toward Teutschbrod on the river Sazawa. The town of Czaslau, in whose ancient church lie the bones of Zisca, the brave hussite captain, was occupied by the Prussians; and with it fell into their hands great quantities of stores, ammunition, guns, and many of the Austrian wounded. Among the latter was general Pallandt,

Retreat of the Austrians.

[1] Frederic has two accounts of this battle: one hastily drawn up on the spot, and sent to Berlin for publication in the newspapers; the other, written several years later as part of the "Histoire de mon temps." The former is in *Polit. Corresp.*, ii. 168–172; the latter, *Œuvres de Frédéric*, ii. 145–150.

[2] Droysen, V. i. 451; Orlich, i. 254, 255.

[3] The insinuation of Frederic, *Œuvres*, ii. 124, that the Austrians lost no battle-flags because they left them all in the rear with the baggage, seems to be unfounded. Cf. Grünhagen, ii. 260.

who died soon afterwards, and was buried by his captors with military honors.[1]

Immediately after the battle the negotiations for peace were resumed by the king's order.[2] But lord Carteret at London and Hyndford at Breslau Negotiations resumed. had both anticipated these overtures by urgent appeals to the court of Vienna, those of Hyndford being subsequent to Chotusitz, and emphasized, therefore, by its lessons.[3] He informed Podewils on the twenty-seventh of May that he expected the early return of a courier with the queen's propositions. But she had just been confined, and it was difficult to approach her with such painful matters of business.

Beyond moving his headquarters to Kuttenberg the king made no military changes, and left the Austrians complete freedom to operate in any direction except that of Prague. Prince Charles began, therefore, to work his way slowly toward Broglie. A small force under Lobkowitz even laid siege to Frauenberg, a strong post which had a French garrison; but he was attacked Battle of Sahay. at Sahay on the twenty-fourth of May, and after a sharp engagement forced to retire. It pleased Frederic to ridicule the importance of this victory, and to say that it made as much noise at Paris as the battle of Pharsalia at Rome.[4] Yet by increasing the queen's de-

---

[1] The touching story, accepted and embellished by Carlyle, iii. 453, that Pallandt on his deathbed revealed to Frederic certain alleged overtures which Fleury had made to the queen, and which confirmed the king's belief in French treachery, is without a particle of evidence to support it. See Droysen, V. i. 455 n.; Broglie, *Fr. II. et M. T.*, ii. 338, 339; Arneth, ii. 481, n. 30.

[2] Eichel to Podewils, 22 May, Frederic to the same, 23 May, 1742. In the latter the opinion is repeated " qu'une paix separée me convient mieux que la paix générale."

[3] 23 May, 1742. Grünhagen, ii. 275.

[4] *Œuvres de Frédéric*, ii. 127.

sire to make terms with Prussia, the repulse of Lobkowitz unmistakably served his purpose.[1]

Two marshals of France, Belleisle and Broglie, witnessed and directed the battle of Sahay. But this harmony was of brief duration. Belleisle soon repaired to Prague, leaving Broglie to arrange for his departure to his new field of activity. From Prague he made a flying visit to Frederic in his camp. His nominal object was to concert a plan for further joint operations; and there was accordingly much solemn discussion between the fiery marshal and his royal host about lines of advance, bases of supply, and all the common interests which bind faithful allies together. Frederic threw out the suggestion that a general peace was possible, and Belleisle inquired on what terms. " On the basis of the beatus est posedendi," was the reply in Ciceronian Latin.[2] Proceeding to details, the king explained that France ought to have at least the duchy of Luxemburg, as a return for all her outlays. Belleisle was too sagacious to fall into this trap, even when set so adroitly; and at once replied that France still adhered to the policy, which she had announced at the beginning of the war, of making no conquests for herself. But Frederic refused positively to move his own troops before the fifteenth of July, not even when he himself announced, as he did the next day, that prince Charles was marching to effect a junction with Lobkowitz. The news prostrated the marshal for several minutes. When he recovered his faculties, and asked for council, Frederic advised that the Saxons be again called into the field. Belleisle then departed for Dresden on this mission.[3]

Belleisle and Frederic.

[1] See Frederic to Podewils, 26 May, 1742.

[2] Meaning, of course, the well-known phrase " beati possidentes," which was lately used by another great Prussian statesman, on an occasion which has also become historical.

[3] Vide Frederic to Podewils, 4 June, 1742 ; Ranke, xxvii., xxviii.

Frederic says in his own account of this interview that the marshal chose a bad time.[1] It was bad Retreat of simply because he himself was again negotiating Broglie. for a separate peace, and, as is now known, was resolved to obtain such a peace even at the cost of some reduction from earlier demands. This anxiety was intensified immediately after Belleisle's departure by the actual union of the Austrian armies, and their triumphant advance upon Broglie. Attacked by this superior force, which acted with unusual celerity, the marshal retired precipitately behind the walls of Prague.

This turn of affairs, to which his own inaction after the battle of Chotusitz had contributed its part, was Frederic and skilfully used by Frederic for the ends which he the emperor. himself had in view. It gave him of course new proof of the incapacity of Broglie, and of the desperate outlook for the imperial cause. But the new situation had other facilities, which he hastened to seize. He had already, by a solemn treaty, obtained from the elector of Bavaria, as titular king of Bohemia, the cession of Glatz, on condition of the payment of two hundred thousand thalers. On one pretext or another the payment had been delayed. Now Frederic took advantage of the practical abandonment of Bohemia by the French to treat the kingdom as no longer belonging to Charles Albert, and the stipulated price for Glatz as no longer a binding debt;[2] thus by an act of open repudiation closing a transaction, which is only made less discreditable than it at first appears by the probability that none of the parties could ever have taken it seriously. Even more than money the emperor needed military support, which Frederic was also forced to deny

531, 532 ; Valori, i. 161 ; Broglie, *Fr. Il. et M. T.*, iii. 288–297 ; and for Belleisle's memoir, written in 1743, ibid. pp. 407, 408.

[1] *Œuvres de Frédéric*, ii. 127.

[2] Frederic to Schmettau, then on a mission at the imperial court, 10 June, 1742.

him. But he promised that he should still have the aid of his pen, and this promise he kept.[1] If the duty which a historian owes to truth has made it necessary to describe without reserve the duplicity, selfishness, and cynicism that marked much of Frederic's conduct during the first two years of his reign, it is pleasant to recognize, if only by contrast, the invariable sympathy, personal as well as political, which he showed for the unfortunate prince, whom designing diplomatists had elevated to a position far beyond his own resources, whether mental, or moral, or material.

In regard to Broglie's retreat it is also intimated, by a French writer, that prince Charles began his offensive movement because he had learned that the response of Maria Theresa to Frederic's demands was such as to render improbable any interference from the Prussians.[2] A comparison of the dates yields some support to such a hypothesis. But letters from French officers at Prague make it seem at least possible that the retreat might have been avoided if Broglie had taken the advice of Belleisle, and sharply followed up the advantage gained at Sahay.[3] Such energy was not, however, in his nature, and the opportunity was lost.

In the mean time the answer from Vienna showed that Maria Theresa was prepared to yield as a last resort everything which Frederic had demanded before Chotusitz, except the two Bohemian counties, and rather than part with those she would perish, she said, in the ruins of Vienna.[4] Her reply, which consisted of a preliminary proposition and a maximum con-

The Austrian propositions.

---

[1] Frederic to the emperor, 18 June, 1742.

[2] Broglie, *Fr. II. et M. T.*, ii. 297.

[3] Luynes, iv. 176 et seq. The material furnished by Luynes, who had a son with the army, deserves the careful study of military historians.

[4] Arneth, ii. 71.

cession, seems to have reached Hyndford on the second of June. Two days later he had a conference with Podewils, but refused to state the terms which he was empowered to offer until the two negotiators should have exchanged their credentials. This involved on Podewils' part a reference to the king; and the ceremony was delayed until the ninth. On the tenth another conference took place. Podewils then renewed his demands for the presentation of the Austrian terms, and received, of course, only the tentative proposals, which in respect to territory conceded only Lower Silesia, with a strip east of the Neisse, and Glatz. Podewils lost his temper at this, which he said his master would never accept. But Hyndford, thus pressed, incautiously showed the order authorizing him, in the last extremity, to yield Upper Silesia. The Prussian minister then undertook to procure the king's assent.[1]

It so happened, however, that the day before this consultation Frederic, ignorant of the queen's concessions, but alarmed by the sudden success of the Austrian arms, sent peremptory instructions to Podewils to close the negotiations. The unexpected disaster which has overtaken the French arms, wrote he, "compels me to inform you in the most positive manner that on receiving this you are at once to exchange full powers with lord Hyndford. As to terms, try to make them as favorable as possible for me, either on the side of Bohemia or on that of Upper Silesia. But it is my express will that, after doing your best for twelve hours, and without making any report, without asking or awaiting my decision, you regulate such points as you shall be able to agree on with lord Hyndford, reduce them to writing, and sign them with him immediately in the form of preliminaries of peace." The papers when completed were to be dispatched to the king for his signature by the same mes-

Instructions to Podewils.

---

[1] Arneth, ii. 77, 78 ; Grünhagen, ii. 283.

senger who carried the instructions. Podewils was further charged to intimate to Hyndford the propriety of sending the courier, who should bear his report to Vienna, by way of the Austrian camp, in order to inform prince Charles that affairs were adjusted so far as Prussia was concerned.[1]

To this formal letter the king added a postscript in his handwriting that Silesia and Glatz were an indispensable condition; beyond that the minister was to obtain as much as he could.[2] But in any event the treaty was to be finished in twelve hours.

Podewils described himself, in reply, as appalled by the responsibility put upon him by these peremptory instructions. It is hard to see why he should have had any other feeling than relief and exultation. He had the king's express authority for concluding a peace on the lowest terms proposed by the queen, and yet his own diplomatic skill had extorted from Hyndford's indiscretion a premature disclosure of even greater concessions which, in the last instance, she was prepared to make. By simply insisting on these, in the final conference of June eleventh, he won therefore an easy victory. It is with justice that a Prussian writer gives Podewils the main credit for the favorable terms that Frederic obtained, even if his suggestion, that the towns of Upper Silesia ought to erect his statue in the marketplace, is not likely to be carried into effect.[3]

Adroitness of Podewils.

Two days after the dispatch of these instructions, and on the very day of their arrival in Breslau, Valori made a last attempt to move Frederic. Prague was threatened; and this created a cri-

Valori appeals to Frederic.

[1] Frederic to Podewils, 9 June, 1742.

[2] "La Silésie et Glatz sine qua non, et du reste tout ce que vous leur pourrez extorquer." Grünhagen, ii. 287, thinks Silesia here means only Lower Silesia.

[3] Grünhagen, ii. 288.

sis for which Belleisle had succeeded in obtaining assurances of Prussian aid. The king did not absolutely deny the engagement, or refuse to keep it. But he urged the usual complaints against the French, with which Valori was already familiar, and positively insisted on a delay of two days before making his decision. The term, though wholly unintelligible to the envoy, was profoundly significant and momentous. In two days the messenger would return from Breslau, and the report of Podewils, not the critical situation of his allies, would determine the king's next movements.[1]

The report which arrived on the thirteenth was therefore a great relief. Podewils and Hyndford had signed the preliminaries on the evening of the eleventh, and the king added his own signature immediately after their arrival in camp.

By the articles of Breslau, Maria Theresa ceded to the king of Prussia and his heirs, male or female, in full sovereignty, the territories of Upper and Lower Silesia, except the principality of Teschen and the district beyond the river Oppa and the high mountains, and in like manner the city and county of Glatz; the king assumed so much of the so-called Silesian debt as was due to English subjects,[2] and promised to make no further demands upon her majesty; the Prussian troops were to evacuate Bohemia within sixteen days; the Catholic religion was to remain in statu quo; England, Hanover, Russia, Denmark, Holland, Brunswick, and Saxony were included in the treaty, the latter on condition of renouncing the hostile alliance, and withdrawing her troops from Bohemia. No mention was made of France or the emperor. Podewils offered indeed a draft of an

Preliminaries of Breslau.

---

[1] " Que n'ai-je point eu à souffrir ! " cries the unhappy Valori, *Mémoires*, i. 154, recalling his treatment by Frederic before and after Chotusitz.

[2] Vide infra, p. 185.

article giving Charles VII. a chance to make peace with
the queen on the basis of mutual restitutions; but it was
opposed by Hyndford, and does not seem to have been
seriously pressed.[1] The demand for the assistance of
Prussia against the other enemies of the queen was not
included in the Austrian proposals.

Frederic wrote to his minister in terms of calm satisfaction over the progress which the negotiations
had made.[2] But the end, though now in view,
was still somewhat distant; and many vexations
arose, which had to be evaded or overcome, before the
preliminaries could be changed into a definitive treaty of
peace. Belleisle wrote letters urgently demanding the
promised succor. Valori came again to the king's headquarters, and was met with the same imperturbable cynicism, the same careless hypocrisy, the same outbursts of
theatrical indignation at the conduct of the French; and
in the end accomplished nothing.[3] A more serious cause
of uneasiness was the continued progress of the Austrian
arms. Prince Charles had drawn daily nearer to Prague,
and, while the two marshals were quarrelling about plans
of action, was preparing to render action impossible by
shutting them up under the walls of the city; an Austrian detachment occupied Pilsen, and threatened Eger,
which was the key to their communications. Frederic
felt great alarm lest the military situation should encourage the queen to repudiate the convention of Breslau,
and was nervously anxious to receive her ratification.[4] But
this arrived on the twenty-first, two days earlier than the
stipulated term, and warrants the conclusion that the

The queen ratifies them.

[1] Droysen, V. i. 464. Yet according to Arneth, ii. 79, the Vienna
cabinet was at the time seriously considering the expediency of a
reconciliation with the emperor on the condition of the election of
the grand-duke Francis as king of the Romans.

[2] Frederic to Podewils, 13 June, 1742.

[3] Valori, i. 284–289.

[4] Frederic to Podewils, 20 June, 1742.

queen had not even thought of a breach of faith. The interpretation which the court of Vienna gave to some of the articles, and the amendments which it reserved for the final treaty, were still, however, suspicious. The king was reluctant to leave Bohemia; at Königgrätz he even threatened, in a letter to Podewils, to arrest the homeward march of his troops unless prompt concessions were made to his scruples.[1]

The principal points of difference were two. One concerned the limits of the proposed cession, and involved questions of grammatical construction.[2] *Points of difference.* The other had to do with the debts of the ceded territory, or the debts which were hypothecated upon its revenues, and was of a different nature. The debts were the result of a loan which had been advanced by English and Dutch capitalists. To the English share of it Frederic offered no objection, though he took care to treat his assumption of it as a species of reward for the efforts of English diplomacy to bring about a peace, and not as an obligation having any basis in equity. But the Dutch portion he refused to bear. He urged that it was a debt of the house of Austria, secured indeed to the creditors by a species of mortgage upon Silesia, but still a debt of the state, not of the province. The queen took the opposite view that it was essentially a provincial loan, and undoubtedly had logic on her side. For a time Frederic remained immovable, and it was his exasperation over this controversy that mainly inspired the fierce letter of the twenty-sixth of June.

[1] Frederic to Podewils, 26 June, 1742.

[2] Upper Silesia was to be ceded " à l'exception de la principauté de Teschen, de la ville de Troppau, et de ce qui est au delà de la rivière d'Oppau et des hautes montagnes ailleurs dans la haute Silésie," etc. The question was whether the mountains themselves were excepted, that is, reserved to Austria, or only the territory beyond the mountains. The construction is awkward, but the arguments of Grünhagen, ii. 303, seem to me conclusive for the Prussian view.

This letter contained, besides the threat addressed to Hyndford, a passage of more personal interest to Podewils. In writing of the difficulties yet to encounter, the minister had suggested that more rapid progress could be made if he, Frederic, would remain for a time in Silesia, instead of proceeding to Berlin, whither it was proposed to transfer the final negotiations. He urged, in perfectly respectful language, that it would thus be easier to get the queen's decision on such points as might arise. But the suggestion threw Frederic into a passion. "Attend to your own affairs, sir," was his dignified reply, " and do not presume to dictate whither I ought or ought not to go. Negotiate as I order you, and do not be the weak tool of English and Austrian impudence. That is what I take the liberty of advising, reminding you at the same time that your language is not suited to the minister of a king, who gained a battle only a fortnight ago." But what is to be thought of language like this addressed to the man whose dexterity had just won Upper Silesia for his master?[1]

A royal compliment for Podewils.

The ill-humor of the king, which had again filled Eichel with consternation, eventually passed away; and as a better prospect for settling all difficulties in the final negotiations at the capital appeared, the homeward march of the Prussians continued. Part of the troops were distributed throughout the annexed territory in garrisons. The rest were assigned to quarters in the leading cities, and military centres of the older provinces; and the entire establishment was soon reduced to its normal footing of peace.

[1] Podewils made a dignified yet humble defence of his presumption, which is given by Grünhagen, vol. ii. p. 299.

CHAPTER VI.

THE PEACE OF BRESLAU.

THE king arrived in Berlin on the twelfth of July, finding his treasury nearly empty, but his subjects full of enthusiasm for the conqueror of Silesia. Three days later he learned that England had formally undertaken the guaranty of the treaty of Breslau.[1] It now remained only to adjust the terms of the definitive peace, and these, as finally adopted, were somewhat more favorable to Austria than the preliminary articles. Frederic agreed reluctantly to assume the Silesian debt of Holland in addition to that of England, making in all about four million thalers; the third claim, that of the estates of Brabant, was adopted by Maria Theresa. The frontier was drawn, on the demand of Austria, in such a way as to reserve both Teschen and Jägerndorf to Bohemia. And the stipulations in regard to the status of the Catholic religion in the ceded province were slightly, though not essentially, changed to suit the scruples of the queen. The text of the treaty was adopted on the twenty-sixth of July; on the twenty-eighth it was signed at Berlin.[2]

As soon as the final treaty was signed, the scruples of Hyndford about accepting a pecuniary return for his labors seemed to vanish. He had refused a bribe, and to that extent his conscience was clear. In the negotiations just completed he had supported the

The definitive treaty.

Hyndford's reward.

[1] Declaration of Kensington, 24 June, 1742.
[2] Wenck, i. 739–747.

interests of the queen as earnestly as if they were his own; and Frederic, who did not share Podewils' opinion that the envoy was an honest and well-disposed person, afflicted only with the vices of his race, and had already written that it was not out of love for Prussia that England had undertaken the mediation;[1] who besides was not inclined by nature or policy to spend money in gratuities, readily assented to Podewils' suggestion to give Hyndford as a present a sum equal to that which had been paid on previous occasions. The archives declared that ten thousand thalers was the usual recompense, and this sum Hyndford received in good coin of the realm. Besides this he obtained from his own king the vacant order of the garter. Frederic himself undertook the investiture; and the ceremony was duly performed on the second of August. By special permission the envoy added the eagle of Silesia to his coat of arms.[2]

Common decency required, as Frederic writes, that the conclusion of the peace should be duly notified to the allies of Prussia. This delicate task was performed not unskilfully in letters to Louis the Fifteenth, to the emperor, to cardinal Fleury, and others, — letters in which frankness is curiously mixed with dissimulation, and in which even the frankness is not without art. The line of reasoning is the same in all. The affairs of the allies were becoming desperate; Prussia had done more than her share for the common cause; the future was ominous; and, as the queen had offered him all he demanded, he felt constrained to consult his own safety by withdrawing from the enterprise. A favorite figure by which he described his policy was taken from a shipwreck at sea, where each person saves himself as best he can.[3] That kind of selfishness often

Frederic to his allies.

---

[1] *Polit. Corresp.*, ii. 279.
[2] Grünhagen, ii. 321.
[3] Frederic to Fleury, 18 June, 1742.

characterizes, it is true enough, the conduct of passengers on a shipwrecked vessel. Is it not also true that the world generally reserves the title of hero, not for the man who in the hour of danger seizes the first boat and escapes, but for the faithful captain who remains at his post until all the others are saved, and is the last to leave the sinking ship?

In the passage where Frederic admits the propriety of announcing the peace to his allies, he adds that although he had good reasons for his course, one His defence. class was not of a nature to be made public, and the other class could not have been stated without covering France with reproaches.[1] From this it may be inferred that he honored his allies only with excuses, which either were not good or were not genuine. He wrote in vague generalities, and his correspondents replied in the same style; but Fleury's letter, though perfectly decorous in form, and almost pathetic in tone, managed to convey a subtile and pointed rebuke, which would have pierced the conscience of a very sensitive person.

"Your majesty can easily judge," wrote the aged states-man, "of the painful impression made on me Fleury to Frederic. by the letter of the tenth of this month, with which you deigned to honor me. The sad event, which has deranged all our plans in Germany, might have been avoided if your majesty had been able to support marshal Broglie, and save at least the city of Prague; but since you did not find that possible, we must submit to your wisdom and prudence. Great faults were indeed committed, which it would be useless to recall; but if we had united all our forces the evil would not have been irreparable."[2]

---

[1] Œuvres de Frédéric, ii. 131.

[2] Flassan, v. 159, 160; Œuvres de Frédéric, ii. 132–135. Both writers err in respect to dates. Frederic's letter was written on the 18th, not the 10th of June, and the cardinal's reply must have been a week later.

The reasons which it was impolitic to make known are easy to divine. Those which were withheld out of consideration for France were drawn from the incapacity of her generals, and from the suspected or alleged faithlessness of her diplomacy. To the first of these charges I have already referred. Frederic is clearly entitled to all the defence which the weak and vacillating tactics of marshal Broglie offered him ; but it is a singular circumstance that he abandoned the alliance just at the moment when Belleisle, in whom he professed to have confidence, and who certainly had abundant faith in him, arrived to take the command in Bohemia.

The other count in the indictment is of a more serious nature. The king seems to have believed that *His unjust suspicions of France.* the cardinal had agents at Vienna and St. Petersburg secretly laboring for peace, and for a peace which would sacrifice him, his conquests, and even his hereditary dominions. At Vienna, Defargis was the supposed agent of his offers for reconciliation with the queen. In St. Petersburg, the resident envoy, the marquis de la Chétardie, was said to be charged to pacify Russia and Sweden, and turn their united arms upon Prussia in a campaign of partition. But the evidence does not justify either of these suspicions. There was indeed a Frenchman of the name of Defargis at Vienna in 1741 and 1742 ; but there is no proof that he ever transmitted any overtures of Fleury, while it is known that overtures from the queen were often received, and as often rejected, at Paris.[1] The alarm about Russia seems to have had no better foundation. It was largely the work of the Prussian envoy Mardefeld, who, knowing his master's humor, was perhaps not unwilling to establish a

[1] The fact that the queen's overtures to France had been invariably rejected was stated to Belleisle by the Austrian marshal Königsegg, and even made a ground of complaint. Cf. Broglie, *Frédéric II. et Louis XV.*, Paris, 1885, i. 12.

reputation for vigilance by daily reports of imaginary plots. The duke of Broglie has examined in the French archives all the dispatches of La Chétardie. He declares that there is in the entire correspondence no allusion, direct or indirect, to any scheme for pacifying Russia and Sweden at the cost of Prussia.[1]

Fears of French treachery did not, then, afford a reason which Frederic could have justified to Fleury, or which he himself probably regarded as very solid. Those which he gave, though plausible and indeed convincing up to a certain point, were not the only or the principal ones. The treaty of Berlin must rather be referred, according to the king's own confession, to considerations which their own nature made it inexpedient to reveal.

If there were several of these working together in Frederic's mind it might be a pleasant exercise of ingenuity to search them out, to find which were the stronger and which the weaker, at what points they conflicted with one another, and how their combined force led to a final decision. But in reality no such labor is required by the nature of the problem. It is enough, and possibly it exhausts the subject, to say that Frederic made peace because his object in the war was attained. That object was, first and last, the conquest of Silesia ; and since all the combinations, military or political, or both, into which he entered, — the alliance with France, the patronage of Saxony, the support of the emperor, — were only auxiliary to the principal end, he abandoned them all as soon as they had served their purpose and were no longer of any value. He had all the advantage which comes from simplicity of aim and unity of action. He knew that Bavaria was a broken reed, on which it was dangerous to lean. He had little confidence in France, and France had little in him. She had indeed set an

His reasons for peace.

---

[1] *Frédéric II. et Marie Thérèse*, ii. 342. Grünhagen, ii. 340, admits that the dates overthrow Frederic's theory.

example of fidelity; but it was only a fidelity of form, and would perhaps have ended earlier than his own, if circumstances had made that possible.[1]

For, that simplicity and directness of end, which enabled Frederic to escape from the war at the proper time by a separate peace, France notoriously wanted. She was hampered by engagements which, instead of being subsidiary to a single, clearly defined purpose, were essential parts of her programme; nay, were even ends in themselves. To make Charles Albert emperor of Germany was to strike a blow at the prestige of the house of Austria. But that blow would not be effective without others, which should further disable the great rival; which should crush her armies, seize her territories, reduce her revenues; degrade her to the second rank of powers, and permanently impair her influence in the Empire. This was a large and complex object, difficult to realize, difficult even to sketch in precise outlines. So long as Austria offered resistance in the field, the court of Versailles could not retire from the struggle without an irreparable loss of honor. Even a treaty of peace without the most exact and far-reaching guaranties for the position of the new emperor would be little more than a truce; and these guaranties the queen, even while offering reasonable terms for a military pacification, had never been willing to give. So long at least as Prussia was still in the field, and Silesia was not formally ceded by the queen of Hungary, self-interest alone made France adhere to the path of honor. But now the situation was abruptly changed by the defection of Frederic. While French diplomacy and French generalship, equally ambitious, feeble, and heartless, were pursuing a scheme far beyond their powers, he made his own terms with the common enemy, secured precisely the object of his efforts, and returned to Berlin with the title-deed to Silesia in his pocket.

[1] Cf. *Œuvres de Frédéric*, ii. 93.

On the receipt of the preliminaries of Breslau, Frederic wrote to his faithful minister that a happy tranquillity ought for some time to be the basis of their policy.   Several years of peace were *Programme for the future.* needed to consolidate the state ; and Podewils was charged to make it his study to avoid alliances which, on one pretext or another, might involve the king in war against his wish.   A few days later his majesty explained how this end could be secured.   " The safety of our new possessions rests," he wrote, " on a large and efficient army, a full treasury, powerful fortresses, and ostentatious alliances,[1] which easily impose on the world.   The worst thing which can happen to us in the future is a league between France and Austria ; but in that case we shall have England Holland, Russia, and many other powers on our side.   It is only necessary to reconcile the cabinets of Europe to the situation in which the war has placed us, and I am convinced that moderation and courtesy toward our neighbors will make that possible." [2]

This extract fairly illustrates the class of communications, half didactic, half speculative, which Frederic was in the habit of sending to his ministers.   One will search them in vain for anything like a system of political conduct, or political philosophy.   They reflect as a rule only the momentary impulses, or impressions, or humors of the writer, and in many cases seem even to exhibit little more than his morbid literary restlessness.   Hence the treatise of one day is often in flat contradiction to that of the next.   Every change in the aspect of affairs brings forth a fresh budget of conjectures and hypotheses, so that the bewildering variety of views makes it hard to determine how much credit for prevision Frederic really deserved. It was impossible that all the predictions which he made at this time should prove true, and it often happened that

[1] Alliances de parade.
[2] Frederic to Podewils, 20 and 23 June, 1742.

in a series of speculations, which had nothing intrinsically absurd or self-contradictory, one part proved true while the other shot wide of the mark. This was the case with the letter to Podewils. The gravest crisis which Frederic had to face arose, indeed, from the union of Austria and France in a hostile alliance against him; but it did not happen that the crisis rallied to his support Russia and many other powers besides England. And so with other productions of the kind. Podewils filed them carefully away in the archives, whence the editors of the "Political Correspondence" have properly exhumed them, for they belong to history. But it does not appear that the minister regarded them as needing reply, or even serious attention, unless they had in view some specific change of policy, or course of action.

The letter of the twenty-third of June was not of this class. The programme contained nothing which was revolutionary, and little which might not properly have been announced before the parliament of a constitutional monarchy. A well-disciplined force, strong fortifications, and an annual surplus are the just precautions of every prudent state; and the present age is also not unfamiliar with alliances which have had a moral effect out of proportion to their actual cohesion. If this were all that the king's schedule contained, the critic might be inclined to condone the original invasion of Silesia as an impulse of unreflecting youth, succeeded by a sincere desire to live at peace with the world, to study the happiness of the Prussian people, to set mankind the example of a wise, humane, liberal, and philosophic ruler. But there is a significant reserve implied in at least one of the royal communications. It is there distinctly intimated that the few years of peace were to be only an exception to the normal state of war, that at an early day the doors of the temple of Janus would again stand open, and the Prussian hosts be hurled once more upon the

Its fatal defect.

enemy. The events to be narrated in this chapter will show that the programme was held strictly subordinate to this ominous condition.

The execution of the treaty of Berlin required, first of all, that the limits of the new acquisition be clearly ascertained. To this end commissioners were appointed by the two contracting powers, — Nüssler, an experienced and ill-paid person, skilled in topography, as the chief Prussian agent; and one Dorsch, supposed to have much local knowledge of Silesia, to represent Maria Theresa. Some frictions necessarily arose in the progress of the work. But while Dorsch was indolent and dull, Nüssler proved fertile in the discovery of compromises which favored his master, and in twenty days the task was completed.[1] The frontier thus drawn still divides the Prussian and Austrian possessions. The territory ceded to Prussia comprised about sixteen thousand square miles, being the larger and by far the more valuable part of Silesia, with a population of one million and a quarter souls.[2]

Execution of the treaty.

The adjustment of the administrative machinery in the new province had made great progress even before the formal conclusion of peace. In March, 1742, the system temporarily set up as a part of the military occupation, and with a view mainly to collecting the revenues for the support of the army, was entrusted to the direction of a single official, the privy councillor Münchow. From chief of the civil service for the district of Glogau, he became president of the province of Silesia. The importance of the office was emphasized by the provision that its affairs should pass directly to the king, and not, as was the case with the other provinces, through the general directory.[3] Münchow's jurisdiction

The civil service in Silesia.

---

[1] The result in Wenck, i. 748–777.

[2] Ranke, xxvii., xxviii. 545 n.

[3] Ranke, xxvii., xxviii. 554 ; Isaacsohn, *Gesch. des pr. Beamtenthums,* iii. 211.

included at first only Lower Silesia. Its extension over the other acquisitions followed as a natural consequence of the final treaty of peace.

No little space has been given by Prussian writers to the discussion of the blessings which this change of rulers and systems brought to the people of Silesia. I am not prepared to say that such congratulations are wholly without basis. In respect to many things which belong to the mere science of administration, such as uniformity, promptness, impartiality, the change was clearly an improvement. The conduct of the revenues, of justice, of police, was thenceforth regular, strict, and uncompromising. Under Prussian rule, no citizen of Silesia, whether he wore the frock of a peasant, or sat in the castle of a noble, or said mass in a cathedral of the church, could escape the fulfilment of his duties to the state. These duties were known and fixed, and, according to every rule of prudence, ought to have been discharged more easily, and more willingly, than the less onerous but also less definite ones which had been imposed by the Austrian authorities. But the Austrian rule, though capricious, was easy. Much as it fell below the highest standard of efficiency, it may be that a people familiar with it looked with dismay upon a new system, in which there were no delays, no evasions ; and which was characterized mainly by a cold, stern, forbidding inflexibility. It cannot be affirmed indeed, on the evidence, that this was the attitude of the Silesians. But it is also rash to interpret random pledges of loyalty, or the addresses of bodies of Protestant clergy, as proof that the whole province heartily welcomed the change of rule. Such transfers of territory are often followed by profuse expressions of satisfaction from individuals, and even classes. The calculated subservience of the few is, however, no more evidence of a hearty approval of the new order of things than is the forced acquiescence of the mass of the population.

Prussian and Austrian rule contrasted.

In one respect, too, Prussia was able to learn a lesson of impartiality from the system which it found in Silesia. In Silesia, under Austrian rule, the nobles had paid, like the other orders, their share of the public contributions, while in Prussia they were practically exempt from taxation. It was natural that on the introduction of the Prussian system in Silesia, the introduction with it of this exemption should be demanded by those who would be its chief beneficiaries. But in this matter Frederic wisely sacrificed consistency to fairness. He insisted on a principle which he hesitated to apply in the older territories, and perhaps enforced in Silesia only because it was already an accepted part of the political system.

The apportionment of the fiscal burdens among the several social orders proved, however, to be a perplexing problem, which was solved only after much debate with indignant deputations, and much wrestling with tables of statistics. The first step was to take a census of the population and of real property, with the average annual yield of each agricultural holding. Since the Austrians had themselves begun a new census some years before, Frederic's officials were able to use the completed part as a basis for their own work, and thus to have the entire survey for Silesia and Glatz finished by the end of the year 1743. The estimated yield in cash value of each holding formed, then, its assessment for purposes of taxation. On this as a basis, the crown domains and the estates of the nobles paid twenty-eight per cent., the peasants thirty-four, and church lands from thirty-three to fifty, according to their character. These rates, though high, especially that of the peasants, were somewhat less exorbitant than they seem. The assigned average yield was usually low, and the assessed value of products was under their market value. It must be kept in mind, too, that each owner's or tenant's contribution was fixed once for all, and independently of what his land might actually bring him in from year to year, so that his tax would relatively decrease as the productivity of his acres increased.

A small capitation or trade tax on farm laborers and others who lived in the country but owned no land, and an octroi, or tax levied on commodities at the gates of cities, completed the system. The aggregate annual return from these several taxes was estimated at about one and one half millions, of which the towns contributed approximately one fifth, the peasants two fifths, and the lands of the clergy and the nobles the remainder. But the total revenues of Silesia exceeded this amount by over one million. For the fiscal year 1743–1744 they amounted to nearly three millions, and continued to rise steadily for several years. The many sources of revenue not included in the above classification, such as the rental of the domains, the profits of the mines, the salt works, the post, and other royalties, account for the excess. Nearly four fifths of this amount was needed to support the military force in Silesia.[1]

The revenues from the other territories show no essential increase before the year 1755. They continued at about seven millions. It does not appear that any systematic attempt was made at this time to improve them, or indeed to introduce sweeping reforms in any branch of civil administration. Either because he did not yet see his way clear, or because he felt that the state needed rest from agitation of every kind, or because he was reluctant to engage in enterprises which war might at any time interrupt, Frederic gave up the next two years to the routine work of drilling the army, restoring the military fund, and healing the wounds left by two costly campaigns. A spirit of general improvement prevailed. Some personal changes were made in the different branches of the

[1] Cf. Grünhagen, ii. 348, 349 ; Riedel, *Staatshaushalt*, Beilage, xiv.; Ranke, xxvii., xxviii. 561.

service; functions here and there were created or abolished; the morale of the service was raised by sharp admonitions. But the hour was not yet come for comprehensive measures of reorganization.

The truth is that so long as the pragmatic war continued between the other combatants, Frederic's attention was necessarily preoccupied by that. For a time, indeed, it was the attention only of an observer. But the observer had an interest in the progress of events scarcely less strong than that of the belligerents themselves. Silesia had been conquered, ceded, and annexed. It was now necessary to watch lest some new turn of fortune imperil the security of the acquisition; for Frederic constantly assumed that the treaty of Berlin would be no restraint upon Austria, if an opportunity should arise for the recovery of the lost province. This hypothesis, again, dictated the direction which his sympathies continued to take. One of his alleged reasons for abandoning his allies was an unwillingness to see the house of Austria completely crushed; and there was every reason to suppose that after his defection the scale would incline in the queen's favor. But if it should incline too far, she might feel strong enough to reopen the struggle for Silesia, and Frederic was resolved to anticipate this danger whenever it seemed likely to appear.

The immediate point of interest was the remnant of the original French army, which with Broglie and Belleisle was left shut up in the city of Prague. Disaster had embittered rather than composed the differences of the two marshals; and each could find some justification for his own course, or at least some ground for complaint against his rival, in the events which led to the disaster. Broglie was of course convinced by Frederic's defection that Belleisle's blind confidence in the king of Prussia was the source of all the trouble. Belleisle could not exactly defend Frederic,

The pragmatic war.

Dissensions of the French generals.

but he would have wanted one of the qualities of human
nature if he had failed to use the Prussian separate treaty
of peace to point a moral at his colleague's expense. To
add to these grounds of discord, there was the still unsettled question of military rank. Broglie had nominally
been assigned to the command of the French reinforce-
ments in Bavaria ; but no term had been fixed for the
transfer, and he showed no haste to depart. Belleisle
was anxious to be relieved of his rival, but had no
authority to dismiss him. There were quarrels about the
number and character of the troops which should be
transferred to Bavaria, and about the plan of operations
to be pursued after the separation. In short, nearly everything except brave soldiers was wanting to a united and
effective defence.

The alarm caused by the withdrawal of Prussia, and
the critical condition of the French army in Prague, led
cardinal Fleury to make overtures for an accommodation. He had intimated such a purpose to Frederic as
soon as he heard of the Breslau convention. " We must
now think only of peace," he wrote, " since your majesty
deems it necessary, and my own master desires it not less
warmly." [1] The agent chosen by Fleury, in perhaps a
slight vein of malice, was Belleisle, who, on the second of
July, had an interview at the castle of Komorzan with
marshal Königsegg of the Austrian army. The
interview was fruitless. But the cardinal, disposed to make one more attempt, wrote an autograph letter to the Austrian marshal in support of the
negotiation. The letter contained not only assurances of
the French desire for peace, but also, as its most remarkable part, a plaintive defence of the writer himself against
the charge or suspicion of being the principal author of
the war. Many people knew, wrote Fleury, how strongly
he had opposed the resolution which was taken, and that

*Fleury's
peace over-
tures re-
jected.*

[1] In the letter above cited, p. 189.

he was in a certain sense forced to give his assent by the cogent reasons that were alleged ; the marshal was well enough informed of what had passed to be able to divine easily the real person who persuaded the king to enter upon a line of action so hostile to his, the cardinal's, tastes and principles. The response of the Austrians was the immediate publication of this letter, and the exposure of Fleury to the derision of Europe.[1] Frederic, too, made an adroit use of Fleury's indiscreet avowal of his opposition to the war. He inquired whether he could justly be blamed for withdrawing from an engagement, which the statesman who governed France confessed that he had undertaken with the greatest reluctance, and against his real inclinations.[2]

The efforts of Belleisle for other interviews with Königsegg proving fruitless, nothing was left for the French except to try again the fortune of the sword. Yet the circumstances were far from discouraging. They had a strong defensive position at Prague ; a respectable force, with some advantage of situation, in Bavaria ; and the army of Maillebois on the Lower Rhine. The queen was inferior in respect to the number, and possibly the quality, of her troops. They were still made up in large part of rude levies, hastily summoned, irregularly armed, and imperfectly disciplined. But the queen

The military outlook.

[1] In a second letter the cardinal protested against this dishonest disclosure of a confidential letter, and Königsegg explained it by the indiscretion of other parties to whom he had been obliged to communicate it officially. Flassan, v. 165, condemns the Austrian proceeding in point of form, but admits that Maria Theresa had reasons for neglecting the strict rules of good faith in her relations with France. For Belleisle's report of the affair, see Broglie, *Frédéric II. et Louis XV.*, i. 10–16.

[2] Frederic to Fleury, 12 September, 1742. But the person to whom the cardinal alluded as the real author of the war was, it is now supposed, Belleisle, not Frederic. Cf. Broglie, *Fr. II. et Louis XV.*, i. 19, 25 n.

herself displayed a courage worthy of her position, and conveyed some of her enthusiasm to her ministers, especially Bartenstein and Stahremberg. This courage had, too, a large element of offended pride, of personal resentment, which with women may easily become the stimulus of a petty revenge, but may also supply the inspiration for noble and heroic deeds. Encouragement of a more substantial nature was found in the active participation of England. The concentration of a British force for a diversion upon Dunkirk had begun even before the withdrawal of Prussia; but after the treaty of Berlin it proceeded more rapidly. In August an army of nearly forty thousand men, English, Hanoverians, and Hessians, was ready for action. The English had attempted to engage Prussia in an offensive alliance against France, and lord Stair at the Hague was specially charged with negotiations to that end. But Frederic repelled all overtures with promptness and emphasis. What Hyndford did with one thousand pounds, which at his own request he obtained for the purpose of bribing Podewils, does not appear. He had no reason to suppose that the minister was purchasable. And he ought to have learned even from his short acquaintance with Frederic's system of government that the bribery of the minister would have little or no effect upon the decision of the king.[1]

A factor of much apparent importance in the situation which now shaped itself was the army of Maillebois. The English commander, lord Stair, had expected that it would be sent to the defence of Dunkirk, and was prepared in that case to give battle. But the army of Harcourt in Bavaria had been practically dissolved. A small contingent joined Broglie some months before, and the rest was turned over to Maurice of Saxony, while count Seckendorf superseded

Maillebois ordered to relieve Prague.

[1] See Eichel to Podewils, 10 July and 17 August, 1742; Droysen, V. ii. 17, 18; Ranke, xxix. 24; and, for Hyndford's reports, Raumer, ii. 183, 184.

the old and incompetent Törring in the command of the
Bavarians; so that it became necessary to employ Maillebois' corps for the relief of Prague. The army of the
Mathurins, the wits of Paris called it, because the Mathurins were monks, whose special mission it was to rescue
Christians from captivity. It deserved the name for
another reason : its general directed it more like the
prior of an abbey than the leader of an army. It had
been arranged that both Maurice and Seckendorf should
join him on the march. The former did actually effect a
junction at Vohenstrauss, on the nineteenth of September,
but Seckendorf halted with the Bavarians at Regensburg.
Without these Maillebois had, however, an army of over
fifty thousand men.

The Mathurins finally reached the entrance to the Bohemian forest, a region offering obstacles formidable even
to an energetic general, and almost insurmountable to
one like Maillebois. Yet the besieged gained a certain
respite by his advance. The grand-duke Francis, who
now commanded before Prague, hastened to raise the
siege, and set off to meet the new enemy, whereupon
Broglie seized the opportunity to make his escape with
eight or ten thousand men, including all the cavalry.
Belleisle was left with the remnant.

The result of the marching and manœuvring was that
Broglie, Maillebois, and all the rest gave up the
relief of Prague as an enterprise which the
difficulties of the country, the exhaustion of
the troops, the want of supplies, and the presence of a
strong hostile army seemed to make impossible ; and the
various detachments, turning southward, reunited as a
new army of Bavaria.[1] The unfortunate emperor found

But joins
Broglie in
Bavaria.

---

[1] Maillebois was sharply criticised for leaving Prague to its fate,
but justified himself in a measure by his orders. " J'avais lettre du
11 September," he wrote, 16 October, 1742, "qui me défendait de
me livrer à aucun événement qui pût être douteux." Luynes, iv. 362.

consolation only in the energy and temporary success of Seckendorf. This officer had seized the opportunity afforded by the withdrawal of the Austrians to occupy Munich, and Charles was enabled once more to visit his capital. The grand-duke followed Broglie closely, and took up a position which covered Austria against any advance from that quarter. Seckendorf and the emperor wished to attack the enemy with the combined French and Bavarian forces. But Broglie, in pursuance, he said, of orders from Paris, refused. The winter thus passed in inaction, except that the Austrians now and then attacked exposed outposts of the allies, and nearly always with success.

The situation of Belleisle had now become desperate. Belleisle's retreat. He had barely eighteen thousand troops, many of them unfit for duty ; the weather was severe ; supplies were scarce ; and there was no hope of relief. But the investment was loosely conducted by Lobkowitz, who had taken his position east of the city and across the river. The chance thus offered, desperate as it was, Belleisle determined to seize. Silently and swiftly completing his preparations, he slipped out unperceived in the night of the sixteenth of December, leaving only some five thousand men under general Chevert to guard the city. His immediate destination was Eger, a place about one hundred miles distant, but practically made twice as far by the fearful obstacles that had to be overcome. The cold was intense ; the roads were heavy with ice and snow ; the troops were in bad condition ; the horses were few ; and the Austrian hussars hung closely upon their rear, picking up stragglers, and cutting off isolated parties. If there was something of the charlatan in Belleisle he had also his heroic side, and it is everywhere conspicuous during this famous retreat. On the twenty-sixth of December the exhausted remnant of the army, which sixteen months before had entered Bavaria with such imposing prospects, arrived at Eger. The frozen corpses of fifteen hundred men marked the line of march. After a few days' rest, the little force continued its retreat, and early in February crossed the Rhine into France.[1]

Chevert was not dismayed by the perilous situation in which he was now left at Prague. When summoned by Lobkowitz, he replied that unless he were granted the privilege of freely withdrawing with his troops, he would fire the city, and die with every man. This firmness secured him his own terms, and eventually the last group of survivors reached Eger.

Fall of Prague.

The enemy was thus practically expelled from Bohemia without a battle, and the kingdom, sadly impoverished by the many armies that it had had to support, returned to its original allegiance. A wise policy on the part of Maria Theresa would have been to grant an indemnity for the past, and begin at once to repair the ravages of war. This was the course required by good faith, at least in respect to Prague ; for one of the conditions exacted, and obtained by Chevert, was that no punishment should be inflicted on such citizens as under constraint had taken the oath of allegiance to Charles Albert. But the queen suffered herself to be controlled by her resentment. She named a commission of inquiry, at the head of which was placed, singularly enough, a man who had himself sent instructions to his son to render homage to the usurper ; and this commission entered upon a deliberate policy of expulsions and confiscations. At the end of it, on the twelfth of May, the queen was solemnly crowned in Prague.[2]

[1] The duke de Broglie, *Fr. II. et Louis XV.*, i. 125, 126, has brought to light the curious fact that Belleisle owed the plan of his retreat to the learned chevalier Folard, the commentator of Polybius, who himself borrowed many of the details from the retreat of Xenophon's Ten Thousand.

[2] Arneth, ii. c. vii., makes no attempt to conceal the pain with which he writes this portion of his history.

The English army under Stair had in the mean time accomplished little except to make plans, and in plans the general was rich. He had served under Marlborough. From that great soldier he had learned what he considered the true rules of strategy; and when the army of Maillebois set out for Bohemia, he advised an immediate invasion of France. But while the hesitation of the Dutch made any movement uncertain, a movement into France suited neither the military nor the political plans of the English ministers. It was thought that the cause of the pragmatic sanction could best be served in Germany; and as soon as Carteret had overcome the reluctance of Holland, preparations were made to march up the Rhine.

The king of Prussia looked upon this movement with much disfavor and some anxiety. He was for one thing uneasy about an enterprise which might give the French a pretext for invading Hanover. He feared, too, that the active assistance of the English would give the Austrian arms too great a preponderance, and thus destroy that equilibrium between the belligerents which it was his policy to maintain. Finally, he was unwilling to see the emperor completely crushed. To avert this result he had already sounded the court of Vienna upon the possibility of a reasonable peace with Charles VII., but found the terms offered by the queen little favorable to an accommodation.[1] The queen insisted on three conditions: that her right to cast the electoral vote of Bohemia should not in the future be contested; that her husband, the grand-duke Francis, be made king of the Romans; and that she be permitted to continue the war against France.[2] Charles, for his part, demanded that for the benefit of his successors in the

[1] Instructions of 28 October, 1742, for count Dohna, Prussian envoy at Vienna.

[2] Droysen, V. ii. 52; Ranke, xxix. 28.

electorate and in return for the renunciation of other claims, Bavaria should be made a kingdom, and so enlarged by cessions of territory that it would have an additional revenue of six millions guldens, and be able to maintain an army of forty thousand men.[1] But it required time to find a plan for reconciling these rival demands, and the English movements threatened to disturb the most sincere diplomacy.

To meet this preliminary danger, Frederic advanced the proposition that if an English army should invade Germany to attack the lawful emperor, it would be the duty of every prince of the Empire, his own first of all, to oppose such a movement.[2] The elector-palatine having appealed to him for aid against a threatened violation of his territory by the Anglo-Hanoverian army, the king replied with assurances of support, and at the same time addressed an urgent remonstrance to George II. on the subject.[3] Other protests were made from time to time, some of them by the king in person, and with extraordinary violence of manner, which Hyndford and Podewils agreed to attribute to wine.[4] But they remained without effect. The English ministers gave assurances that they meditated no attack upon the emperor, and would respect the liberties of the Empire. The French, they said, were the real invaders of Germany; and the duty of England, as prescribed alike by her treaty engagements and her own interests, required her to aid in repelling them.[5] With these delightful fictions on the one side and on the other, the controversy was enlivened. But the English preparations

Frederic's intercession.

[1] Droysen, V. ii. 16.

[2] Rescript addressed to the department of foreign affairs, 16 December, 1742. Andrié, at London, was instructed accordingly.

[3] *Polit. Corresp.*, ii. 319, 321, 322.

[4] Raumer, ii. 186 et seq.

[5] Hyndford to Frederic, 29 January, 1743, in *Pr. Staatsschriften*, i. 360–363 ; the Prussian reply, ibid. pp. 363, 364.

kept on without interruption; and the diplomatic advantage rested decidedly with England. The original protest against the English march was withdrawn and Frederic finally gave orders, though with great reluctance, to sign the long-pending treaty of defensive alliance with Great Britain.[1] Even the conciliatory explanations which Hyndford gave in a note were apparently suggested only by considerations of formal courtesy. For Carteret had conducted affairs so adroitly that Frederic seemed to be threatened with the prospect of a combination, which would expose him to the united vengeance of all the powers that he had successively offended.

The efforts of Frederic to effect a compromise were, however, not relaxed. But, while one class of obstacles arose from the unnatural association of French and Bavarian interests, with the prejudice which that created in the Empire, others not less serious were found in the uncompromising temper of Maria Theresa, and the inflated, irrational expectations of Charles himself. If not blind to the dangers which threatened his ruin, he seemed at least indifferent to the labors of those who were trying to save him. He clung to the demand for six millions revenue, and forty thousand troops, as if those figures had some peculiar charm; as if the men and the money could be had for the asking, or picked up without effort in the market-place.[2] But more practical men, approving the end, set out to find the means. One plan was to assign to the unfortunate prince certain imperial cities which should be mediatized, and certain bishoprics which should be secularized, after the

Plan of pacification.

[1] Eichel to Podewils, 12 November; Frederic to same, 16 November, 1742. The treaty was signed at London on the 29th of November. The text in German is given by Adelung, iii. 313 et seq. Broglie, *Frederic II. et Louis XV.*, i. 265, seems hardly justified in calling this treaty a triumph for Prussia.

[2] Thus Frederic to Klinggraeffen, envoy to the emperor, 2 February, 1743.

example of the treaty of Westphalia. It is difficult to say with whom this project in its concrete form first originated. Podewils suggested something of the kind in a memorial to Frederic as early as February, 1742; but it seems to have passed unnoticed.[1] It again comes up in a report of Klinggraeffen from Frankfort-on-the-Main in November of the same year.[2] Two months later, Frederic himself proposed it as an original plan, and apparently with some confidence in its success. For he added, as a warning to the emperor, that it was all which he would be able to obtain for him. If the plan met the approval of Charles, he was to indicate the cities and bishoprics which he desired.[3]

In reply Klinggraeffen sent the propositions which Haslang, the imperial envoy at London, had already submitted to Carteret, and which Carteret had at once revealed to the court of Vienna. *Its failure.* Charles still offered to treat for peace with the queen only on the condition that Bavaria be raised to a kingdom, with additions of territory equal to a revenue of six millions. Half of this increase was to come from districts ceded by Austria. The other half would be furnished by annexations which could be agreed on later, pending which, however, it should be charged on the revenues of the Netherlands.[4] In London the report was circulated that Haslang had actually specified certain free cities and bishoprics, which his master desired. The public prints were soon full of the scheme. The archbishop of Salzburg issued a fiery protest; the papal nuncio made formal representations at Frankfort-on-the-Main; and Maria Theresa, quick to seize the advantage offered by Charles's error, published a declaration to the effect that no extremities to which she might

[1] Droysen, V. ii. 23; Grünhagen, ii. 134.
[2] Ranke, xxix. 30 n.
[3] Frederic to Klinggraeffen, 21 January, 1743.
[4] Droysen, V. ii. 56.

be reduced would ever tempt her to purchase peace at the cost of the church.[1] Under the storm of reproaches which poured in upon him, the emperor was forced to disavow the project of confiscating the bishoprics. His envoy, Haslang, even procured from Carteret a written statement that such a proposal had not been made formally, but was only thrown out incidentally in the course of conversation.[2] Frederic himself did not approve the entire scheme, and hesitated especially to support the demand for cessions of territory by the queen. The proposed secularization he held to be the best plan.[3] But as this plan was swept away by the first breath of publicity, the result cannot be called a triumph for his well-meant efforts.

Into the multitude of schemes for treaties of peace and treaties of alliance, into the countless projects for mediation and compromise and readjustment, into the intrigues of Frankfort, Paris, Berlin, Vienna, and London, it seems unnecessary here to enter. They are alike bewildering in their variety and their obscurity, and offer little that can gratify a friend of upright political methods. A word must, however, be said by way of characterizing the leading features of the situation, which presented itself on the resumption of hostilities.

The French for their part were active in negotiations, and were perhaps as ready to desert the emperor as he was to desert them. But France the queen was determined to chastise. She had been forced to yield to Prussia, and her revenge for Silesia had to be reserved, however reluctantly, for a later and better opportunity. The emperor alone would be an object only of contempt; he was, besides, a kinsman, and had at least been guilty of

Death of Fleury.

[1] Ranke, xxix. 35 ; Adelung, iv. 35, 36.

[2] Carteret to Haslang, 15 March, 1742. *Heldengeschichte*, ii. 848, 849.

[3] Echel to Podewils, 3 February, 1742.

no treachery. But the conduct of France was without any palliation, and the fortune of war seemed now to put it in the power of Maria Theresa to administer an effective lesson to a wanton aggressor. While Frederic was in the field she had been a suppliant at the court of France. Now the French were suing for peace, and she took a characteristic delight in treating their overtures with derision. The death of Fleury on the twentieth of January, 1743, two years too late, as was justly said, for his fame, removed an antagonist whose skill in diplomacy was always a dangerous factor.[1] The young king announced, in a sudden outburst of independence, that the cardinal would have no successor. He proposed to take the government into his own hands.[2]

Louis lacked, however, the force of will necessary to carry such a purpose into effect. He was intelligent, and in his own way sincerely patriotic; *Le secret du roi.* but it was easier to declare that thenceforth no one minister should wield the power of Fleury than to make all the ministers and all the favorites support his own crude and feeble schemes of policy. He adopted, therefore, a system of intrigue and deception. Without openly disavowing his ministers or his mistresses, he tried to escape the just demands of the first and the fond importunities of the others by opening secret communications with a small band of trusted confidential agents selected from the diplomatic service and the army. In this way began the famous secret correspondence of Louis the Fifteenth. The first confidant was marshal Noailles, a survivor from the reign, and an interpreter of the

---

[1] Frederic says with some neatness of the cardinal, " on dit trop de bien de lui pendant sa vie, on le blâma trop après sa mort." *Œuvres de Frédéric*, iii. 2. The cases of Fleury and Walpole may point a moral against statesmen, who to keep office adopt a policy opposed to their convictions.

[2] D'Argenson, *Mémoires et journal inédits*, vol. ii. p. 270.

statecraft, of Louis the Fourteenth. He was a good soldier, a fair politician, and probably an honest man, but
something of a doctrinaire, and full of confidence in himself. The correspondence with him began about the time
of Fleury's death, and continued many years. After his
fall, the king formed a complicated network of secret
agents, in which figured such persons as prince Conti,
Tercier, a subordinate in the ministry of foreign affairs,
count Broglie, a son of the old marshal, the chevalier
d'Eon, and many others of high and low degree. The
state thus maintained two policies, often opposed the one
to the other. The cabinet represented one policy, to
which the king gave outward signs of approval. The
secret correspondence was the medium of the other; and
it often suggested to an envoy, or an ambassador, a line of
conduct opposed to that which had been prescribed by his
recognized official superior. This state of things explains
in part much of the weakness of French policy during the
rest of Louis' reign.[1]

In England Carteret's power was now at its height, and

Activity of Carteret.

his colleagues only essayed to moderate an ardor
which they found it impossible to quench. The
connection with Hanover took on an importance never
before known. Hanover had troops, but no money; and
the minister risked his popularity at home by taking
twenty thousand Hanoverians into the British service,

[1] The secret correspondence of Louis XV. forms the subject of
several interesting publications. Extracts from that part of it in
which he was concerned are given in the *Mémoires politiques et militaires* of Noailles, and the more complete work of Camille Rousset,
Correspondance de Louis XV. et du maréchal de Noailles, Paris, 1865.
The subsequent correspondence has been published by E. Boutaric,
Correspondance secrète inédite de Louis XV., Paris, 1866. In *Le
secret du roi*, Paris, 1878, the duke de Broglie adds some further information drawn from the family archives. Count Ségur had already given as early as 1793, in his *Politique de tous les cabinets de
l'Europe*, some of the letters addressed to the king.

and thus enriching the electoral purse of his master at the cost of the tax-payers of England. His dashing diplomacy even broke down the barriers of Dutch caution and obstinacy. After lord Stair had failed to overcome the scruples of the United Provinces, Carteret himself visited the Hague, and by his eloquence and energy secured the promise of Dutch coöperation with a liberal subsidy, and twenty thousand troops, in support of the pragmatic sanction.

Frederic was justly suspicious of Carteret, for he gave English diplomacy a tone and a direction which threatened danger. But he was also suspicious of the currents that prevailed in Russia, in Saxony, in all the countries with which he was nominally at peace; he and his ministers were alarmed by every new phase of the diplomatic situation. An unauthorized intimation by a high official in Holland that the question of Silesia was still open, threw the Berlin politicians into a panic. An explicit disavowal of the sinister words was required, and readily given. The Dutch greffier explained away his imprudent language; the courts of London and Vienna disclaimed all responsibility for it; and Frederic gave orders to let the matter drop.[1] The attitude of Russia also caused uneasiness. Mardefeld was fertile in the discovery or invention of plots of the French envoy, the marquis de la Chétardie, or the Austrian envoy, marquis Botta, to lead the empress into schemes aimed at the later conquests, and even the original possessions of Prussia. The instructions to count Dohna, on the occasion of his appointment as resident at Vienna, pointed out the part which he was to play in frustrating such designs.[2] In the spring of 1743 Mardefeld reported the leading features of a quadruple alliance to be formed between Rus-

Frederic's uneasiness.

[1] Frederic to O. von Podewils, and to Andrié, 4 March, 1743; the same to Podewils, 21 March, 1743; Droysen, V. ii. 66, 67.

[2] *Polit. Corresp.*, ii. 287.

sia, England, Austria, and Saxony against Prussia, but Frederic seems not to have treated it seriously.[1] At Dresden it was as usual the intrigues of priests and confessors that gave great concern to Podewils, and even to the king. From Vienna no cordiality, or anything except the most formal and indifferent courtesy, was to be expected in any circumstances ; and the Prussian diplomatists were nervously watchful for contingencies which might lead to the renewal of hostilities. Once at least a very precise report was submitted of an alleged effort of France to obtain peace even on the condition of aiding the queen to recover Silesia.[2] But Frederic's military sympathies were in general with France and the emperor, rather than with their enemies. He resisted, indeed, earnest entreaties to reënter what was called the anti-pragmatic alliance; yet in one noteworthy communication he intimated that he was keeping quiet because the time for action had not arrived, leaving it to be inferred that a serious crisis would not find him wanting.[3] He was evidently prepared, all through the year 1743, to interfere whenever his interference should seem required by his interests.

In the mean time the English — or the combined force The English in Germany. of English, Hanoverians, and Hessians, which I shall designate by that name — broke camp, and early in March proceeded slowly up the Rhine. In Luxemburg they were joined by a few Austrians under Neipperg, who had been transferred to that region. Toward the end of April the force crossed the river at Neuwied, and then continued its march, on the right bank, toward

---

[1] Frederic to Mardefeld, 1 June, 1743 ; Droysen, V. ii. 115, 116 ; an extract from Mardefeld's report, 7 May, *Polit. Corresp.*, ii. 369 n.

[2] Cf. in Coxe's *Pelham*, i. 469, 470, Mr. Stone to lord Harrington, 31 July, 1743 ; and *Polit. Corresp.*, ii. 395–397.

[3] Frederic to Schmettau, 27 April, 1743.

Frankfort. Lord Stair was yet in command, but George II. was expected to arrive before the opening of actual hostilities. The English troops were the objects of marked attention. They were the first which had been seen in Germany since the eventful season forty years before, when Marlborough set out to meet the French on the Danube, and returned with the spoils of Blenheim. The showy uniforms and splendid physique of the men, the luxurious appointments of the officers, and the easy air of aristocratic superiority which characterized them, led sceptics to doubt whether the ability of the strangers was equal to their splendor, and whether they could face troops which had learned the lesson of serious war in Bavaria and Bohemia, on the Danube and on the Moldau. But when the trial came it appeared that these fine gentlemen could march up to the cannon's mouth as steadily as the tattered veterans of Khevenhüller and Seckendorf.[1]

At Wiesbaden a junction was effected with the duke of Ahremberg, who was commander-in-chief in the Austrian Netherlands, and who early revealed a tendency to oppose everything that lord Stair proposed. What Stair proposed was to march toward Bavaria, and cut Broglie's communications with France, or intercept his retreat. This could be done, it was thought, without regard to the large French army which under the duke of Noailles was manœuvring on the other side of the Rhine. But Ahremberg refused, and for reasons which, as the sequel will show, were not contrary to the policy of England.

The see of Mayence had lately become vacant, and the choice of a new archbishop and elector was a matter of no little moment to both the contending parties. Frederic sent a special envoy, colonel von Bornstedt, to work in behalf of the Bavarian candidate, a

The see of Mayence.

[1] Frederic himself was one of the sceptics, as appears from Hyndford's report, 9 July, 1743. Raumer, ii. 190.

younger brother of the emperor.[1] But the pragmatic army — as that of Stair was called — proved to be an even more powerful canvassing agent. When the chapter met on the twenty-second of April, the choice fell upon count Ostein, a strong Austrian partisan. He had lately been the queen's envoy at London; and if his character was not exactly that which a strict advocate of the ecclesiastical proprieties would demand, he was a good politician, and the office was mainly political. The archbishop of Mayence was chancellor of the Empire, and in dignity the first of the electors. The result was thus a decided victory for the queen.

The Austrians began to move somewhat later than their allies. But they moved with the energy and the rapidity which the enterprise of their generals and the confidence of their soldiers had already made so effective. Early in May prince Charles drove the French back upon the Isar. On the ninth he cut off a Bavarian corps of nine thousand men, and forced it to surrender, while the town of Braunau, before which the army had lain, was at once invested. The important post of Dingelfingen was captured a few days later by general Daun, the French garrison and covering force making a hasty escape across the Isar. Landau and Deggendorf fell in rapid succession; and the lesson of concentration, which Seckendorf and the emperor had vainly tried to teach Broglie, was thus learned in a thorough though costly manner. By the end of May the Austrians had three columns converging upon the enemy, that of prince Charles from the east, that of Lobkowitz from Prague, and that of Khevenhüller from Salzburg. Broglie, who had steadily refused to fight, now wrote that fighting could no longer save him. A force of twelve thousand men detached from the army of Noailles was on the way to his relief; but without awaiting its arrival,

French expelled from Bavaria.

[1] Instructions of 6 January, 1743.

the marshal drew his divisions together, and set out on his homeward march. Seckendorf again protested, and another altercation took place. But as Broglie's purpose could not be changed, the Bavarians were forced to follow him, and leave their country again to the enemy. The unhappy emperor fled first to Augsburg, and thence to Frankfort. Broglie continued his retreat swiftly, harassed only by the irregular Austrian cavalry; met his expected reënforcements, which he swept along with him in his flight; and finally took refuge across the Rhine. Seckendorf retired with the Bavarians into Suabia, and on the twenty-seventh of June concluded a temporary convention for a suspension of hostilities, and the neutrality of his army. Eger was the only important Austrian town still left in the enemy's hands, and even Eger held out but a short time.

The defence of Broglie was that he had received orders to avoid a hazardous engagement, and, if necessary, to abandon the country. Such may have been his private instructions. Maillebois made the same excuse for his failure even to attempt the relief of Prague; and in truth the principal rivalry of the French generals seemed to show itself in giving the most liberal extension to the term "hazardous engagement." In one sense all battles are hazardous; otherwise none would be fought. The general who runs no risks may of course escape open defeat; but he is also not likely to win many victories, and may lose a campaign which less caution and more boldness would have saved. The French court was indeed timid. Its orders were weak and contradictory, and its own irresolute conduct may explain in part the apparent timidity of its generals. But it was not the policy even of that court to sacrifice position after position, advantage after advantage, and to incur the derision of Europe, without striking a blow. In private, at least, Louis censured the hasty abandonment of Bavaria, and

Broglie soon fell into disfavor. Marshal Noailles even proposed that he be cashiered for misconduct.[1]

The old marshal had the right to give such advice because his own more energetic and more skilful movements had roused the pragmatic army from its lethargy. The force under his command had been collected for the purpose of thwarting the projected invasion of France, and originally numbered, before drafts had been made upon it for the relief of other corps, some seventy thousand men. When the English changed their plans and moved up the Rhine, he changed his own accordingly, crossed the Rhine, and seized the line of the Neckar. Lord Stair then pushed his army toward the southeast, with a view to joining prince Charles. But this purpose was frustrated by the French marshal, who gained possession of the upper waters of the Main, and barred all further progress in that direction. The pragmatic army then took position at Aschaffenburg, on the right bank of the river. There it was joined on the twentieth of June by George the Second and his son, the duke of Cumberland. But it was impossible for the army to remain shut up in this narrow valley, with no hope of supplies, and a superior force surrounding it on all sides. To move in any direction permitted by the nature of the ground, it would be necessary to cut a way through the enemy ; and the choice of plans was to retreat down the Main, because that route led toward the store of supplies, and the few thousand Hessians guarding them, at Hanau. In the night of the twenty-sixth and twenty-seventh of June this critical march began.

The English march arrested.

The English followed closely the course of the stream, but, as Noailles had planted batteries along the opposite or left bank, they were exposed to a murderous fire without any opportunity of replying. At Seligenstadt the marshal had thrown bridges across the

Battle of Dettingen.

---

[1] Louis to Noailles, 13 July, 1742. Cf. Luynes, vi. 66.

river, and stationed a force near the village of Dettingen
to arrest the retreat. All these dispositions of the French
were admirably made ; it seemed impossible for the pragmatic army to escape. But at the most critical moment
the fatal impetuosity of a French officer, the duke of
Grammont, opened a way out of the difficulty. The duke
commanded the mounted portion of the force at Dettingen ; and when the English approached, he, instead of
holding his horse in reserve, and allowing the batteries on
the other side of the river to do their work, fiercely
charged the enemy, and forced the guns to suspend a fire
which would have been as destructive to friends as foes.
The battle thus became practically one between the whole
of the pragmatic and a part of the French army. It was
desperately contested, but the steadiness of the English in
the end prevailed. The French retreated over the river,
while the victors, without attempting any pursuit, and even
leaving their wounded to be cared for by the enemy,
hastily continued down the valley, and at length reached
Hanau in safety.

It is evident that this could be called a victory only in
the sense that it was a close escape from a grave
disaster. But it gave encouragement to the
queen, and caused unbounded exultation in England,
where Handel commemorated it in a solemn and noble Te
Deum. Among the friends of the emperor it caused a
corresponding depression. Even Frederic was for a moment alarmed by the supposed magnitude of the calamity,
and drew a gloomy picture of its expected consequences.
He predicted the complete superiority of Austria and
England in the Empire, the election of the grand-duke
Francis as king of the Romans, and an alliance between
England, Austria, Saxony, and Russia.[1] But in a few
days he recovered confidence, and wrote, more correctly,
that the triumph reduced itself to the maintenance of

*Its signifi-
cance.*

[1] Frederic to Podewils, 3 July, 1743.

the field of battle by the English, with equal losses on both sides.[1]

This was the only important achievement of the English arms during the war of the Austrian succession. Lord Stair, offended at some slights which he had received, threw up his command, and retired to England. He was succeeded for a time by marshal Wade, an old and brave but unskilful soldier, totally unfitted to conduct a campaign. A partial reorganization of the English cabinet, which took place in August, was also not advantageous to the Austrian cause; for when, on the death of lord Wilmington, the nominal premier, in July, a contest arose over the succession to the place, the candidate of Carteret's enemies, Henry Pelham, prevailed over Carteret's own favorite, and the elements of opposition to that minister's policy and methods received a formidable accession. The dissensions which had long reigned in the cabinet became now more violent than before. Carteret still kept his place, but his vehement and dictatorial style was no longer so effective, and a visible reaction set in from the energy and ardor with which he had supported the Austrian cause.

The military situation continued, however, favorable to the queen. Prince Charles collected a formidable army east of the Rhine; and although he did not immediately succeed in crossing, he at least kept the French out of Germany, and the emperor out of Bavaria, and threatened eventually to carry the war into the very heart of France. In Italy, too, the Austrians were admirably handled by Traun, and achieved a number of striking triumphs over the Spaniards.

This seemed to George the Second and Carteret a favorable time for new efforts in diplomacy. In July they agreed with prince William of Hesse-Cassel, acting for the emperor, upon the so-called project

The English cabinet.

Success of the Austrians.

Project of Hanau.

[1] Frederic to Rothenburg, 13 July, 1743.

of Hanau, a scheme of pacification between Charles and Maria Theresa. By its terms there were to be mutual restitutions of territory and renunciations of claims; but Bavaria was vaguely promised some future extension of her frontiers, and, in return for abandoning France, was to receive from England subsidies equal to those which it was then drawing from Louis the Fifteenth. But when the project with the last-named stipulation reached England, it was at once denounced by all parties as an act of apostasy dictated by Hanoverian influence. Carteret at once disowned it, and the negotiations ceased. The queen, too, was little disposed in the hour of triumph to accept an agreement which recognized the pragmatic sanction indeed, and her right in the future to cast the electoral vote of Bohemia, but otherwise made no concession to her outraged pride, and took no account of the arduous conquests of her gallant armies.

Even the final treaty with Sardinia involved sacrifices which she made with the greatest reluctance. The temporary alliance of the year before with Charles Emanuel expressly provided that he might withdraw from it at any time, and was therefore of too frail a texture for security. He had indeed co-operated against the Spaniards, and successfully. But, with the proverbial dexterity of the house of Savoy, he still held one ear open to the voice of French diplomacy; and in the summer of 1743 it became clear that his defection could only be averted by the prompt adjustment of the compensations, which were already promised in general terms. He demanded the Italian principalities of Finale and Placentia, and part of Pavia. England acted again as the benevolent friend of Austria, and in the treaty of Worms the queen was compelled, against her protest, to make the required cessions.[1]

Treaty of Worms. September, 1743.

[1] Wenck, i. 677–679. Cf. Coxe, *H. of A.*, iii. 296 ; Ranke, xxix. 50–52, etc.

The narrative now reaches another point at which the historians are accustomed to pause and moralize upon the unreasonable obstinacy of Maria Theresa. Yet the case is by no means so clear against the queen as it is often made to appear. She had been deeply wronged. She would have denied not only her sex, but even her species, if she had too readily forgiven the powers which had invaded her dominions without cause, and spread the lurid flames of war over the fair valleys of the Danube and the fertile plains of Bohemia. By the surrender of Silesia she had bought off the most dangerous of her enemies. She had been led to make this sacrifice in part by the consideration, of which England was the persistent advocate, that it would give her the necessary freedom of action in other directions. To be invited, in addition to this, to purchase the friendship of the king of Sardinia, and to grant Charles VII. a complete indemnity for the past, seemed to her the most cruel irony; nor is it surprising that she became indignant at English diplomacy, since its support seemed to consist only in extorting fresh sacrifices from her, either of honor, or of territory, or of both.[1] And it is superfluous to urge that it was impossible for her to foresee the event which soon gave a new shock to her confidence. That event was indeed shut out of consideration by the universal principles of good faith and the solemn obligations of a treaty.

[1] Cf. Raumer, ii. 161.

CHAPTER VII.

THE UNION OF FRANKFORT.

THE failure of all his efforts to pacify the belligerents, and the rising prosperity of the queen's fortunes, led Frederic to consider carefully the state of his pecuniary and military resources. He had begun, immediately after the treaty of Berlin, to replenish the war fund, on which the two campaigns had made such heavy drafts. By the end of 1744 it was expected to reach six millions. The army was to be enlarged by May of the same year to the extent of eighteen thousand men.[1] The arsenals, gun-foundries, and powder-mills now began to increase their activity; the repairs on the fortifications were accelerated; new defensive works were planned; new facilities for an offensive campaign were provided in every branch of military organization. It might not be quite correct to say that the king already foresaw his renewed intervention in the struggle. But there can be no doubt that the contingency seemed so near in the summer of 1743, and especially after the battle of Dettingen, that it became prudent to have everything ready for the crisis.

Another reason which led to this augmentation of the Prussian army was the king's profound distrust of the policy of Russia. "He fears Russia more than his God," was the blasphemous report of Hyndford.[2] If the Russians had come to the relief of

Frederic makes preparations.

Continued distrust of Russia.

[1] Frederic to Rothenburg, 27 August, 1743.
[2] 18 July, 1744, apud Raumer, ii. 194.

Maria Theresa in 1741, as at the time seemed not unlikely, and had invaded Preussen, they would have found
the province stripped of all its troops, and nearly defenceless. It was mainly to avoid a similar peril in the future
that, as Frederic himself wrote, the new regiments were
formed.[1] But the real state of affairs at St. Petersburg
was not always correctly understood either by Frederic or
by Mardefeld. They knew, indeed, that Bestuschef was ill-
disposed toward Prussia, and that English influence was
for the time paramount in the councils of the empress.
This influence had brought about a treaty of peace
between Russia and Sweden, and a defensive alliance
between Russia and England; while other schemes and
intrigues were suspected to be equally favorable to the
cause of the pragmatic sanction. And the Russian guaranty for Silesia still awaited ratification.

One of these intrigues, if such it may be called, proved,
The Botta
incident.
however, of no little service to the king of Prussia. On the discovery of a supposed plot to
dethrone Elizabeth, and restore the exiled Ivan, one of
the conspirators deposed under torture that the marquis
Botta, formerly Austrian ambassador at St. Petersburg,
but then at Berlin, was implicated in it. He had pledged
himself, so the story ran, to secure the coöperation of Austria and Prussia. Frederic promptly disavowed the part
attributed to Prussia, and had apparently no difficulty in
satisfying the empress. But the general charge against
Botta he was able to use adroitly for the furtherance of
his own interests. There is no evidence that he believed
in the envoy's guilt. Yet he promptly demanded his recall, out of consideration, as he said, for the Russian
court,[2] and even denied him the usual courtesies on his
departure. Then, by Frederic's orders, Mardefeld proceeded to make the most judicious use of the incident at

[1] To Mardefeld, 1 June, 1743.
[2] *Polit. Corresp.*, ii. 444.

St. Petersburg. He was to take advantage of the favorable impression, created by this abrupt dismissal of Botta, to press the Silesian guaranty, to effect the removal of Bestuschef and his brother, and to secure a suitable bride for the young prince of Holstein-Gothorp, whom Elizabeth had chosen for her successor.[1]

The overthrow of Bestuschef was not effected, but the rest of this programme was soon carried out successfully. The accession of Russia to the treaty of Berlin was signed on the twelfth of November.[2] About the same time the Prussian party succeeded in carrying their candidate for the hand of the future tsar, and thus administered a severe check to the schemes of Bestuschef.

Frederic's candidate was the young daughter of the prince of Anhalt-Zerbst, a general in the Prussian service and commandant at Stettin. A plain, simple, straightforward man, he preferred *The future Catherine II.* a soldier's work to the idle life of a petty German court, and had few plans for his own advancement, or that of his family. But the princess, his wife, had larger views. She was a member of the reigning family of Holstein-Gothorp, and, with high culture and considerable force of intellect, was full of ambition, which she was not unwilling to gratify even at the cost of great sacrifices, and by the use of the most vigorous measures. Frederic knew her character well, and believed that her delight at the prospect of a great career for her daughter would easily overcome any hesitation on the part of her less enterprising husband. And the event proved that he had judged wisely. When the scheme was broached to her cautiously, as a secret known only to half a dozen persons, not including

---

[1] The history of the Botta incident will be found in Martens, *Causes célèbres du droit des gens*, vol. i. The marquis was placed in arrest at Vienna, on a peremptory demand from Elizabeth, but subsequently released after a humble apology had been made.

[2] Wenck, i. 782–784.

Bestuschef, she adopted it with enthusiasm, and gladly accepted an invitation to visit Russia with her daughter. The rest was easy. Elizabeth was delighted with her choice; the betrothal took place in February, 1744; and a year later, the princess having in the mean time, after a little coquettish hesitation, entered the Russian church, and taken the name of Catherine, the marriage was celebrated. It is probable that Frederic had little insight into the character of the girl whom he thus sent to St. Petersburg to be an instrument of his policy at the Russian court. She was only fifteen years old when she was invited to visit Elizabeth; but she was developed beyond her age, both in mind and body, and her acquiescence in the change of religion early showed that scruples of conscience were not likely to interfere with her worldly interests as she understood them. The germs of the future Catherine the Second were already present in the young girl, who, in the winter of 1743–44, set out to seek her fortune at the court of Russia.

This achievement of Frederic was more than a defeat of Bestuschef: it was also a victory over the court of Saxony, which in the princess Marianne had its own candidate, warmly supported by the chancellor, for Peter's hand. The problem was, besides, made more delicate by the fact that Elizabeth had at first fixed her choice upon Frederic's own sister, Ulrica. But an indirect intimation to this effect was adroitly parried by various excuses, mainly by putting forward the question of religion as an obstacle. The real reason was, however, a different one, as appears from Frederic's own subsequent account. "Nothing," he says, "would have been more unnatural than to sacrifice a princess of the royal blood to such a fate." This was true fraternal prudence and humanity; but as the religious obstacle was not treated as insuperable in the case of the young princess of Zerbst, so there seemed no impropriety in sending

Better relations with Russia.

her to the sacrificial altar in the interest of Prussian diplomatic policy. In any event, the efforts of Frederic and Mardefeld were for the time crowned with success. Warm compliments were exchanged between the two courts; decorations were freely dispensed; and Mardefeld received twenty thousand thalers with which to reward his friends at the imperial court. The envoy even reported that it was a matter of general remark that the king had the preference over all other princes in the mind of the empress, and that she expressed the utmost indifference to the attitude of the rest of the powers so long as she was on friendly terms with Prussia.[1]

These opportune incidents made it easier for Frederic to treat with indifference the overtures which about this time were again made in behalf of France. The medium of the overtures was Voltaire.

The king and the poet had not ceased to correspond even during the most trying days of the Moravian campaign. When Frederic made the separate peace of 1742, which caused such indignation in France, Voltaire alone sent him an ardent letter of congratulation.[2] It is true that he afterwards tried, though without much success, to disavow the unpatriotic proceeding.[3] But the circumstance that by his zeal for Frederic he had compromised his credit at Paris seemed likely to give him strong claims upon the confidence and gratitude of his royal friend, and to make him a useful advocate of French interests at Berlin. There were, besides, other reasons which led him to seek for a time a voluntary exile abroad. He had lately been a candidate for the

Troubles of Voltaire.

[1] *Polit. Corresp.*, ii. 480 n. For the facts connected with the choice of Catherine, the marriage, etc., I have consulted Brückner's *Katharina die Zweite*, Berlin, 1883, and Schlözer's *Friedrich II. et Katharina II.*, Berlin, 1859.

[2] Voltaire to Frederic, July, in reply to one from the king, 18 June, 1742.

[3] Cf. Broglie, *Fr. II. et M. T.*, ii. 328–333.

academy, with the acquiescence of Louis, the sympathy of madame de la Tournelle, and the support of all who justly appreciated the splendor of his literary genius. But the fauteuil left vacant by the death of Fleury was not to be occupied by Voltaire. The hatred of the priests, whose sacred office he had held up to ridicule, the malignity of wretched versifiers, whom not even flattery could call his rivals, and the resentment of all those, in high station or low, who had writhed under his terrible satire, again defeated his aspirations; and the academy fixed its suffrages upon an abbot of the church, whose writings may have had the good fortune to escape the Index, but are not otherwise counted among the masterpieces of literature. This defeat threw the sensitive poet into a violent rage, which Piron, Boyer, and others further increased by their cries of triumph and derision. Voltaire replied with epigrams, which convulsed the salons, and showed that anger had not dulled the edge of his wit. Some of these were too pointed and indecent for publication, but they were all sent faithfully to Frederic. The king hastened to condole with the disappointed candidate on his defeat, yet no doubt secretly rejoiced that the incident seemed likely to give Voltaire a fresh aversion to Paris.

Yet Voltaire had a thrifty power of self-command even in his moments of greatest irritation. He resolved, indeed, to leave Paris for a time, but before leaving he obtained from Louis a species of authorization to act as secret agent of the French government. In this capacity he hoped to keep up useful relations with the ministers, to render some signal service to the state, and thus to change the temporary exultation of his enemies into feelings of shame and remorse. His vanity permitted him to believe that he could probe the purposes of Frederic, and persuade him to another alliance with France. It was given out accordingly that the persecu-

His mission to Berlin.

tions of Boyer had driven him away, and, tearing himself from madame du Châtelet, he set out in July, by way of the Hague, for Berlin.

Frederic at once prepared not only to receive, but also to retain the illustrious traveller. He reasoned that it would be easier to make Voltaire remain in Berlin if it were first made difficult for him to return to France; and the circulation at Paris of the vicious pasquils, in which the rage of the defeated candidate found too free expression, seemed admirably adapted to this end.[1] It is true that these had been communicated to Frederic in the strictest confidence. But Voltaire, who was himself not too scrupulous in guarding the literary secrets of others, was also no ordinary acquisition to the royal circle; and Frederic had the whole batch of verses conveyed by a private channel to Paris.[2] The scheme proved a complete failure. Voltaire himself states that the king of France, to whom his performances were reported, explained with great simplicity that they were only devices to conceal more effectually the poet's diplomatic character.[3]

The reception which Voltaire received at Berlin was, of course, not the less warm after this piece of flattering treachery. He was lodged in the royal palace, fed at the royal table, and permitted to share, in the closest intimacy, the entire daily leisure of his host. The pretty sisters of Frederic fluttered about the poet with charming feminine delight; while he repaid this not

His reception.

---

[1] Frederic to Rothenburg, 27 August, 1743.

[2] In an earlier letter to Rothenburg, Frederic characterized this proceeding by a term more accurate than elegant. Dr. Preuss, the editor of the *Œuvres de Frédéric*, does not scruple to give, vol. xxv., one of these poems, of which the following lines may serve as a specimen: —

> Loin de ton ignorante clique,
> Loin du plus stupide des rois,
> Je vais oublier à la fois
> Et la sottise de Mirepoix
> Et la sottise académique.

[3] *Œuvres de Voltaire*, lxiv. 207.

unwelcome adoration with verses, which expressed with
incomparable felicity his respect, his admiration, and perhaps, on one occasion, even more audacious sentiments.
"A little truth," he writes to Ulrica, "is often mixed
with the grossest fictions. Last night, in the illusion of a
dream, I rose to the rank of kings; I loved you and
dared declare my love. When I awoke the gods left part
of what my sleep had given me. I only lost my kingdom." [1] When royalty thus set the example of homage,
and permitted such freedom, the poet's place at Berlin
was of course assured. At the theatre, or the ballet, he
divided public attention with the king himself. "Nothing is spoken of here, but Voltaire," reports Hyndford to
his court; "a man does not pass for educated unless he
has this poet's verses in his head or his pocket, or speaks
in rhyme." [2] It is not strange that the saturnine envoy,
and Valori, his French colleague, were impatient of such
a rival, and, in the confidence bred by common hardships,
even compared notes upon their experiences with the
king, whom each was trying to gain.

In the mean time Voltaire found no hearing for his
His diplo-   political recommendations. He came, as Fred-
macy.   eric afterwards wrote, without credentials, and
his mission became a simple pleasantry.[3] But it was a
pleasantry which Voltaire himself, with a dullness to be
explained only by his vanity, failed to perceive. Not even
the famous memorial which was submitted in categorical

---

[1] The original of this well-known madrigal can alone render its
exquisite delicacy : —

À LA PRINCESSE ULRIQUE.

Souvent un peu de vérité
Se mêle au plus grossier mensonge,
  Cette nuit dans l'erreur d'un songe
  Au rang des rois j'étais monté.
Je vous aimais, princesse, et j'osais vous le dire.
Les dieux à mon reveil ne m'ont pas tout ôté;
  Je n'ai perdu que mon empire.

[2] Raumer, ii. 192.

[3] Œuvres de Frédéric, ii. 23, 24.

form to the king, and returned with his marginal comments, part in prose, part in verse, flippant, ironical, evasive, — that memorial over which the whole world has laughed, and which is truly one of the most curious documents in political literature, — not even that opened the eyes of a man usually so keen, so quick to see the ridiculous; and the amateur envoy carefully preserved it among the records of his visit.

The original paper contained nine propositions or theses which, as the best product of the writer's adroitness, were intended to incite Frederic to some kind of action, or at least to extort some revelation of his secret views and intentions. Hence they took the form of doubts or queries suggested by the infirm condition of the imperial cause, and the rising prospects of the pragmatic alliance. Was it not clear that France was showing vigor and wisdom? If the king of Prussia should assemble an army of neutrality, and adopt the tone of a master, would he not bring the English and Dutch to terms, and become the benefactor of Europe? Had he not a vital interest in preventing the English from making the grand-duke Francis king of the Romans? What would he do if the Austrians, with their allies, successful against France, should open the next campaign in Silesia? Would he not now march his troops into Cleves, and thus encourage the peace party in Holland? Finally, would his majesty be pleased to make his humble visitor forever happy by confiding to him some morsel of news agreeable to the court of France? But Frederic parried these ingenious efforts with almost cruel facility. He admired the wisdom of France, he said, but he hoped God would prevent him from imitating it. He concerned himself little about what the English and Dutch said of him, for he understood not a word of their patois. The election of a king of the Romans required the unanimous suffrages of the Empire, so he himself had

An annotated memoir.

an absolute veto on the scheme; though it is not certain that his constitutional law was much better than Voltaire's. If the Austrians should invade Silesia, he would receive them in the manner of Barbari.[1] The proposition to send troops to the Dutch frontier produced more doggerel, and so with the rest. Even a child ought to have understood the king's response to be an intimation that a poet should stick to his verses, and not expect a prince burdened with affairs of state, at a most critical juncture, to give ear to the unofficial diplomacy of an amateur.

The only utterance of Frederic which had any element of the serious was in reply to Voltaire's plaintive request for some bit of information to carry back to France. Even this was malicious, but it was not altogether frivolous. " I have no alliance with France," — " liaison " is the word, — " and nothing to fear or hope from her. If you wish," he said, " I can make a panegyric of Louis XV., in which there shall not be a word of truth; but as to political affairs we have nothing in common, and if we had, it is not for me to speak the first. When propositions are made to me I will answer; but you, who are so reasonable, must see how ridiculous it would be for me to offer terms to France, and especially to put them in writing. . . . The only commission which I can give you is to advise the statesmen of France to be more prudent in the future than they are at present. That kingdom resembles a strong body without soul or nerves."[2]

It is to be presumed that Frederic put these strong expressions in the paper because he felt certain that Vol-

[1] On les y recevra,
　　　Biribi,
　À la façon de Barbari,
　　　Mon ami.

[2] The document is in *Œuvres de Frédéric*, vol. xxii. pp. 141–144, and a translation in Carlyle, iii. 553–556. See Broglie, *Fr. II. et Louis XV.*, vol. ii., appendix, pp. 419–437, for such of Voltaire's reports to Amelot as are not contained in his published works.

taire would not expose himself to ridicule, and proclaim the failure of his mission, by laying it before Amelot. He was evidently unwilling, too, at the time to help France out of her difficulties. But that he did not really feel the optimism so jauntily expressed to Voltaire is abundantly proved by his correspondence with his ministers and envoys, by the negotiations which he soon began with France and the emperor, and by the treaties which were concluded in the spring of the following year.

Early in September Frederic, accompanied by Voltaire, paid a visit of pleasure, which was also one of business, to the court of his sister Wilhelmina, at Bayreuth. For him, indeed, the social festivities were probably only a mask. While Voltaire entertained the ladies with epigrams and sonnets, he himself was sounding the neighboring princes, and the agents of others more distant, about the feasibility of a union or association between the members of the Empire, for the defence of the chosen head of that frail commonwealth. The emperor himself grasped at it eagerly. But it soon appeared that there were grave differences of opinion among the leading parties in regard to the participation or exclusion of France. Count Törring, the Bavarian minister, insisted on the necessity of taking France into the scheme, at least through troops to be loaned to the union. Frederic affected, on the other hand, to prefer a purely German demonstration.[1] It would carry, he thought, a greater moral weight than a movement hampered by complications with a foreign power; and toward its success he was willing to contribute thirty thousand troops. The negotiations continued for several months, but this particular phase of them led to no result. It gradually became apparent that the Austrian influence was unexpectedly strong with the leading princes, both

More efforts for the emperor.

[1] Ranke, xxix. 61; rescript addressed to the department of foreign affairs, 10 February, 1744.

temporal and spiritual; and English diplomacy, supported by English gold, was active in increasing the number of the queen's adherents. The plan of saving the emperor without the aid of the French necessarily gave way, therefore, to a plan by which Prussia should reënter the Franco-Bavarian alliance.

A number of circumstances concurred to effect this change. One was the treaty of Worms between Austria, England, and Sardinia, in the second and thirteenth articles of which Frederic professed to see a possible danger, if not an intended menace, for Prussia.[1] These articles contained renewed guaranties of various earlier treaties, to which some of the contracting powers might be parties, but conspicuously omitted the treaty of Berlin, by which Prussia held Silesia. The provision, too, for subsidies, which England agreed to furnish "during the war, or as long as necessity might require," could be interpreted as permitting, if not distinctly authorizing, the aid of English money and Sardinian troops for restoring the entire integrity of the Hapsburg dominions. In a paper prepared by Frederic in February, there is a curious balancing of reasons for and against taking alarm at the treaty. But the conclusion was that it created a danger, which ought to be anticipated by prompt measures. Podewils took, however, a more favorable view."[2]

Treaty of Worms.

A more direct, though also more trivial cause of offence was the formal recording by the imperial diet, at the instance of Austria, of the queen's protest against the election of Charles VII., and all official acts since done in his name. The protest was couched in language unnecessarily offensive to those who had participated in the election, and especially to Fred-

Austria and Prussia in the diet.

[1] See Eichel to Podewils, 10 February, 1744.

[2] *Polit. Corresp.*, iii. 35–42 ; Droysen, V. ii. 209 ; *Œuvres de Frédéric*, iii. 33, 34.

eric.   Much correspondence ensued, and a bitter feeling long survived the unfortunate incident.[1]

Finally a treaty between Austria and Saxony gave en- couragement to Frederic's fears.   The body of the instrument had an innocent look, being little more than a renewal of former treaties of alli- liance and guaranty.   But in one separate, and three secret articles the republic of Poland was admitted as a party ; concessions were made in regard to the right of passage through Austrian territory from Dresden to War- saw ; and the promise of eventual assistance to be given by Saxony, though expressly made inapplicable to the powers engaged in the war then pending, was applied to any other power which should interfere against the queen of Hungary.[2]   The last article was evidently aimed at Prussia.   The progress of the negotiations had been known vaguely to Frederic and his ministers ; and five days after their conclusion the fact was learned at Berlin.[3]   On the twentieth of January, 1744, Seckendorf was able to send the king a copy of the second secret article.[4]   Frederic's information was thus indeed scanty, but it was enough to arouse the liveliest solicitude.

Treaty between Austria and Saxony.

The convention had, besides, a direct practical bearing on the proposed union, or association, for guarding the neutrality of the Empire.   Such a scheme could not leave Saxony out of account; and in fact Seckendorf was at Dresden, laboring to secure the adhesion of August, at the very time that the latter was concluding the treaty of Vienna with the queen of Hungary.

Baffled in this direction, Frederic now turned seriously toward France.   A sketch in his own handwrit- ing, and probably datable the seventeenth or

Frederic surveys the field.

[1] The so-called Dictatur-streit, further details of which I shall mercifully spare the reader.

[2] Treaty of Vienna, 20 December, 1743.   Wenck, i. 722–733.

[3] Podewils to Frederic, 30 December, 1743.

[4] Acknowledged in Frederic to Seckendorf, 26 January, 1744.

eighteenth of February, discusses the terms of a possible treaty with that power, and enumerates as leading conditions six articles, which show conclusively the course and tendency of the recent negotiations. The king requires that he be aided in forming a defensive alliance with Russia and Sweden; that France declare war as a belligerent against Austria; that Bohemia be wrested from the queen; that cardinal Tencin, the French minister, be put in charge of German affairs; that Hanover be attacked by twenty thousand Swedes; and that the allies continue the war until the queen shall be forced to cede Bohemia and sue for peace.[1]

A further step was taken at the same time in the dispatch of count Rothenburg on a secret mission to the court of Versailles. Rothenburg was one of those young and accomplished soldiers who enjoyed the personal friendship, as well as the confidence of Frederic, and whom he often employed in such delicate services as, for various reasons, he was unwilling to entrust to his regular diplomatists. The missions of Camas and Truchsess, in 1740, belonged to this description. Rothenburg was the peer of either of these as a soldier, and probably their superior in the tact, versatility, and personal bearing which make the successful negotiator. He had travelled much, had visited Voltaire, was connected by marriage with the French aristocracy, and was universally popular. His journey was concealed even from Podewils, but was apparently known to Valori.[2]

Sends Rothenburg to Paris.

The instructions to Rothenburg, and the parallel negotiations which went on at the same time with the emperor, show that Frederic now contemplated, not the mere maintenance of the Em-

Rothenburg's instructions.

[1] *Polit. Corresp.*, iii. 43. On Frederic's partiality for cardinal Tencin and marshal Noailles, see Frederic to Chambrier, 18 February, 1744.

[2] Valori, i. 188, 189; Frederic to Chambrier, 18 February, 1744.

pire's neutrality, or even the restoration of Charles VII.
to his hereditary possessions, but a new war of spoliation
upon the queen, and new acquisitions for Prussia. He
was ready to rescue the imperilled emperor on certain
conditions. But the most important of these was the one,
not often found in books of chivalry, that he be liberally
paid for the service. He demanded that part of Silesia
which still remained with Austria, and a strip of Bohemia
along the Elbe; the rest of Bohemia, including Prague,
was offered to the emperor.[1] He required also that the
treaty with France be kept secret, in order that the world
might accept as genuine the pretext that Prussia was taking up arms only to preserve the neutrality and independence of the Empire, and not in consequence of an
express engagement with France.[2] The other conditions
were not essentially different from those contained in the
king's memorandum as above given.

Rothenburg's neglect of the dissimulation and tortuous
devices, which Frederic in his earlier years His nego-
seemed to regard as essential to diplomacy, drew tiations.
forth several sharp rebukes from Berlin. But he acquitted himself of his task, as the result showed, with success and credit. Very soon after his arrival he put himself on good terms with the reigning mistress, madame
de la Tournelle, lately created duchess of Châteauroux,
and obtained her powerful support for his cause. Cardinal Tencin justified the good opinion which Frederic had
formed of him. By the aid of these two, and the connection which he had in high society, with Noailles, the duke
of Richelieu, and others, Rothenburg was able to form a
strong Prussian party, which succeeded, as its first triumph, in overthrowing Amelot, the lukewarm, if not

[1] *Polit. Corresp.*, iii. 44 n.; Frederic to Eichel 24, and to Rothenburg 30 March, 1744.
[2] Frederic's own words to Rothenburg. *Polit. Corresp.*, iii. 72.

positively hostile secretary for foreign affairs.[1] This obstacle removed, the affair proceeded more smoothly. The formal conclusion of the treaty was still delayed, but some of the conditions laid down by Frederic were fulfilled at an early day. On the fifteenth of March France declared war upon England, and a few days later upon Austria.

It would be a mistake, however, to regard this action as a mere compliance with Frederic's demands. The truth is, rather, that it was the tardy abandonment of a wretched fiction, which, originally invented to satisfy the scruples of Fleury, had never served any useful purpose, and had long since been effectually exposed. Yet the statesmen of that age found a singular charm in such feeble devices. Even Frederic put forth, at the time of his invasion of Silesia, the fiction that he entered the province as a friend of the queen, to defend it against her enemies. This pretext never convinced a single person, gained him no time, and was in no way whatever of the slightest advantage; yet he clung to it until its absurdity became incompatible with any further maintenance of his dignity and self-respect. All parties were now wise enough to see that Fleury's sophism, that France was only an auxiliary, not a belligerent, ought also to give way to an attitude of sensible and manly frankness.

In throwing off the mask, by which she had hitherto tried to conceal the character of her measures, France also revealed the real issue lying beneath all the minor antagonisms, that the art of diplomatists had so skilfully yet so unnaturally enlarged. For there can be no doubt that the more correct and more honest statesmen were those who refused to regard the war as a paltry dispute over the interpretation of a will, or the

Meaning of the war.

[1] Cf. Flassan, v. 202, 203; *Œuvres de Frédéric,* iii. 40; Frederic to Klinggraeffen, 7 May, 1744. But Ranke, xxix. 96, questions whether Rothenburg was not rather a dupe than a principal.

legality of an imperial election. It was rather a struggle, which had remote historical antecedents, and strictly
obeyed the traditions of a hundred years. The real secret
of the war was the ancient rivalry of France and Austria,
of Bourbon and Hapsburg; and though Prussia, by the
adoption of a new policy, had utilized that rivalry for her
own aggrandizement, England was simply faithful to the
lessons of William III. and Marlborough, and to her interests as they were still understood, in supporting the house
of Austria on the continent. But her part was gradually
ceasing to be that of an ally, and becoming that of a principal. Austria was only a European power, and her aim
was to maintain her ascendency on the continent. But
France and England were commercial, naval, and coloni-
zing powers; and their rivalry, being felt in every part of
the world, soon dwarfed the ancient duel between Bourbon and Hapsburg, and prepared the way for a contest
of vastly more imposing proportions. The declaration of
war by France was thus an act of defiance to both the
rival powers. In March she challenged England to a battle for the supremacy on the sea and on the land, in Europe and in America. In April she notified Austria that
the leadership in the politics of the continent was again
an open issue. The line between the belligerents was thus
clearly and honestly drawn, and all parties prepared more
intelligently for the impending struggle.

The promise given by France to open the next campaign with greater vigor was faithfully kept.[1]
It is true that this vigor did not reach the standard proposed by Frederic. The French did not
cross the Rhine and besiege Freiburg, as he had suggested, nor could they well force a passage in the face of
the large army of prince Charles. But they still pre-

New energy
of the
French.

---

[1] Klinggraeffen to Frederic, 4 February, 1744. Chavigny, the
French envoy at Frankfort, spoke to Klinggraeffen of 350,000 French
troops under arms.

vented the prince himself from crossing, thus holding his force in check, and inactive. The scheme for a descent

Jacobite plans. upon England in the interest of the pretender was indeed a military blunder, though entrusted to Maurice of Saxony. It was a hopeless enterprise from the first; and the indirect consequences of the plan itself were unfortunate. It disarmed the opposition in parliament by making it seem the duty of all Englishmen to support the king, and the Protestant cause, against the unscrupulous designs of France; and it so alarmed the prince of Hesse-Cassel, whose contingent of six thousand troops was about to pass into the pay and service of France, that he threatened to transfer them to England. But this project had the approval of Frederic himself. He had earnestly supported the efforts of France to hire the Hessian troops, and he labored quite as earnestly to calm the scruples of prince William, when the discovery of the purpose for which they might be used, or might at least indirectly aid, led him to cancel the contract.[1] The precautions of France and the fear of England were, however, alike unnecessary. A storm dispersed the French fleet, and as the channel was patrolled by an English squadron, the enterprise was for the time abandoned.[2] Maurice then joined his troops to the formidable army which was preparing to carry the war into the Austrian Netherlands. Under his lead, and in spite of the presence of Louis in the field, the campaign opened vigorously. The allies were not only far inferior in numbers and equipment, but they were also weakened by the jealousy of the higher officers, the incompetency of marshal Wade,

[1] Frederic to prince William of Hesse-Cassel, 19 and 30 March, and to Seckendorf, 31 March, 1744.

[2] Cf. Noailles, *Mémoires*, p. 330 ; St.-René Taillandier, *Maurice de Saxe*, pp. 244–246 ; Espagnac, *Histoire de Maurice Comte de Saxe*, Paris, 1775, i. 448–451. Maurice was created field-marshal at this time.

and the indecision of the Dutch. One after another the chief fortified places of the Netherlands — Courtray, Menin, Ypres, Furnes — fell into the hands of the French.

Frederic watched the progress of Maurice with placid satisfaction. While the French were fighting in the Netherlands he himself, though preparing indeed for war, was busily pursuing the work of peace. *Life at Berlin.* For his new opera-house, finished and opened the year before, his agents at the different capitals were incessantly active in procuring the best singers, dancers, actors; and on terms which were beyond the dreams of a general of the army, or a privy councillor of the civil service. The greatest acquisition was Barbarina, the danseuse. If her engagement was a species of diplomatic triumph, her arrival in Berlin was celebrated like a victory in the field; and the chronologist of Frederic's reign is careful to record the date of her first appearance on the stage.[1] The repertoire of the new theatre was mainly confined to French comedy of the lighter kind, and Italian opera. Occasionally a tragedy of Voltaire's was rendered. The classical music of Germany, then just beginning its noble career, was recognized as early as 1740 by the appointment of Graun as director of the royal orchestra; in December, 1741, his opera "Rodelinde" was put on the boards.[2] But the national drama found no hospitality or encouragement.

The academy of sciences, reorganized shortly before, and under its new organization reopened in January, held regular sessions for reports and debates, *Reorganization of the academy.* and had open doors for eminent scholars from every part of the world. Maupertuis was present at the opening. He had returned to Paris after his release by the Austrians in 1741, and it appears with the intention of remaining. He was a member of the French academy

[1] Rödenbeck, *Tagebuch*, i. 102.
[2] Preuss, i. 276.

of sciences. But his old rivals renewed their hostility, and, again yielding to the urgent appeals of Frederic, he returned toward the end of the year 1743 to Berlin. But he disapproved of the new form given to the academy. It was divided into classes, with a curator at the head of each; and these curators, who were high officials civil or military, not men of science, acted in rotation as president of the general sessions. Maupertuis carried through, therefore, a reform by which he was made perpetual president, with a French refugee, Formey, as secretary.[1] The institution then resumed its learned labors on a broader and more scientific basis. The proceedings were, however, all conducted in French, and even papers submitted in German were translated before they were read. The king himself frequently attended the sessions; now and then he sent in contributions of his own, in the presence of which criticism was silent.

A domestic incident, on which some political calculations were also based, enlivened at this time the court and society of the capital. Frederic had long been anxious to establish closer relations with Sweden, chiefly indeed as a means of restraint upon Russia. An alliance with the northern court was, we have seen, one of the conditions which Rothenburg had to present at Paris; and it was supposed that the influence of France, which was still powerful at Stockholm, would easily meet the requirement. But he did not neglect a more direct opportunity, which enabled the resources of his household to aid the efforts of diplomacy. He had just refused to send Ulrica, his oldest unmarried sister, to the sacrificial altar, as the bride of Elizabeth's chosen successor; and this decision was a praiseworthy act of prudence, though, as now appeared, not at all inspired by scruples about marriages of utility for the female members of his family.

Marriage of Ulrica.

[1] Statutes of 24 January, 1744. Mylius, *Corp. Const. March.* Cont. Suppl., pp. 258–266.

When a more tempting offer was made on behalf of the crown prince of Sweden, he gave a ready assent. To the choice of Ulrica he offered indeed the objection that she already had a good establishment as abbess, or rather prospective abbess, of Quedlinburg, and was not inclined to marry; but the younger sister, Amelia, was equally desirable as a bride, and would make less difficulty about adopting the Lutheran religion. A political alliance with Sweden, it was also intimated, would be welcome.[1] Further negotiations led, however, to the removal of the obstacles to Ulrica, and an agreement was reached.[2] The betrothal was celebrated in May, the marriage in June. By the fate which often overtakes spinsters, the discarded princess Amelia succeeded her sister in the rich establishment of Quedlinburg.

At this juncture another piece of good fortune fell to Frederic. Charles Edzard, prince of East Friesland, died on the twenty-fifth of May; and since he left no male representatives, his death introduced precisely the state of things which gave Prussia the right to claim the province, under the expectancy granted by the emperor in 1686. It is true that Hanover also had claims to the succession, and they had been for many years the subject of litigation; while Holland, as a creditor of the province, asserted a species of lien upon the revenues. Various dispositions of the territory, which none of the claimants yet possessed, had been from time to time proposed. Frederic himself was once ready, it appears, to cede his own rights to the elector palatine, as part of a general scheme of pacification.[3] But when the fief became vacant he acted with his usual promptness. A small force, which had been awaiting the event, at once occupied Embden, the capital; officers of the civil service received

Acquisition of East Friesland.

---

[1] *Polit. Corresp.*, iii. 5.

[2] Frederic to Podewils, 12 March, 1744.

[3] *Polit. Corresp.*, iii. 66 ; Frederic to Klinggraeffen, 11 April, 1744.

the oath of homage in the king's name; and Cocceji, the minister of justice, began to reorganize the administration on a Prussian basis. But the local institutions were left mainly unchanged, and Frederic wisely contented himself with the surplus revenues, which were long inconsiderable. The new acquisition was held to be chiefly valuable on account of the fine port of Embden on the North Sea, to which Frederic warmly desired an independent outlet. The hopes which he had formed for Prussian commerce proved, however, delusive, for Embden failed to become a rival of the free cities of Bremen and Hamburg, or of his own towns on the Baltic. Even the seizure of the province itself, though formally ratified by the emperor, was only the beginning of a new and weary course of litigation.

This event coincided in time with the successful close of the negotiations for adding Prussia a second time to the enemies of Maria Theresa. They had been conducted simultaneously, and on parallel lines, at Paris and Frankfort. The efforts of Rothenburg to secure from France the pledges which Frederic required, in regard to the military and diplomatic measures to take, were supplemented at the imperial city by conferences between the agents of Prussia, of the emperor, and of such minor German princes as it was desired to bring into the coalition. The mediator was Theodore de Chavigny, the French envoy at the itinerant court of Charles the Seventh. Chavigny was one of the most active, enterprising, and ambitious diplomatists in the service of Louis. His aims were as extensive as Belleisle's, his ardor not less great, his methods far more subtle. He was unscrupulous in intrigue; and Frederic, though using him now as an ally, and even urging his appointment to succeed Amelot in the French cabinet, was often suspicious of his activity, and watched his proceedings with the greatest care. Klinggraeffen, his own

Progress of the negotiations.

envoy, was an official of some experience in diplomacy, intelligent, industrious, and faithful. But he had little force of initiative, and was not apparently a very acute observer.

Finally the time arrived when the diplomatists could put the result of their labors in shape for formal adoption. The various stipulations between the contracting powers were embodied in three treaties, each of which was devoted to a special subject, or satisfied some scruple raised in respect to form or method. The earliest in date was the so-called union of Frankfort, the meagre outcome of all the ambitious schemes for combined federal action in the name of the Empire. It seemed to aim only at the pacification of Germany, the recognition of the emperor, and the restoration of Bavaria; and there was no hint that to attain these ends other than diplomatic pressure was to be applied to Maria Theresa. The contracting parties were the emperor, the king of Prussia, the young elector-palatine, — for Charles Philip had finally died in the December previous, and the line of Sulzbach had peaceably succeeded, — and the landgrave of Hesse-Cassel, who had recovered from his alarm about the Stuart expedition. But a secret article, which admitted France into the union, if only as a party to the treaty of Westphalia, obviously had in view the use of force. This treaty was signed on the twenty-second of May.[1]

Union of Frankfort.

The second treaty was a tripartite agreement between France, Prussia, and the emperor for a division of the spoils after they should be gathered in. This followed closely the lines laid down by Frederic two

Treaty of partition.

[1] Droysen, V. ii. 272, 273; the treaty in Wenck, ii. 163–169. The denial of Ranke, *Sämmtliche Werke*, xxix. 92 n., that there was a secret article, is founded on a misapprehension. Writing to Klinggraeffen, 13 May, Frederic says: "quant à l'article secret . . . j'ai à la fin résolu d'y condescendre . . . et veux bien que . . . vous puissiez signer cet article secret." But Droysen, V. ii. 273, says it was not signed until the second of June.

months before, at least so far as his own share was concerned. He was to receive the rest of Silesia, the three Bohemian counties of Königgrätz, Leitmeritz, and Buntzlau, as well as Kolin and Pardubitz, with the Elbe as a frontier, — all of which was conceded by the emperor with a reluctance which probably imposed only on himself.[1] In return Frederic promised to guarantee Charles in the possession of the rest of Bohemia and Upper Austria. France was to retain several fortified places in the Netherlands.

The third treaty was a species of military convention between France and Prussia, signed on the fifth of June. By its terms France agreed to operate energetically in the Netherlands, and at the same time to send a second army through Westphalia against Hanover. In August, if his alliance with Sweden and Russia should be concluded, Frederic was to strike into Bohemia with eighty thousand men. Should prince Charles return to meet this new enemy, he was to be closely followed by the French.

Military convention with France.

It will be seen that this was a comprehensive scheme of action, offering to its authors a great advantage of numbers, and, with ordinary management, every prospect of success. Frederic was profuse in acknowledgments to all who had contributed to the complex alliance, to Noailles, Seckendorf, Chavigny, Rothenburg, Klinggraeffen. He even wrote to the mistress of Louis XV., who had effectually aided Rothenburg, in terms of heartfelt gratitude. He was truly flattered, he said, to be in part indebted to her for the disposition which the king of France had shown to accept the bonds of a new and durable alliance. The esteem which he had always felt for her was now strengthened by feelings of gratitude. It was unfortunate that Prussia had to conceal the obli-

Frederic's satisfaction.

[1] Droysen, V. ii. 273 ; Arneth, ii. 398 ; Schoell, ii. 349–353, has the text of the treaty.

gations which she felt, but they would rest profoundly engraved in his heart. And the king remained her affectionate friend.[1]

In accordance with Frederic's demand, these transactions were at first carefully concealed even from his most trusted ministers and generals.[2] Whether this policy was adopted because he feared that they would betray the secret, or because he was impatient of the objections which he knew they would raise, does not clearly appear; but the disadvantages of such a system reveal themselves at once. Podewils and Borcke labored in the dark, and often at cross purposes with the king. Eichel was, doubtless from necessity, admitted to the secret. But Eichel was as voiceless as a sphynx, and in silent amazement copied and expedited orders which involved the lives of thousands of men, the fate of mighty empires, the fortunes of Europe itself.

It is probable that since the proposed alliance with Sweden and Russia was closely connected with the treaties of Frankfort and Paris, it, too, was reserved for Frederic's personal diplomacy. If so, he could not congratulate himself on his success. Sweden offered, indeed, no difficulty. Her interests, and, since the marriage festivities at Berlin, her dynastic connections, were wholly favorable to the Prussian alliance, and made it unlikely that she alone would cause any trouble. But at St. Petersburg the chancellor Bestuschef continued to hold the confidence of the empress, and, supported by the opulent resources of Tirawley, the English envoy, thwarted the most ingenious schemes of Mardefeld. Even the marquis de la Chétardie, who had lately

Failure of the Russian alliance.

---

[1] Frederic to the duchess of Châteauroux, 12 May, 1744; cf. Ranke, xxix. 96. Luynes, vi. 388, says Frederic asked for her portrait after her death. But his interest then could have been only æsthetic.

[2] Ranke, xxix. 98.

returned to Russia, failed to change the prevailing current. He had relied, and not without reason, on his
former popularity with Elizabeth ; but this time he met
with a cold reception, and, having been betrayed by the
accomplices whom he had employed to overthrow Bestuschef, was in June abruptly ordered to leave Russia.
These circumstances caused no little dismay at Berlin.[1]
The value of the chancellor had already risen so high in
the market that Frederic authorized the expenditure of
one hundred and fifty thousand thalers, if need be, to
gain him.[2] Now, too, there are frequent hints in the correspondence about the use which might be made of the
young princess of Anhalt-Zerbst. But Mardefeld reported that he had no hopes of success, although he did
not apprehend any measures of open hostility to Prussia.[3]

The full meaning of the Russian article of the treaty
with France now first appears. Frederic's ostensible reason for insisting on the alliance with
Russia, as a condition without which he would
not consent to take the field again, was that otherwise
he would have no security against an attack by the empress on the province of Preussen. His real motive was,
as he himself avows, a different one. The provision was
inserted as a shrewd tactical device, by which he acquired
the option, in case the northern alliance should fail, of
acting or not acting, as his own interests might decide.[4]
And now the situation had arrived which gave him, under
the treaty of June, an undoubted technical right to refuse
to fulfil its engagements. But instead of claiming the
right, he prepared to execute the treaty. Indeed, he an-

Frederic's purpose unchanged.

[1] Frederic to Mardefeld, 2 and 4 June and 15 July; to Noailles,
8 July, 1744.
[2] Droysen, V. ii. 279. Frederic to Mardefeld, 11 April, 1742,
speaks only of 50,000, though the passage may be read to mean
that this sum was in addition to what had previously been authorized.
[3] Œuvres de Frédéric, iii. 40.   [4] Droysen, V. ii. 283.

nounced such a purpose as early as the twenty-eighth of
June, while the air was still full of sombre reports from
St. Petersburg.[1] Three days later, on the first of July,
Podewils was taken into the secret, which filled him with
amazement and alarm.[2] From that time onward the
king's correspondence has almost daily allusions to the
great scheme. Why, then, did Frederic neglect to make
use of the pretext which he had so carefully reserved?
To this question, also, he himself supplies the answer.
It was, he says, because the military situation made it a
matter of policy, or even necessity, to overlook the unfulfilled condition. He had hoped to postpone the rupture,
but the general turn of affairs obliged him to declare
against the queen of Hungary. The alliance of Prussia
was the most fortunate thing which could have happened
to France, and her own interest at least ought to have
excited her to fulfil her engagements. But what dependence could be placed on the policy of a court governed by intrigues, or on the valor of troops led by timid
and nerveless generals?[3]

The progress of the French in the Netherlands was indeed purchased at the cost of disaster on the
Rhine. Toward the end of June the Austrian
army, which had been destined to cross the river
and carry the war into the enemy's country, was put in
order for the decisive blow. Under prince Charles, its
commander, served, as professional adviser, count Traun,
whose campaign in Italy had been brilliant and successful. He was a cautious soldier, who avoided risks; was
a better strategist than tactician, and to Maria Theresa
often seemed unduly slow. His refusal to advance to

Austrians
cross the
Rhine.

---

[1] "Quand même l'alliance . . . ne réussirait pas le roi . . . ne
s'y arrêtera pas, et il exécutera tout ce de quoi il est convenu avec
la France dans le temps arrêté." Frederic to Noailles, 28 June,
1744. Cf. Broglie, *Fr. II. et Louis XV.*, ii. 322, 323.

[2] Droysen, V. ii. 290.　　　　[3] *Œuvres de Frédéric*, iii. 40.

the Rhine until all his preparations were completed, severely tried her patience. But the ardor of prince Charles was nicely tempered by the measured judgment of Traun, who had for his part the further qualification that modesty, or tact, made him invariably give his nominal chief the credit for any success. The army of the prince numbered nearly seventy thousand men.[1] Against it marshal Coigny, the French commander in Alsace, could muster only fifty thousand, including Seckendorf's Bavarians, whom, the better as he supposed to dispute the passage, he had called to the left bank of the river. But this left the Austrians free to manœuvre on the right bank, where by a series of rapid and skilful movements they completely deceived the enemy, and almost chose their own place for crossing. On the second of July they obtained control of sufficient bridges, by which the whole army passed over in safety. This successful crossing of a river in the face of a hostile force, one of the most difficult of military problems, has always been greatly admired by critics. Frederic compared it to Cæsar's passage of the Rhine, and Eugene's of the Po.[2]

Once safely over the Rhine, prince Charles pressed forward as fast as the state of the roads and the weather permitted. He seized the lines of Lauterburg and Weissenburg. He made a diversion toward Strasburg, and sent cavalry to surprise Luneville in Lorraine, whence Stanislas Lescinski, the father-in-law of the French king, made a precipitate flight. Coigny was too weak to offer battle, and only feebly manœuvred for delay until the arrival of reënforcements.

And invade Alsace.

These had been detached, on the first alarm, from the army in Flanders, which during their absence was of course condemned to inaction. Louis himself accompanied them. He had originally joined the army in Flanders on the advice of madame de Château-

Louis the well-beloved.

---

[1] Arneth, ii. 390.   [2] *Œuvres*, xxviii. 61.

roux, and Frederic assured him that he would have an opportunity to rival the exploits of his predecessor.[1] Now the spirited mistress urged him to seek the new post of danger, and again he obeyed. Again, too, Frederic added his benediction. " How beautiful," he exclaimed, " to see your majesty fly to the rescue of your people! The promptness of your movements is admirable. You command, and an army disappears from Flanders to fall like a thunderbolt upon prince Charles. Your blows are those of a master." [2] This ardent panegyric was intended to welcome Louis to Metz, where he arrived, with a vast train of male and female attendants, on the fourth of August. But at Metz he was taken violently ill, and military measures, like all others, suffered from the general panic which ensued. All France resounded with prayers for the " well-beloved king." The priests cried for joy over the profound piety which the patient displayed; over his revived moral sense; over the works meet for repentance. The Châteauroux was rudely dismissed. The queen herself, poor Marie Lescinski, was called to the royal bedside; and, taking his violent remorse as a pledge for the future, gave an embrace of forgiveness to the wretched libertine. In all the life of this basest of kings there is no more ghastly episode than this.

What the prayers of priests, and the tears of women failed to effect was, however, soon accomplished Turn of by a sensible physician; and the disease, which fortune. was only an acute attack of indigestion, passed away as rapidly as it had come. But Louis recovered too late to lead his army against the invader. His generals had already collected a force sufficient to check the progress of the Austrians, and to shatter the fond dream of their commander. To carry out his project of wresting Alsace and Lorraine from France, the prince needed not only a

[1] Frederic to Louis XV., 9 July, 1744.
[2] Same to same, 5 August, 1744.

field army superior to that of the enemy, but also a reserve strong enough to keep open his lines of communication and bases of supply. These he did not possess, and
the enterprise soon came to an end.

The immediate cause of prince Charles' retreat was not,
however, the formidable preparations of the French, but
the movements of the king of Prussia.

The common account, which represents Frederic as renewing hostilities in consequence of the alarming progress
of the Austrians in Alsace, has already been described
as more faithful to dramatic effect than to historical
truth. His resolution to intervene was formed, and made
known before prince Charles crossed the Rhine. But it
is not less inexact to say that the court of Vienna was
wholly deceived and surprised. The efforts of Frederic
to embroil the queen with the empress of Russia by means
of the Botta incident, certain ill-defined rumors of his
intrigues at Constantinople,[1] the tone which his envoy at
Vienna began in the spring to assume, the union
of Frankfort, the concentration of Prussian
troops, — these were symptoms of coming danger which
it was impossible to overlook. Maria Theresa was not
too well served by her diplomatists abroad; but the indiscretion of the imperial court repaired their defects, and
the treaty of the twenty-second of May was early known
in every European capital.[2] It was likewise easy to read
the meaning of the union through the frail disguise in
which it was draped. The queen took, indeed, no earnest
measures to meet the danger, but this omission was not
due to ignorance or carelessness. Nearly all her available
troops were in the west. She was naturally reluctant to
recall prince Charles from the Rhine, and reopen Germany to the French, an hour earlier than supreme necessity should require. There was, besides, a chance that

Feeling at Vienna.

[1] Arneth, ii. 407 ; Droysen, V. ii. 233 n.
[2] Frederic to Chambrier, 3 July, 1744.

some unforeseen event would change Frederic's purpose. One or two of her advisers even believed that he was simply trying to intimidate her, and had no intention of proceeding to hostilities.[1]

Early in August Frederic's purpose became, however, so clear that it could no longer safely be ignored. General Batthyany was accordingly ordered to collect such Austrian troops as were still in Bavaria, and march immediately toward the Bohemian frontier, whither it was intimated prince Charles might soon be compelled to follow. Three days after this dispatch the cruel reality was laid bare. The Prussian envoy, Dohna, read to the Austrian chancellor a declaration to the effect that while the king, his master, had faithfully observed, and intended still to observe, all the articles of the treaty of Berlin, he could not look with indifference upon systematic attempts to overthrow the lawful head, and subvert the constitution, of the Empire; and that he had decided to furnish the emperor with a certain number of auxiliary troops, in order that he might be rescued from his enemies, and restored to the enjoyment of all the dignities and privileges of his office.[2]

Frederic declares his purpose.

The same reason, with others in addition, were given in a long manifesto, which was prepared by the Prussian king himself, and, after being translated into several languages, was made public on the tenth of August.[3] Although unnecessarily violent in tone, it was arranged with considerable art, and if unanswered would have made no little impression. The document begins by recounting the barbarous crimes of the Austrian soldiery, directed as they were by the boundless ambition

Prussian manifesto.

[1] Arneth, ii. 409.

[2] Instructions for Dohna, 28 July, 1744 ; cf. Eichel to Podewils, 26 July, 1744, and Adelung, iv. 155.

[3] "Exposé des motifs qui ont obligé le roi de donner des troupes auxiliaires à l'empereur." *Pr. Staatsschriften*, i. 442–447 ; *Polit. Corresp.*, iii. 242–245.

of the court of Vienna, and serving its pernicious designs. Germany had been inundated with foreign troops. The queen of Hungary had formed alliances, which proposed to indemnify her supporters for their outlays by sweeping confiscations of secular and ecclesiastical estates. Her generals had tried to seize imperial cities, had intimidated electors, and had planned the subversion of Germanic liberty. These things were insulting to the honor and dignity of every prince of the Empire; and it would be unpardonable for the members of the sacred college, endowed since time immemorial with the power to name the head of the commonwealth, to endure the arrogant policy which aimed to rob them of their rights. The king himself, the manifesto continued, had no quarrel with the queen of Hungary. He had no personal grievance, no demands; he took part only as an auxiliary in a dispute which deeply concerned the liberties of the Empire. Every effort had been made by him to reconcile the parties. The emperor had offered great sacrifices for peace, provided only that his title and the dignity of his office were assured respect. But all these labors had been frustrated by the arrogant exactions of the Austrian court, and now the dormant spirit of patriotism was aroused. The ancient race of Germans, who had defended their country for so many centuries against all the majesty of the Roman Empire, still survived, and would defend it today, in the same manner, against any who should presume to attack it. In this spirit the king of Prussia was leading his armies into the field. He had no other motive than to secure liberty for the Empire, respect for the emperor, and peace for Europe.

Such were the ostensible reasons which Frederic published for his course. Yet these were accompanied, in several cases, by other more private ones, which suggest curious reflections upon his real character and motives. To the empress of Russia he wrote gallantly that his chief object was to avenge the insults which she had received at the hands of Maria Theresa in the Botta affair.[1] But the court of St. James was honored with a special communication, which had a tone radically different. It severely criticised England for interfering in a quarrel that concerned her in no respect, and aiding one of the members of the Empire to overthrow its constitutional head; and hinted that this policy was due to the evil counsels of certain influential statesmen.[2] This was an indirect, yet sufficiently intelligible, way of describing lord Carteret.

But Frederic's enmity was rather to be desired than feared by an English minister. The British nation was aroused to renewed indignation by what was called the third treason of Prussia, and Carteret obtained a fresh lease of power. On the eleventh of August he signed an engagement to give the queen, in addition to the regular subsidy of three hundred thousand pounds, a further sum of one hundred and fifty thousand for the support of prince Charles' army in France. The Pelhams opposed this transaction, but too late to prevent it. They were equally suspicious of Carteret's scheme for subsidizing Saxony from the English treasury, and even of the negotiations for a quadruple alliance against Prussia. But the immediate though brief effect of Frederic's move was undoubtedly favorable to George the Second and the resolute minister who supported his continental policy. It must have required no little courage for lord Chesterfield to publish, even anonymously, a pamphlet in defence of the character, policy, and measures of the king of Prussia.[3] *Indignation in England.*

Finally, explanations were made even to France, though

---

[1] Frederic to the empress of Russia, 10 August, 1744.

[2] Instructions for Andrié, 8 August, 1744. *Pr. Staatsschriften*, i. 577–580. See, also, Adelung, iv. 177, for Hyndford's representations at Berlin, and Frederic's replies.

[3] *Natural Reflections on the Present Conduct of his Prussian Majesty,*

these are of course to be judged by a different standard.

If not more sincere, they were naturally less formal; and they had a particular object in view, or rather objects, for there were two of them, as Frederic's letters clearly show. The one was to correct any impression which yet remained — and, since the death of Fleury, scepticism on this score had been much less active — that the king of Prussia was an untrustworthy ally, that he sought only his own advantage, and would betray his best friends without scruple at any convenient moment. Hence Frederic laid emphasis on the fact that now he had no personal ends to gain, leaving it to be inferred that he could have no motive for treachery. Self-interest and ambition had no part, he declared, in his decision. It was a necessity for him to sustain the emperor; it was a necessity for him to have allies, and he hoped, by plucking the thorn from the foot of France, to make her glad to count herself among them.[1] After this convincing demonstration, the general assurances of loyalty, which of course were not withheld, seem, as it were, superfluous. A prince, who shows conclusively that the iron law of necessity will compel him to keep a particular engagement, gains little in point of credit by adding assertions of his respect for the law of good faith.

Even more important to Frederic at this time was the

other object which his active correspondence with Louis and Noailles had in view, namely, to secure from France the same degree of fidelity,

etc., London, 1744. The concluding panegyric is interesting: "To take the king of Prussia in every light," says the writer, "I think his character is amiable; . . . he is sincere, because he has acquainted the combined courts with his intentions; he is punctual to his engagements, because he assures our English adventurers that he will pay off their debt to a farthing; he is a politician, because in securing the rights and liberties of his country he secures the balance of power," etc.

[1] Frederic to Noailles, 9 August, 1744.

both political and military, that he promised from himself. An open breach of faith he hardly feared, and said as much in reply to the doubts raised by Podewils.[1] In letters to Noailles he mentioned the probability that his intervention would be the signal for specious overtures to France only to express his confidence that they would be promptly rejected.[2] But he assured his minister that his principal reliance was upon the interest which his ally would have in keeping faith; and although he could not be equally frank with the marshal, and wrote nobly about the honor of France, he was not the less careful to make it appear for her advantage to be governed by her honor. The king of France could no more afford than he himself, he said, to abandon the emperor. Unless the war were continued until the ambition of the queen of Hungary was completely crushed, and her posterity forever excluded from the imperial throne, a peace would be a mere interval of rest, to be followed, on the death of Charles VII. by the reopening of the whole question, by new struggles and new sacrifices. The interests of the two allies were identical, and their motives to good faith the same.[3] On the military side Podewils expressed even graver doubts about the safety of the French alliance. According to his view France had everything to gain and nothing to risk. The Prussian armies once in the field, she would conduct the war according to her own convenience; would take such places as she desired in the Netherlands; and remain on the defensive in Germany, while the entire Austrian force marched to the defence of Bohemia. Prussia would thus have to bear the whole burden of the war, and, once engaged, would be unable to withdraw. For the queen would not offer Frederic a second separate peace, after the first had been broken

[1] Droysen, V. ii. 290, 291.
[2] 5 August, 1744.
[3] Frederic to Noailles, 5, 9 August, 1744.

in such a manner. She would have no more confidence in treaties with Prussia.[1]

These views, which in the light of subsequent events seem almost prophetic, were in a measure shared by Frederic, and explain the persistence with which he urged upon the French court the need of promptness, energy, and audacity; of executing strictly the military stipulations; of carrying out to the letter the formulated plan of campaign. The prince of Lorraine should not be suffered to escape. A French army should threaten Hanover. Freiburg should be invested only by a small force, leaving the rest free to operate in the field. No more Broglies, who retreated two hundred leagues, without pausing for breath, when they saw the enemy, should be employed, but men of zeal and energy, — such, for instance, as Belleisle. To these repeated, and perhaps rather tiresome appeals, plenty of assurances were given in reply. Belleisle was duly assigned to command the army of Bavaria, the mission of which was indicated by its name, and all the indications seemed to point to a cordial and successful coöperation.[2]

Yet in spite of his pretended faith in the power of self-interest to hold the French to their engagements, and inspire them with the requisite energy, Frederic took the precaution, late in July, of sending a trusted military agent to reside at their headquarters, and accompany them on their campaigns. For this delicate duty he selected field-marshal Schmettau, who, though a soldier, was no novice in diplomacy. In many respects this officer's mind resembled Frederic's, in its suppleness, facility, and boldness; in the ease with which it formed combinations, and the contempt with which it swept away objections. To high culture and accomplished manners he added a plausible eloquence,

Schmettau's mission to Metz.

[1] Droysen, ubi supra.
[2] Frederic to Noailles, 5 August, 1744.

the gift of persuasion, and the power to convey his own enthusiasm to others. Without these qualities, or some of them, he would never indeed have acquired the position which he held with Frederic. A soldier of fortune, he left the Austrian service in 1741 to join the Prussian, making his own bargain in advance;[1] and yet in a short time he was taken into the king's most secret councils, and employed on the most confidential missions. But none of these required more tact, foresight, and prudence than the embassy to the camp of Louis the Fifteenth. He arrived at Metz early in August, with credentials stating that he was sent to explain more clearly his master's plans and expectations.[2] His private instructions were to enforce, by all the arts in his power, the points which Frederic had so often urged in his letters to Noailles; and to this end he was charged to caress the duke of Richelieu, in order through him to gain the confidence of Louis, and then to speak to him face to face and read to the very bottom of his soul.[3]

One formality yet remained. To carry out the fiction that he was only acting as an auxiliary, Frederic had early solicited for himself a commission as general in the service of the emperor;[4] and he now obtained from Charles VII. a requisition upon the elector of Saxony to permit the passage of Prussian troops through his territories. August was absent in Poland, and the officials to whom application was made insisted on the necessity of consulting him. But the Prussians were inclined to suffer no delay. The regent, the duke of Weissenfels, bewildered and helpless, made the best terms possible, and saved the capital from occupation by giving a forced assent to Frederic's principal demand.[5]

Demands upon Saxony.

[1] *Polit. Corresp.*, i. 236 n. ; Droysen, V. i. 325.
[2] Frederic to Louis XV., 29 July, 1744.
[3] Instructions to Schmettau, 29 July, 1744.
[4] Frederic to Klinggraeffen, 26 May, 1744.
[5] Adelung, iv. 170.

CHAPTER VIII.

THE SECOND SILESIAN WAR.

THE Prussians marched in three columns. Two of
these traversed the territory of Saxony, — the
larger under the king himself by the right, and
the smaller under prince Leopold by the left bank of the
Elbe. The third section, some twenty thousand strong,
under Schwerin, set out from Silesia, and marched southward through Glatz. The rendezvous was Prague. A
reserve force, with general Marwitz in command, was left
in Upper Silesia, whence it could make a diversion into
Moravia, if necessary, and take possession of Olmütz.

The march was made without serious opposition, or
any very striking incidents, and by the second
of September the three columns were reunited
at Weissenberg, near Prague. The garrison of
the city consisted of only a regiment or two of troops of
the line, with several thousand militia and irregulars, in
all not more than fourteen thousand men.[1] The corps of
Batthyany, though within marching distance, was too
weak to attack eighty thousand Prussians. But the commandant, count Harsch, refused to yield the city when
summoned, and made the best possible preparations for
defence. The population gave him a hearty support.
The citizens worked on the walls, the students of the
university patrolled the streets, the militia was drilled
day and night. It was hoped to hold the city until the
arrival of prince Charles, and that event seemed to de-

March of the Prussians.

Movements of prince Charles.

[1] Droysen, V. ii. 305.

pend only on the rapidity with which his troops could march. For the principal Austrian army, having successfully recrossed the Rhine, was now on the way to Bohemia. Feeble attacks upon the rear guard, which were easily repulsed, were the only opposition which the French offered.

Frederic received this news, just before reaching Prague, with feelings of dismay and indignation. Already apprehensive lest Batthyany should throw his force into the city, and thus prolong the defence, he now saw the possibility that prince Charles would gain the strong position of Budeweis while the siege was still in progress. He would never have believed, he wrote, that the French could fail him at such a serious crisis. Their king indeed was blameless, for he was prostrate on the bed of sickness, but the affair would cover Noailles with disgrace. The most energetic demands should be made upon the French authorities to show more vigor in their own measures, and to put the army of the emperor, under Seckendorf, in pursuit of the enemy.[1] The rage of Frederic was natural and justifiable. Although he had had little confidence, perhaps, in the ability of Noailles to detain the Austrians in Alsace, he was surprised at the ease with which they recrossed the river, and the little energy shown in following them.

In the mean time the capture of Prague was delayed, even after the completion of the investment, by the want of heavy siege guns. These were expected on the sixth, but were not in position until the ninth, when the bombardment began. For three days the fire was steadily maintained. On the twelfth Schwerin carried by storm the commanding Ziscaberg, east of the city, where the besieged had a strong redoubt, defended, however, only by militia. The loss of this important position, and the breaches made in the walls by the Prus-

Anger of Frederic.

Fall of Prague.

[1] Frederic to Schmettau, 31 August, 1744.

sian batteries, soon determined the fate of the city. On the sixteenth it surrendered at discretion. The citizens were required to pay a heavy contribution, and to swear allegiance anew to the emperor, while the garrison were sent to Glatz as prisoners of war.

This seemed an auspicious opening of the campaign. Early diffi-culties. But the joy of the Prussians was of short duration, for while they were celebrating this preliminary triumph enemies were rising up on every side. The Saxons turned a deaf ear to Frederic's specious appeals, and had a treaty which bound them to furnish troops to the queen. Batthyany was falling back, indeed, but only to make an earlier junction with prince Charles. The prince was hastening by forced marches to the scene of danger; and while Seckendorf, whose part it was to recover Bavaria, and then advance into Upper Austria, moved with inexcusable slowness, the French were even more dilatory. When they finally advanced into Germany they made no effort to pursue the Austrians, but turned off with their whole army toward Freiburg, before which place they sat down for a systematic siege. Deserted thus by his allies, and threatened by the regular armies of the enemy, Frederic soon found himself confronted by other foes, whose prowess he indeed despised, but whose tactics were not the less annoying.

The anguish of soul with which Maria Theresa saw Enemies thicken. herself compelled to recall her principal army, in its full career of triumph, may well be conceived. But to England the retreat of the prince was scarcely less embarrassing. The cabinet had just granted the queen a large additional subsidy for the express purpose of maintaining her army in Alsace, and now, by the sudden close of the invasion, the French were left free to pour a large force again into the Netherlands.[1] But in

[1] See in Coxe's *Pelham*, i. 168, the letter of Pelham to the duke of Newcastle.

the face of this new invasion of her territory, and not-withstanding the disappointment of her ally, the courage of the queen only rose the higher, and shone with a deeper glow. Again, as in 1741 and 1742, she flew to Press-burg, and appealed to her Hungarian subjects. Once more the insurrection was proclaimed, and the magnates resolved to raise and equip a force of one hundred thou-sand men. " People call our levies irregulars," said one of the speakers at the diet; " but every nation has its own military customs, and the insurgents deserve a better name. The Hungarian troops have hitherto done far more than those who march upon the enemy in fine uni-forms, and with regular step. Who can insist that the pandours, feared as they are by all their foes, shall fol-low the discipline of the grenadiers?" [1] The old palatine, Palfy, also made a fiery address, which was printed and circulated throughout the country. Not less enthusiasm was shown by the people themselves, and soon the fron-tiers were black with horsemen. While prince Charles and Batthyany were converging from the west in strict mili-tary order, the wild tribes of the lower Danube were clos-ing in upon the Prussians from the east, seizing their trains, snatching up their scouts, cutting their communi-cations, and obstructing every foot of their march.

The plan of campaign adopted by Frederic, after the fall of Prague, facilitated the measures of the enemy. Out of several courses which were open to him he chose the one which led nearly due south, into the districts of Tabor and Budeweis, and thus, as he himself afterwards declared, committed a serious military blunder. But he deferred to the judgment of the em-peror and Belleisle. It was urged by them that an ad-vance toward Budeweis would at once threaten Vienna, and open communications with Bavaria, two allied and equally desirable objects. The distances were, however,

The plan of campaign.

[1] Adelung, iv. 173–176.

great; the country was wild and mountainous, difficult to invade and easy to defend; and every march carried the Prussians farther from their supplies. The supplies, too, were deficient, both in quality and amount. A magazine had been formed at Leitmeritz, but the pandours effectually isolated it, while the field commissariat, which accompanied the army, was wretchedly incompetent; "that," says Frederic, "was the principal cause of all the misfortunes which afterwards arrived." [1] But there were so many other causes, so many gross blunders, that the execution of the plan must be pronounced as faulty as the plan itself. Even the policy of leaving only six battalions in Prague is stigmatized by the king as inexcusably reckless.[2]

The campaign beyond Prague was thus doomed to failure almost before it was begun. For the first few days, indeed, no enemy of consequence appeared. General Nassau, who had the advance, occupied one after another, and without resistance, several important towns, — Tabor on the twenty-fourth, Budeweis on the twenty-ninth, of September, and Frauenberg on the first of October. But the ease of these achievements was wholly delusive, and by the time the main army reached Tabor the state of affairs compelled a halt.

As soon as the Prussians had advanced far enough from Prague, the light horse of Batthyany fell in behind them, and so effectually cut off their communications that for days at a time they were without intelligence from the rest of Europe.[3] The natives were hostile, the pandours grew daily more bold, and prince Charles was rapidly approaching. On the second of October he effected a junction with Batthyany, and learned that a Saxon corps, twenty thousand strong, had set out

Preliminary successes.

The Saxons in the field.

---

[1] *Œuvres de Frédéric*, iii. 59.   [2] Ibid., iii. 58.

[3] Frederic himself says, *Œuvres*, iii. 60, for four weeks, but the statement is not to be taken literally.

to reënforce him. Its expenses were defrayed from the English treasury.[1] Frederic knew that this action was required by the terms of the defensive alliance between the courts of Vienna and Dresden, and that it also suited the inclinations of the ministers of August. But he had hoped to delay it until the following spring, and then to prevent it by massing troops under the Old Dessauer on the Saxon frontier.[2] The reality, when it burst upon him, was a serious blow to his hopes, and led to bitter complaints of his own folly in venturing so far from Prague.[3] But he still endeavored to avoid a breach. He could hardly refuse to accept the explanation of the Saxons, that they were merely furnishing auxiliaries to the queen of Hungary under the terms of an existing treaty, since he himself was invading her territory only as an ally of the emperor; and diplomatic relations between Dresden and Berlin were still continued, not without some outward signs of friendliness.

The situation now made it more than ever necessary that the measures which Frederic had repeatedly urged upon his allies, the increase of the im- *The allies.* perial army to forty thousand men, and the dispatch of a French corps equally strong to Westphalia, be at once executed. This now forms the leading theme of his letters to Noailles, Louis XV., Schmettau, and others. But although Seckendorf succeeded in driving the Austrians from Munich, and compelled Batthyany, who had been transferred to that command, to fall back upon the Inn, the French were still detained by the siege of Freiburg, and spared no troops for other service. In the mean time, too, the Prussians had been forced to give up their advance, and turn their faces homeward.

The movements of the enemy were long wrapped in

---

[1] Arneth, ii. 413.

[2] Frederic to Leopold of Dessau, 25 September, 1744.

[3] Vide Frederic to Podewils, to Louis XV., etc., 20 October, 1744.

mystery, and Frederic was led by false reports to under-

take a number of costly and useless marches. But it was finally learned that prince Charles had struck the river Moldau below Tabor, that is, between the Prussians and Prague. At Beneschau, on the Sasawa, he had begun to collect a store of provisions, and his evident intention was to cut off the retreat of the Prussians, and leave them to perish in the trap which they had foolishly entered. Schwerin was, therefore, sent back with fifteen thousand men to seize Beneschau, and reopen the lines of retreat. The duty was performed with the usual skill of that accomplished soldier. On the fourteenth of October the king joined him there, with the rest of the army, and the garrisons of Tabor, Budeweis, and Frauenberg, now left without support, fell into the hands of the enemy. The situation was thus gloomy enough. It was some little satisfaction to the imperialists, though of little benefit to the common cause, that Charles the Seventh reëntered Munich in triumph, as it was called, on the twenty-third of October. The exploit even called forth bitter reproaches from the French. They had supplied Seckendorf with German troops, which they were paying, and added others of their own, and loudly demanded that he should follow prince Charles in fulfilment of the bargain made by them with Frederic. The field-marshal retorted with counter-charges, more or less valid, and pursued his own course. Schmettau, who was now with the emperor, now with Louis, offended both by the vivacity of his language; and, after repeated rebukes at the hands of Frederic, was finally recalled in disgrace.[1]

There now remained to the Prussians only the hope of

improving their fortunes by an open engagement, in which their discipline and tactics would give them the usual advantage. But it was no part of the policy of prince Charles, or rather of his effi-

[1] Frederic to Schmettau, 22, to Louis XV., 23 November, 1744.

cient lieutenant, Traun, to give or accept battle so long as hunger, disease, and fatigue were serving their cause so well. All of Frederic's efforts to draw them into action proved fruitless. As often as he approached their neighborhood he found them posted on impregnable heights, where it would be folly to attack them, and from which they refused to descend. When he moved onward they followed on parallel lines, fortifying their position wherever they stopped. They felt their advantage, and were too wise to sacrifice it.[1]

The position taken by Frederic near Beneschau was not permanently tenable, and a further retreat to the line of the Elbe became imperatively necessary. But this, also, was not without its difficulties. The watchful Traun had prepared for it by seizing Kuttenberg, so that Frederic, instead of defending himself south of the river, was forced to take a position on the other side. Everything now depended on barring the passage of the river to the Austrians. If that were done, the army could pass the winter in the enemy's country, restore its condition, draw reënforcements, and be ready for early operations in the spring. But even this plan failed. In spite of the watchfulness of the Prussians, the valor of single detachments, and the heroism of individual officers, the strategy of Traun baffled all precautions; on the nineteenth of November he succeeded in forcing a passage at Teinitz. The situation of Frederic thus became desperate. His force was greatly reduced by disease and desertion; Franquiny, the Hungarian partisan, was at Chrudim, whence he threatened the Prussian supplies at Pardubitz; Schwerin had been driven from the army by the jealousy of Leopold; other

Retreat of the Prussians.

---

[1] Cf. Frederic to Seckendorf, 14 November, 1744, being an account of events since the fourth of October, or the complete "Relation de ma campagne 1744," which was prepared in December and sent to France. *Polit. Corresp.*, iii. 343 et seq.

officers were beginning to criticise the generalship of the campaign; and the morale of the men was greatly impaired. It became evident that the campaign must be abandoned.[1]

The Prussian army next took a position near König-

The campaign abandoned.

grätz, where, in Frederic's opinion, it could have maintained itself against the enemy had not the impossibility of obtaining adequate supplies compelled a further retreat.[2] This was begun on the twenty-seventh of November. The king led the way with the greater part of the army, and, molested only by Nadasdy's hussars, reached Silesia by way of Braunau, Trautenau, and Glatz. General Nassau was ordered to collect certain outlying detachments, and pursue a parallel course. This proved, however, more difficult. The weakness of the force encouraged the pandours; and such were the obstructions of every kind thrown in the general's path that he had to make long detours, and frequently lost all communication with Frederic. But he skilfully overcame his many obstacles, and, without serious loss, eventually rejoined the king.

The Prussian garrison in Prague escaped even less

Loss of Prague.

easily. It was too weak to hold the city after the retreat of the principal army from König-grätz, and, in pursuance of orders from Frederic, the commander, general Einsiedel began his homeward march. The authorities at Dresden offered a passage through Saxon territory only on condition that he disarm and disband his force, — terms which he indignantly refused. But he was obliged to leave his heavy guns behind, to destroy a large amount of material, and to divide the army funds among the officers. The enemy, who entered the city on one side as he passed out by the other, followed him sharply on the march. Led astray by hostile

[1] Droysen, V. ii. 369.

[2] Eichel to Podewils, Nachod, 28 November, 1744.

peasants, the little force wandered into the Isar Mountains, where it would have perished from cold and hunger if it had not been opportunely rescued by Nassau. On the sixteenth of December this last remnant of the Bohemian expedition reached Silesia. Einsiedel was arraigned for misconduct before a court-martial, but the tribunal had the courage to refuse to make him a scapegoat, and he was fully acquitted.[1]

Baffled in its purpose to pass the winter in Bohemia, the Prussian army now went into quarters in Silesia. But it was a different army from that which, splendidly equipped and full of enthusiasm, marched up the Elbe four months before. Though it had not fought a battle, its numbers were reduced by nearly one half. It had simply wasted away. The pandours counted, indeed, many victims, but hunger, exhaustion, and disease were far more fatal agents of destruction, and the worst enemy of all was desertion. There are various accounts of the loss which the army suffered from this cause, and none of them can be absolutely trusted. A Hungarian officer wrote of nine thousand deserters during the retreat from Königgrätz; and a careful computation, made from official data by another writer on the same side, fixed the total for the entire campaign at not less than thirty thousand. In the Prussian archives no precise statement has been found. But the indirect evidence fully sustains the reports which were current at the time, and the results which have been reached by Austrian inquirers, that desertion raged like a disease among the rank and file of the army, and that the losses attained to proportions almost without a parallel in history. A large share of the deserters, among whom were noticed with surprise many native Prussians, passed, too, into the service of the enemy.[2]

Cost of the campaign.

[1] Cogniazo, ii. 103, thinks the force might have been destroyed, or captured by more energy on the part of the Austrians.

[2] Droysen, V. ii. 366, 367 ; Arneth, ii. 440.

The material losses were on the same scale. Sixty heavy guns were left, it was said, in the hands of the Austrians. Horses, wagons, small-arms, were lost in great numbers in the daily skirmishes with pandours, or purposely destroyed as impediments to the army on its retreat. The magazines of supplies, which it was impossible to carry away, were gladly seized by the pursuers. The officers lost great quantities of private baggage. Of the large war-fund, which was in the treasury in July, hardly enough remained to repair the losses of this single campaign ; [1] and yet the means had to be provided for maintaining the army through the winter, and renewing operations in the spring.

Worst of all was, however, the blow to Frederic's prestige. The Moravian campaign of 1742 was quite

Moral effects of the disaster.

as unwise, and, up to a certain point, nearly as disastrous ; but it ended in a victory which erased a long record of errors, and left the king's credit higher than ever. In 1744 there was not even the partial solace of an honorable defeat in the field. An enterprise begun in the greatest confidence, and with every preparation for success, ended in an ignominious retreat, with losses such as two pitched battles would not have caused, and a demoralization beyond the power even of the iron discipline of Prussia to resist. And the responsibility for this disaster rested mainly on the king's own shoulders. No general, he himself wrote, had ever committed so many blunders in a single season. But the strategy of Traun was a model of perfection, and ought to be studied by every soldier who loved his profession. As for himself, the Bohemian campaign was his school in the art of war, and the Austrian marshal was his teacher.[2]

It is true that this frankness was the product of many years of reflection, for the words which I have quoted are

[1] Droysen, V. ii. 367, 368.
[2] Œuvres de Frédéric, iii. 76, 77.

found only in the revised version of 1775.[1] But even the letters which the king wrote under the immediate impression of the catastrophe hardly warrant the excuses often put forward in his behalf. It is true that he was justly indignant at the ease with which prince Charles succeeded in crossing the Rhine, almost without opposition from the French. But he either fully approved their plan of campaign, or had confidence that any original errors would be repaired in the future; for, while there are passages in his correspondence which support each of these hypotheses, there are none which make it clear that he absolutely charged the failure of his own campaign to his allies, or even that his forbearance was simply due to an unwillingness to offend them by useless reproaches. Policy would undoubtedly, in the circumstances, have prescribed such a forbearance. The issue of the Bohemian campaign left the king's affairs in a precarious state, and he could afford to overlook the lukewarmness of an ally who, if provoked by injudicious censure, might make his separate peace with the common enemy. The recall of Schmettau might be attributed to this form of prudence. The approval of Seckendorf's march into Bavaria, and Coigny's siege of Freiburg, are also, though less easily, explicable on the same grounds. But there is evidence to show that this attitude of confidence in his allies was not artfully assumed by Frederic; and that after his return from Bohemia, under the stinging exasperation of defeat, he hesitated, even in his most confidential correspondence, to hold the French responsible. His letters are marked rather by the absence, or at least the infrequency of such flippant expressions of doubt and distrust as were common in 1741 and 1742. Yet the French continued as slow and irresolute as at the beginning of

---

[1] The original MS. of 1746 ascribes a larger part of the failure to the caprices of fortune. But see Preuss, i. 209, for earlier tributes, oral and written, to Traun.

the campaign. They formed, indeed, a second army, which under Maillebois crossed the Rhine in November; but it was too weak for effective work, and greatly embittered the princes through whose territories it took its leisurely march. Freiburg surrendered on the twenty-eighth of November, and its capture set free the army which had been engaged in the siege. But, instead of reënforcing Seckendorf or Maillebois, it went into winter quarters in Suabia.

Even the services of Belleisle were for a time lost to Capture of Belleisle. France and the emperor by an accident which had some elements of the ludicrous. The marshal had not taken the command of the army of Bavaria, as originally planned, but on the contrary was sent to Berlin on a military mission from the French king. His object was to concert with Frederic a scheme of operations for the coming year. Nominally he was an ambassador from the emperor, and thus clothed with a diplomatic character; but he was also a French officer, and wore the uniform of his rank. It happened now that the Prussian post, which he took for the last stage of his journey, crossed a corner of the Hanoverian territory, and stopped at Elbingerode for a change of horses. But here, when it was too late, the marshal learned the wisdom of those who had advised him to take a safer route. Travelling as usual in great state, and with a brilliant suite, he was easily recognized by the local officials, and, thoughtlessly giving up his sword as a prisoner of war instead of claiming his diplomatic character, was sent under guard to Hanover. From there he was transferred as a precious prize to London. All the complaints of the emperor, the threats of France, the representations of Frederic, failed to secure his release; and for a time the incident caused no little dismay to the allies. Chavigny wrote from Munich that it fell upon the emperor like a thunderbolt. Frederic, too, was considerably vexed, though his natural scepticism made him feel, or at least express, some doubts about the real secret of the transaction. Writing to Louis on the subject, he observed significantly, after asking for the appointment of another agent in the place of the unlucky prisoner, that he would suspend his judgment on the affair; it must be known better at Paris than elsewhere what interpretation to put upon it.[1] He suspected, possibly, that the whole was a prearranged plan to give Belleisle access to the British ministers with secret overtures for peace.[2]

In the military part of the marshal's mission Frederic had shown little interest. But he was at times Dreams of peace. hopeful that his presence in Berlin might be made useful in arranging terms of peace, for which he was again ready and even anxious. As early as the twenty-ninth of October he had sounded Mardefeld upon the possible willingness of Russia to undertake a mediation.[3] Two weeks later he suggested the terms of an agreement, by which he thought peace could be established that winter, at least in Germany. They proposed that the emperor should be recognized by the queen of Hungary; that, besides the restoration of Bavaria, he should receive Upper Austria as well as the Upper Palatinate and Neuburg, for which the queen should indemnify the elector; that, in return for Prague, the king of Prussia should have the rest of Upper Silesia with the high mountains, and the enclaves of Moravia; that France should be promised a slight rectification of her frontiers; and that a general amnesty should be proclaimed.[4] This scheme was submitted to Podewils in confidence for his opinion.

[1] Frederic to Louis XV., 26 December, 1744. For a piquant account of Belleisle's arrest, with some rather unfriendly comments on Frederic's treatment of it, see the duke de Broglie in the *Revue des Deux Mondes*, 1 May, 1887, pp. 51 et seq.

[2] Droysen, V. ii. 403.

[3] Frederic to Mardefeld, 29, to Podewils, 30 October, 1744.

[4] Eichel to Podewils, 13 November, 1744.

After another fortnight's interval, when his affairs looked even more desperate, the king wrote to Louis XV. in the same sense; though now the demands in behalf of the emperor were somewhat reduced, and the mediation of Holland and Sweden was to be solicited. In any event, so he wrote, he would take no action toward peace except with the full concurrence of his ally the king of France.[1] It was from Belleisle, then on his way to Berlin, that he seemed to expect great assistance in his plan.[2]

The arrest of Belleisle put an end to any hopes based on his mission. His successor, baron Courten, had only a military character. But, with or without Belleisle, the time was ill chosen for offering Maria Theresa such terms as Frederic had in view, or even for asking the neutral powers to present them as mediators.

The bloodless triumph in Bohemia caused at Vienna an

The queen revokes the cession of Silesia.
exultation which almost effaced the memory of the painful check to the campaign across the Rhine, and made the loss of Freiburg or of Bavaria seem at the time of little importance. As Frederic fell back before the irresistible tactics of Traun, the queen's hopes rapidly rose. From merely defensive she passed to offensive plans; and visions of revenge, which included first of all the recovery of Silesia, began to take shape before her eyes. On the first of December she issued a proclamation which announced her purpose. Since the king of Prussia, it was said, had himself broken the peace of Breslau, the cessions made by that treaty were legally cancelled, and the inhabitants of Silesia were free to return to their original allegiance. The oppressions of the Prussian rule would justify them in such a step. The introduction of the cantonment system of conscription had reduced the people to a state of slavery, in which the father had no control over his son; and the

[1] Königgrätz, 26 November, 1744.
[2] Frederic to Podewils, 9 December, 1744.

old liberal constitution had been completely overthrown. With the restoration of Austrian authority the local institutions should be revived, and the conscription abolished.[1] This document was to be carried into Silesia, and distributed by an army of invasion.

It is another curious illustration of the love for fictions, which then prevailed, that Frederic chose to treat this measure, not his own invasion of Bohemia, as the real breach of the treaty of Breslau. He had announced such a theory, though contingently, at the very outset of his campaign. On the first rumor that partisans of the queen might treat his movement as an act of war, and attempt reprisals in Upper Silesia, he ordered general Marwitz to adopt measures of the utmost severity, and threatened that he would take revenge under the very walls of Vienna.[2] The same theory of his innocence he steadily asserted, as we know, in his correspondence with Dresden, with St. Petersburg, and with all other courts. Naturally, therefore, he could not allow the Austrian manifesto to pass unanswered. His first act was to order the arrest and execution of all who circulated it in Silesia, whether natives or aliens.[3] Twenty-four hours later, on the nineteenth of December, appeared his own counter-proclamation, which, after reciting the facts from his own point of view, and in true chancelry style, warned all his subjects to pay no attention to the seditious words of Austrian emissaries, on pain of arrest and punishment for treason.[4] This was followed on the ninth of January by one even sharper in tone.[5]

It would be unjust to Frederic's good sense to suppose that he expected these fiery manifestoes to change in any respect the plans of Maria Theresa.

Protests of Frederic.

Appeal to Russia.

[1] Arneth, ii. 441, 442 ; *Preuss. Staatsschriften*, i. 528, 529.
[2] To Marwitz, 20 August, 1744.
[3] Frederic to Münchow, in Breslau, 18 December, 1744.
[4] *Preuss. Staatsschriften*, i. 530–532.
[5] Ibid., pp. 533–535.

Even their effect upon the Silesians would depend largely upon the military power to enforce them. But at foreign courts, to which they were also indirectly addressed, they were sure to be interpreted, not necessarily in the sense of their author, but rather according to the prevailing interests and sympathies. Even these, however, Frederic still believed to be at least not unfriendly to him or his cause. In Russia Mardefeld had used one hundred thousand thalers to good advantage, as he supposed, in buying the friendship of the grand-chancellor, Bestuschef, and the vice-chancellor, Woronzof;[1] but, if the diplomatic gossip of the time may be believed, he simply poured water into a sieve. "Take it," Elizabeth is said to have replied, when the two ministers consulted her about the bribe; "if the king of Prussia has so much money to spare, take it by all means."[2] They pocketed the gifts, therefore, with protestations of undying devotion to Prussia, and Frederic felt for a time much encouraged by Mardefeld's reports.[3] Although the empress had shown no signs of a willingness to mediate between the parties, the situation now seemed to give him the right, under treaty engagements, to make a more formal demand upon her. On the nineteenth of December this idle ceremony was performed. It was hoped that Elizabeth would not refuse to fulfil her guaranty of the settlements made in the peace of Breslau; that she would warn the queen of Hungary against invading Silesia, and if necessary send a force to prevent it.[4]

England had also guaranteed the cession of Silesia, and had in that respect the same obligations as Russia. Nay, the fall of Carteret, which his persistent enemies finally brought about late in November,

And to England.

---

[1] Droysen, V. ii. 380.

[2] Reports of the British embassy, Raumer, *Beiträge*, ii. 201.

[3] See Frederic to Mardefeld, 18 December, 1744.

[4] Frederic to the empress of Russia, 19 December, 1744.

just before the opening of the session, even encouraged Frederic to hope that the cabinet, now controlled by the Pelhams, might be willing to take an active part in a scheme of general pacification. Parliament met on the twenty-seventh of November. The speech from the throne, though firm enough in its pledges of fidelity to the common cause, was studiously moderate in its single reference to Frederic's intervention.[1] The addresses in reply, which were voted without debate, were equally careful to avoid anything which could give offence at Berlin.[2] Andrié's reports were hopeful and encouraging. Hence, in the case of England, Frederic accompanied the formal demand for the fufilment of the Silesian guaranty by other letters, in which compliments for the Pelhams and for lord Harrington, Carteret's successor, were adroitly mingled with insinuations about the need of a general peace, and the splendid opportunity for a new policy.[3] He also redoubled his efforts to detach Saxony, as a supposed victim of Carteret's statecraft, from the Austrian connection.

It was to what he called the treachery of the Saxons that, after his own blunders, Frederic ascribed the largest part in the unlucky failure of the Bohemian campaign. Against his aspersions they had indeed an easy defence. It has been shown that the excuse, which they gave for taking up arms, was quite as solid as the clumsy fiction, by which he tried to explain his invasion of Bohemia. But this controversy only revives national antipathies, which can now be permitted to slumber. The importance of the Saxon diversion is indisputable. It added a considerable number to the fighting force of prince Charles, and — what was even more grave — it cre-

Position of Saxony.

---

[1] "The queen of Hungary, though attacked and invaded by powers (sic) from whom she had least reason to expect such a conduct," etc.

[2] *Parl. History*, xiii. 976–993 ; Coxe's *Pelham*, i. 192.

[3] Frederic to George II., 19 December ; to Andrié, 20 and 29 December, 1744.

ated a perplexing diplomatic problem, which for a time almost paralyzed the military plans of Prussia. For, since the Saxons had not declared war, and professed to be acting, like the Prussians, only as auxiliaries of a belligerent, it was inadvisable to treat them as actual enemies. Yet they might at any time become enemies, and, owing to the situation of their country, dangerous enemies; it was known that negotiations were in progress looking to such an end. The plan was for a quadruple alliance of Austria, England, Holland, and Saxony against Prussia.[1] It was even hoped to bring Russia into the league; and the anxiety which these movements caused Frederic is attested by the copious diplomatic correspondence of the time.

The connection of Carteret with this project made him
Dismissal of Carteret. rejoice the more heartily over the downfall of that minister. But it soon became apparent that the change was only one of men. The more carefully one reads the history of this period, and especially that part which is furnished by the confidential letters of Carteret's enemies, the more clearly does it appear that he fell a victim to the personal hostility of the Pelhams and others in the cabinet. They were jealous of his talents and influence, and were perhaps justly impatient of his arbitrary methods. The vigor and energy, not to say the recklessness, of his measures alarmed a cabinet of cautious and temporizing mediocrities; made them hold back when he urged forward; and thus placed them in an attitude of acute personal opposition. But in the end they could only captiously criticise his policy, without suggesting anything essentially different.[2] This was plainly shown when, after

[1] See, in Coxe's *Pelham*, i. 170, the letter of the duke of Newcastle to lord chancellor Hardwicke, 28 August, 1744, and supra, p. 255.

[2] Pelham put the matter clearly perhaps when he wrote to Robinson, "We may not promise so much, but we will perform what we promise." Coxe's *Pelham*, i. 207.

Carteret's fall, his victorious rivals were brought face to face with the pending Saxon negotiations.

The project of subsidizing Saxony for the service of the queen of Hungary was warmly advocated by George II. as soon as the intentions of Frederic became clear. Carteret of course supported it. The Pelhams, without openly opposing it, brought forward a variety of objections, which stopped little short of complete condemnation.[1] But they were really helpless in the matter. The negotiations, instead of being dropped on Carteret's retirement, were taken up with equal vigor by lord Harrington, and on the eighth of January, 1745, were brought to a successful close in the treaty of Warsaw.[2] The treaty provided that Saxony should furnish thirty thousand men for the defence of Bohemia, and, that work accomplished, ten thousand for service against the French in Flanders ; while England and Holland were to guarantee her territories, and pay fixed annual subsidies so long as her troops were employed. It was also significantly declared that the elector should participate in any advantages which the arms of the contracting powers might procure for them.[3]

Treaty of Warsaw.

The treaty and the subsequent legislation to carry it into effect revealed a curious device of Carteret's enemies to retain the substance, while rejecting the features of his policy. One of his most unpopular measures was the payment of the Hanoverian troops, as auxiliaries, from the treasury of England ; for it was justly said that, since the war concerned Hanover as much as England, she should furnish her contingent at her own expense, and let England hire her mercenaries of princes

The Hanoverian contingent.

[1] Coxe's *Pelham*, i. 165, 179, 180.

[2] Wenck, ii. 171–179 ; Adelung, iv., Beilage II.

[3] " Art. VIII. S'il plaisait à Dieu de bénir les mesures et les précautions . . . dans ce cas S. M. Polonaise participera aux avantages qui reviendront par les convenances qu'on lui procurera."

who had no interest in the struggle, and were equally willing to accept the subsidies of France. The leaders who had just overthrown Carteret were therefore forbidden to revive this arrangement. But in effect they revived it, in a form scarcely less odious, by adding two hundred thousand pounds to the annual subsidy hitherto paid to the queen of Hungary, with the understanding that the Hanoverians were to be taken into her service, and supported by this sum. The weakness of this subterfuge was promptly exposed by the friends of the fallen minister. They observed with obvious force that the new arrangement was no relief to the British tax-payer, and that if England had to pay for the troops, it would be much better to keep them in her control. But the ministers succeeded without difficulty in carrying the appropriation by large votes. William Pitt, who had failed to get a place in the cabinet, nevertheless came down to the house, writhing under an attack of gout, to make fiery speeches in behalf of the scheme.[1]

It was thus evident that Frederic was not to reap at once all the benefits which he had expected from the fall of Carteret. But a ministerial change which took place at the same time in France, though it excited less attention, was far more auspicious. After the retirement of Amelot, the post of secretary for foreign affairs remained vacant for several months. There were candidates in abundance; and one of them, Chavigny, had, as we have seen, the qualified support of Frederic himself. Louis finally fixed upon the marquis d'Argenson, brother of the secretary of war. The choice was unexpected, and did not escape criticism; but the chief feeling aroused was perhaps that of curiosity. The marquis was one of those literary noblemen who enjoyed the friendship of Voltaire, and through Voltaire he had learned to admire Frederic; his political views were liberal, and for

Marquis d'Argenson.

[1] *Parl. History*, xiii. 1174–1201.

the time even radical; his pen was one of the busiest in France. The fidelity with which day by day for many years he recorded the events, the intrigues, the gossip of court and cabinet, made his journal, when it subsequently appeared, one of the most valuable of all sources for the history of his time. His speculations upon questions of political philosophy, and especially upon the government of his own country, were far in advance of the age. As early as 1733 he predicted the successful revolt of the English colonies in North America. Although his acute and ingenious mind was partly hidden beneath a rough exterior, and a certain brusqueness of manner, the austerity of his morals, the healthy vigor of his convictions, and the nobility of his motives gave him a unique position among the empirics and adventurers who preyed upon the confidence of Louis. The most piquant interest was everywhere felt, among politicians, at court, and in society, to learn what line of conduct the brilliant doctrinaire would adopt. He had originally opposed the war, but was now understood to be in favor of its vigorous prosecution. With him returned, too, madame de Châteauroux, and her spirited sentiments were already known.

The first measures of the new minister gave great satisfaction to Chambrier. He proposed to send the count of Saint-Séverin, then envoy at Dresden and Warsaw, on a special mission to the empress Elizabeth. Ample funds were to be placed at the disposal of the emissary; and it was hoped that with such an equipment, and his own acknowledged ability, he would be able to remove the bad impression left by the Chétardie incident, to cross the efforts of English diplomacy, and recall Elizabeth from her dangerous inclination to the Austrian cause.[1] Frederic deprecated the choice of Saint-Séverin for reasons connected with his earlier career, and without at all reflecting upon his capacity. The project fell, therefore, to the

[1] Chambrier, 4 December, 1744.

ground. But he warmly urged the dispatch of a more suitable person to reënforce D'Aillon, the French resident at St. Petersburg, for the progress of affairs now made it highly important to conciliate the favor of Elizabeth.

The resolution of Maria Theresa to follow up her appeal to the Silesians by a military demonstration, though opposed by prince Charles, was carried out with unusual energy. Scarcely had the last Prussian detachment crossed the frontier, when the enemy began to pour by every avenue into the province. The principal army under Traun entered by way of Glatz, which general Lehwald was unable to defend, and drew a strong cordon about the frontier. The Hungarian insurgents swept into Upper Silesia in so great numbers, and with such tempestuous force, that general Marwitz, who had some ten thousand men in Troppau and Jägerndorf, saw himself in danger of isolation, and, on the advice of a council of war, retired behind the Neisse.[1] Then the Austrians prepared to go into winter quarters. The outlook for the Prussians seemed serious enough; and it was under the influence of the alarm caused by this unforeseen invasion that Frederic issued his second proclamation to the Silesians, and appealed to the guaranteeing powers.

He had himself returned to Berlin the middle of December, supposing the campaign ended for the winter. For reasons of policy, or from native buoyancy of spirits, he gave no signs of discouragement, received the foreign envoys with a cheerful face, and laid out a programme of winter festivities.[2] Then came the news that the enemy had crossed the frontier. Report after report followed, until it was gradually learned that Glatz was lost, that Marwitz had fled to the Neisse, that Upper Silesia was at the mercy of the pandours.[3]

---

[1] Marwitz himself died on the march, and prince Dietrich took the command.

[2] Droysen, V. ii. 395.   [3] Orlich, ii. 110.

Leopold of Dessau had been called to Silesia to take the command for the winter, with headquarters at Neisse. He had expected only a routine life in camp ; but now, much to his delight, he found himself confronted with a problem which roused all his undimmed military ardor. He entered upon the task, however, in his own peculiar way. He soon became involved in a bitter dispute with the civil authorities, whom he accused of defrauding the commissariat. The walls of Neisse being found unsatisfactory, he bluntly arraigned general Walrave, the engineer by whom they had been repaired. The slowness of his movements broke down the patience of Frederic, who sent angry letters of exhortation, command, rebuke, and once returned to Silesia with the purpose of resuming the command in person.[1] But this plan he soon abandoned, finding the danger less serious, and the prince's plans better, than he had supposed.[2] He may have been touched, too, by Leopold's mental condition, which was such as to invite sympathy and forbearance. Not long before this, the veteran had lost his wife, whom he married out of affection from a lower social rank. His three sons were ill. He himself was broken down with age and infirmities, and could only move about painfully in a clumsy coach ; and it was evident that his days of usefulness were nearly over. But he made his preparations with great care and method. On the ninth of January, 1745, he crossed the Neisse and moved upon the enemy.

No very serious resistance was offered. Traun avoided a general engagement ; and only single detachments, having the advantage of numbers or position, attempted to make a stand ; though, when a collision occurred, both the regular and the irregular

The Old Dessauer in the field.

Expulsion of the Austrians.

---

[1] See Frederic to Leopold, 17, 18, 19 December, 1744 ; Orlich, ii. passim.

[2] Frederic to Podewils, 20 December, 1744.

troops of the queen fought with determination. At Ratibor and Habelschwerdt there were spirited encounters,
in which equal courage was displayed on both sides. But
the Prussians were everywhere victorious, and by the end
of February the last Austrian was driven over the frontier. If no great battles were fought, the operations
were not the less useful for exercise and discipline, and
the final result vastly improved the spirits of the army.

The failure in Silesia was, however, a check to only one
feature of the plan of the Austrians, and even
this they hoped to make good in the spring. On
the Danube they were more successful. Without opposition from the imperialists, who were too weak
to face them in the field, or from the French, who remained quietly in their winter quarters, they advanced
into the Upper Palatinate, established connections with
Ingolstadt, and gained control of the river as far as the
circle of Suabia. Even Munich was in danger, and the
emperor remained in his capital only on the assurance of
Maria Theresa that, whatever might happen, his own person would be held inviolate. For the next campaign the
most imposing plans were formed at Vienna. The regiments were recruited up to their full strength, and fresh
levies of irregulars called under the flag. The reconquest
of Bavaria was to be followed by that of Silesia; and
then the victorious armies of the queen were to hurl the
French contemptuously over the Rhine.[1]

The warlike ardor of Maria Theresa was in striking
contrast to the pacific sentiments which seemed
to reign everywhere else in Europe. True, the
allies and friends of the queen exulted over the easy victory in Bohemia; the envoy of Holland at London lay
awake nights from joy.[2] Plans and preparations for the

Progress of the Austrians on the Danube.

Peace sentiments.

---

[1] Droysen, V. ii. 389 et seq.; Frederic to Louis XV., 4 January,
to Klinggraeffen, 5 January, 1745.

[2] Andrié, 25 December, 1744. *Polit. Corresp.*, iv. 5.

next year were not intermitted an instant. The dispatch of lord Chesterfield to the Hague, to induce Holland to declare war against France ; the treaty of Warsaw ; the English negotiations for an auxiliary force of thirty thousand Russians ; the increased subsidy to the queen ; the activity of the French in Flanders ; their two armies in Germany ; the augmentation of the Saxon forces ; the angry conflicts in Silesia, — all this brought no gladness to the white-winged angel of peace. Yet the words and phrases of diplomacy, excepting again that of Austria, showed no little desire to end the war. Frederic repeated, in letter after letter to France, Russia, England ; to the great and little princes of the Empire ; to his ministers and his envoys, the need of a general peace, in which he would ask nothing for himself, and but little for the emperor. He continued his intrigues for the mediation of Russia. He appealed to the humane impulses of George the Second and his ministers. When France threatened to carry the war into Holland, he disavowed in advance any share in such a proceeding ; he had advised against it ; he was anxious to spare the republic the evils of an invasion, which would only postpone the blessed day of peace.[1] The English ministers, so Andrié reported, were equally tired of the war, and anxious to secure honorable terms for all parties.[2] Louis XV. agreed with Frederic that peace was desirable ; if an armistice could be arranged, and Russia would take the initiative, he would not refuse to coöperate.[3] The Saxon court continued to protest that it had only the most friendly feelings toward Prussia, and made private overtures at Paris.[4] Reports of similar efforts of the emperor at the Hague came to the ears of count Podewils.[5] The grand pensionary of

[1] Frederic to count Podewils, at The Hague, 2 January, 1745.

[2] *Polit. Corresp.*, iii. 368, 369, 380 ; iv. 15, 21.

[3] Droysen, V. ii. 399, 400 ; Frederic to Louis XV., 8 January, 1745.

[4] *Polit. Corresp.*, iii. 368.   [5] Ibid., iv. 19, 20.

Holland even suggested the order which the work of pacification should follow, and other leading members of the government frequently approached the Prussian envoy on the subject.[1] Such were the professed sentiments of a great majority of the powers, as well belligerents as auxiliaries ; and by concerted action they could easily have imposed their will upon the queen of Hungary. But their interests were too diverse and too antagonistic for such an agreement. Only vague assurances were as yet exchanged.

Late in January, however, Frederic took the further step of submitting to England a programme for peace in Germany. Part even of this he himself described as somewhat elastic and open to amendment, but he thought it would afford a working basis. The removal of lord Carteret from the cabinet, he continued, and the reports which had been received of the more friendly sentiments of lord Harrington, led him to lay before the latter, not as a minister but as a friend, and in the strictest confidence, an outline of terms on which the proffered mediation of England might be accepted. The first article demanded the recognition of the emperor, the restitution of his hereditary possessions, and the cession to him either of Upper Austria, or the estates of the queen in Suabia. The second included Hesse-Cassel, the Palatinate, and other allies of the emperor, in the peace. The third was less precise, but the substance was that Prussia required, as indemnity for the wanton and cruel invasion of Silesia, at least the cession of the mountains from which the queen's troops had descended into the province, and as much more as Andrié could get. Then followed some suggestions about the possibility of extending the peace to France and Spain, and all the combatants. But the principal thing was the pacification of Germany, and the indispensable condition of that was the

Frederic's scheme of pacification.

[1] Report of Beck, secretary of legation at the Hague, 5 January, 1745. *Polit. Corresp.*, iv. 7.

reëstablishment of the emperor.   He, Frederic, would not even make his own interests an obstacle to the speedy progress of the work, it was added for the confidential guidance of Andrié.[1]

This dispatch left Berlin on the twenty-sixth of January.   But it had no sooner started on its way than Frederic was forced to send another to the same address, announcing the arrival of news which suddenly changed the whole face of the situation.[2] The emperor Charles VII. died at Munich on the twentieth day of the month, and the report of the momentous event had thus tardily reached Berlin.

Death of the emperor, 20 January, 1745.

It is admitted by friend and foe that Charles Albert was a man of some amiable qualities, and no positive faults of character.   But he wanted political ability, and even ordinary firmness of mind, so that, having rashly assumed a part which he was unfitted to play, he fell a victim to circumstances which he made little or no effort to control.   He was now timid, now reckless, but nearly always took, by a fatal perversity, the wrong course at every great crisis of affairs.   When he should have been resolute and manly, he showed a feeble indecision ; when a reasonable moderation would have served his purpose, he became arrogant and exacting. The indiscretion of his court was proverbial throughout Europe.   No secret entrusted to him was safe; and his enemies were nearly as well served as his friends by his unskilful diplomacy.   He had, besides, the great disadvantage of being a helpless tool in the hands of France ; and this circumstance, while it destroyed his own freedom of action, aroused prejudice in the Empire, and seriously

His character.

[1] *Polit. Corresp.*, iv. 21–23.   A curious light is thrown upon Frederic's confidence in Harrington by the complaint of the duke of Newcastle, that he was little more than Carteret's shadow.   Coxe's *Pelham*, i. 198.

[2] Frederic to Andrié, 26 January, 1745.   But the earlier dispatch was not countermanded.

embarrassed the efforts even of Frederic himself. His career was a mournful one in every respect. The moralists drew from it ample lessons about the dangers of excessive ambition. The diplomatists had their oracular deductions; the soldiers, theirs. But to most observers of that age, and for several generations afterwards, the failure of Charles Albert seemed to show the folly of all attempts to wrest the imperial dignity, and the leadership in German politics, from the house of Austria.

With the death of Charles, all treaties and all alliances, all orders and all commissions, which centred about or issued from him as emperor, came of course to an end. The union of Frankfort died a natural death. Seckendorf threw up his command as imperial general, because there was no longer an emperor to serve.

Conse-
quences of
his death.

From Paris Chambrier reported that everybody, except possibly cardinal Tencin, felt that France was now relieved of a burdensome ally, and could make an honorable settlement with Austria.[1] The reputation of D'Argenson for humanitarian views, and the knowledge that he had originally opposed the war, may have encouraged this hope. But the report of Chavigny from Munich, that the dying emperor had solemnly placed his son under the protection of France, made it difficult to throw up the Bavarian alliance, and France had still unfulfilled designs in the Netherlands.[2] Hence, if there was some delay and even hesitation, about which indeed the information is meagre, it was early resolved to adhere to the main lines of the old policy. Louis himself, though he had lately lost by the death of madame de Châteauroux his chief inspiration to brave deeds, showed no disposition to retreat.[3] The

---

[1] Duke de Broglie in the *Revue des Deux Mondes*, 1 May, 1887; Droysen, V. ii. 423.

[2] Especially the recovery of the right to fortify Dunkirk. Vide Flassan, v. 239 ; Droysen, V. ii. 398.

[3] Flassan, v. 241 ; Broglie, ubi supra.

marquis sketched in cogent memorials a plan of action for the future.

One of these was presented to Frederic by Valori on the eighth of February. It contained military as well as political recommendations; and the former were to be explained more at length by the chevalier de Courten, who reached Berlin at the same time. Their principal features were, first, the expression of a hope that Frederic would again penetrate with an army into Bohemia or Moravia; and, next, the intimation that France would probably recall her troops from Germany, or at most keep them on the defensive, and throw her principal energy into the campaign in the Netherlands. Various technical scruples, based on the death of the emperor, were put forward to justify this measure. But the real reason was the direction of Louis' own ambition. In this matter he overruled D'Argenson, who advised strict fidelity to Prussia, another campaign in the Empire, and the defensive in Italy and the Netherlands.[1]

Military plans of France.

The political articles of the marquis' paper concerned chiefly the vacant imperial crown. The maxim so often announced by Frederic, that the two courts ought to insist on the exclusion of the house of Austria from the succession in the Empire, was still an article of faith at Versailles; but the youth and weak character of the new elector of Bavaria, together with the knowledge that his leading advisers were inclined to an arrangement with the queen,[2] seemed to make it necessary to leave him out of account. In this dilemma the French minister proposed to put forward the elector of Saxony as the candidate of the two courts. His ambition was no secret, and if he should enter into the plan the first result would be his withdrawal from the Anglo-Austrian alliance. But his dependence on England and Rus-

D'Argenson suggests August III. for emperor.

---

[1] Flassan, v. 242–245.

[2] Frederic to Louis XV., 30 January, 1745.

sia was great; he was timid; and much adroit management would be needed to draw him into the scheme. As
Saint-Séverin was ill at Warsaw, the marquis proposed to
send Valori to Dresden on this mission, which he hoped
would have the approval and support of Prussia.[1]

The Prussian reply, drafted by Podewils, was justly described by Frederic as an extremely adroit com-

Prussian
reply.

position, which, by leaving all doors open, would
afford easy excuses to France for whatever might happen. It was non-committal, and yet not suspiciously evasive.[2] The king, it said, would continue to fulfil his engagements, so far as the existing situation and the state of
his own affairs permitted. The resolution to retire the
French armies to the Rhine would simply leave the Palatinate and Hesse-Cassel to the vengeance of the queen,
since it was impossible for him to make a diversion in
their behalf with a hostile army at his own gates. But he
was ready to discuss with the chevalier de Courten a plan
of operations for the coming season. In regard to the proposed negotiations at Dresden, he urged that it would be
fatal to the scheme to have it suspected that he was its
principal author; and he would only consent that Valori
should promise the acquiescence of Prussia in whatever
agreement might be made with the Saxon court. It may
be added here, though it was no part of the reply to
France, that, though Frederic looked with some favor on
the project, he was not sanguine of its success. He refused to give Prussian credentials to Valori, and instructed
his own envoy to avoid everything which might look like
active coöperation.[3]

The reason for this cautious policy on Frederic's part,

[1] *Polit. Corresp.*, iv. 39 ; Droysen, V. ii. 430.

[2] Réponse qu'on pourrait faire sur les différents points du mémoire
de M. d'Argenson, 10 February, 1745. *Polit. Corresp.*, iv. 41–43.

[3] Frederic to Podewils, 8 February ; same to count Beess, at
Dresden, 13 February, 1745.

as shown in the reply to D'Argenson, was that he found the death of the emperor at once an embarrass- ment and a relief. It was an embarrassment because Charles the Seventh served, while he lived, as a certain centre about which the enemies of Austria, German and foreign, could rally. On his death, with no available successor in his own family, the chances of the grand-duke Francis were vastly improved. This was understood at Vienna, where orders were at once issued for a vigorous resumption of hostilities in Central Germany. The Austrian troops pushed out again toward the Rhine ; invaded the Palatinate ; threatened Hesse-Cassel ; and, under the policy announced by Louis, met no opposition from the French. Encouraged by her new prospects, the queen was taxing her last energies for a renewal of the struggle over Silesia. In this situation, exposed to an attack from the united forces of Austria and Saxony, with his German allies dropping off one by one, and Russia still in doubt, Frederic was compelled to avoid an open rupture with France. It was, however, equally wise to make no irrevocable engagement with Louis until it was seen whether the emperor's death might not actually help the secret negotiations for peace. In this sense that event might prove a relief. The ultimatum in favor of Charles VII., which had formed a part of all previous overtures to England, could now be dropped ; and Harrington could be assured that, as the connection with France had mainly in view the defence of the emperor, the king could now make his own peace, without regard to his ally. And, as the price of peace, the vote of Prussia might even be promised to the grand-duke Francis. With that alternative in view, it was of course unwise to enter too deeply into the Saxon project of D'Argenson.

Reason of Frederic's caution.

This may seem to be an impossible scheme of treachery. Yet it was so far from being impossible that it actually formed one part, and the larger part, of

The two policies.

Frederic's diplomacy for several weeks to come. The other part consisted of parallel negotiations with France for more effective military operations in the next campaign, while Valori's intrigues at Dresden served as a background.

An intimation of Frederic that he might consent to support the grand-duke for the imperial throne was given as early as the day after he received the news of the vacancy.[1] On the eighth of February he ordered Andrié

A repulse at London.

to renew at London essentially the same propositions as were made in January, except of course the articles in favor of the emperor, and with another referring, though still vaguely, to the grand-duke.[2] Count Podewils, at the Hague, was to support the plan by interviews with lord Chesterfield.[3] The king was still uncertain, however, of his ground, but hoped soon to see his way more clearly.[4] The scheme for a Russian mediation was cautiously pressed. At one time the empress had seemed willing to undertake it, and a note to that effect was handed in by Bestuschef. But her majesty proposed to mediate alone; and, as the pending negotiations with England made such an offer somewhat awkward, Mardefeld was sharply reprimanded for going beyond the king's intentions.[5] Every hour was now precious. The season for active operations was approaching; the French were pressing for the conclusion of the military arrangements; England, by a formal note, had refused to fulfil the Silesian guaranty, on the ground that Frederic himself was the aggressor; and it was feared that Bestuschef would make an evil use of the rejected mediation. But in these

[1] To Andrié, 27 January, 1745.

[2] Eichel to Podewils, 8 February, 1745.

[3] Frederic to count Podewils, 12 February, 1745.

[4] Same to Andrié, 12 February, 1745.

[5] *Preuss. Staatsschriften*, i. 706 ; *Polit. Corresp.*, iv. 34 ; Frederic to Mardefeld, 20 February, 1745.

days arrived the English answer to Frederic's repeated and pressing overtures. In effect it dismissed the whole subject with the cold though civil explanation, that his Britannic majesty could take no measures until he had had time to discover the effects caused by the death of the emperor, and to take counsel with his allies.[1]

This put an end for a time to Frederic's suit for the aid of England; and the Russian mediation, as the last string to his bow, was again taken up with zeal.[2] But the march of events soon left this expedient behind. The Saxon court responded unfavorably to the insinuations of Beess and Valori in regard to the imperial throne; and about the same time the more important articles of the treaty of Warsaw, which showed how close were the ties that bound August III. to England and Austria, were communicated to Frederic.[3] Bad news now came by every post. The young elector of Bavaria was in secret negotiations with Vienna; a Russian army corps was preparing for some unknown service; the army of Maillebois abandoned the line of the Lahn as soon as the Austrians made a move in that direction.[4] Worse than all these, at least in its possible results, was the disclosure to France of the Prussian overtures in London. Frederic promptly assured Louis that there was nothing in them which had not already been made known to him; that he had only sounded the English court on the terms of a general pacification.[5] But his alarm was shown by the order to arrest a clerk whom he suspected of betraying the secret. When

Complications thicken.

[1] Delivered to Andrié 15 February, 1745. *Preuss. Staatsschriften,* i. 641 ; cf. Frederic to Andrié, 27 February, 1745.

[2] Frederic to Mardefeld, 4 March, 1745. The figure is Frederic's.

[3] Droysen, V. ii. 438.

[4] Frederic to Klinggraeffen, 2 March ; to Mardefeld, 9 March ; to Louis XV., 26 February, 1745 ; Ranke, xxix. 140.

[5] Frederic to Louis XV., 13 March, 1745.

Podewils interceded for the innocent victim, as he proved indeed to be, the royal vengeance fell upon him. "You may reprimand your clerks," wrote the king, "but not me. The wrath of Agamemnon [1] at the siege of Troy was nothing in comparison with your rage over the arrest of a beggarly copyist. If the ministers of London and Vienna were as confiding as you, we should be much better informed about their secrets." [2]

In this crisis the least agreeable of several alternative plans was finally adopted. The negotiations with Courten, for the military coöperation of France and Prussia in the campaign which now seemed inevitable, came to a conclusion essentially as Frederic had desired. France promised to aid Bavaria to bring its effective force to fifty-eight thousand, to give Maillebois seventy thousand for operations on the lower Rhine against Hanover, and to place one hundred thousand in Flanders under Louis himself, — a noble scheme, of which only the last provision was at all realized. Prussia, for her part, undertook to be ready for action with one hundred and fifteen battalions, and one hundred and eighty squadrons, approximately eighty thousand foot and thirty thousand horse.[3] The chevalier de Courten then returned to Paris, and Frederic himself, impatient with the long delay, set out for Silesia. On the seventeenth of March he was at Breslau, and a few days later at Neisse. Here he formally took the command of the army.

Military agreement with France.

Yet Frederic's correspondence shows that he still preferred a separate peace, through the efforts of England in the closet, to the doubtful advantage of French support in the field. If he excelled all contemporary rulers in the prudence which prepares

Embarrassments of Frederic.

[1] Sic.

[2] Frederic to Podewils and Borcke, 8 March, 1745. The suspected clerk was released five days later.

[3] Droysen, V. ii. 437.

for war in time of peace, he was not less distinguished by the persistence with which he labored for peace in time of war. He had come to Silesia to begin a campaign. But he still clung tenaciously to the thread of his negotiations for escaping a campaign, — to the hope of English mediation, of Russian mediation, of any kind of a separate accommodation with the queen. "We are in the midst of a great crisis," he wrote; "either we shall have peace through the aid of England, or all the forces of the enemy will precipitate themselves upon us."[1] These forces were already collecting on the frontier. But England still maintained her attitude of reserve. The air at St. Petersburg was full of sinister rumors, and the chances of aid from that quarter became daily fainter. To all these causes of anxiety was added, besides, a pecuniary problem. The Bohemian campaign had again exhausted the surplus in the treasury, and it was feared that the regular revenues would be insufficient to support the large armies, which a renewal of the struggle would necessarily call into the field. Frederic was therefore forced to look abroad for help. France had vast resources, though her treasury was nearly bankrupt; and late in March he resolved, in case the negotiations for peace should fail, to apply to Louis for a subsidy.[2]

The situation in the early spring was thus full of uncertainties, some hopeful, some ominous; and the fate of Prussia seemed to depend on the manner in which they would all be resolved.

The first blow to the Franco-Prussian plans was the defection of the young elector of Bavaria. This event had been preparing for some time, and not

Defection of Bavaria.

[1] Frederic to Podewils, 27, 29 March, 1745.
[2] Eichel to Podewils, 27 March, 1745; *Polit. Corresp.*, iv. 97. According to Droysen, V. ii. 441, the expenses of the coming campaign were estimated at five and a half millions, while the available funds would hardly reach one and a half millions.

wholly without the knowledge of the Berlin diplomatists;[1]
but so long as the step was not actually taken, there was
still a chance that it might be prevented. Maximilian
Joseph acted, however, with a prudence in which there
was no mixture of treachery. On the twenty-second of
April he concluded with Maria Theresa the preliminary
peace of Füssen, and retired on favorable terms from the
struggle. The basis of the agreement was the mutual
restitution of territory and prisoners, and the mutual renunciation of conflicting claims and pretensions. The
elector received back Bavaria, worn and wasted by many
campaigns, from the Austrians. He recognized the pragmatic sanction, and agreed to support the grand-duke
Francis for emperor.[2]

The failure of the attempt to bribe August of Saxony
by the offer of the imperial crown, in support of
Plan for the
partition of which Valori made a second journey to Dresden,
Prussia.
had been foreseen by Frederic from the first,
and caused therefore no surprise at Berlin.[3] But a far
graver matter was the negotiations for changing the defensive alliance of Warsaw into an active alliance of
aggression and spoliation. It was to take the form of a
supplementary treaty between Austria and Saxony, on
which August had insisted as a condition of accepting the
earlier compact.[4] Each state was to enrich itself at the
cost of Prussia ; but, while the queen simply claimed the
territory which she had lately lost, more difficulty was
found in meeting the expectations of the elector. He first
demanded several Silesian counties, in order to open a connection between Saxony and Poland. This was promptly
refused. The two courts then turned to other parts of

---

[1] Supra, p. 289 ; Frederic to Klinggraeffen, 14 April, 1745.

[2] Wenck, ii. 180–190 ; Arneth, iii. c. 1.

[3] Valori, i. 211–218. Brühl, he says, and Guarini both opposed
the project.

[4] Schoell, ii. 359, 360 ; Arneth, iii. 38.

Prussia, and found in the end that a strip adjacent to the Lausitz, and a section from the district of Magdeburg, would nicely round off the Saxon territory. After Austria had promised to add the county of Schwiebus, the scheme of partition was complete. The condition was joint military action, offensive as well as defensive, against Prussia, and each of the contracting powers was to guarantee the acquisitions made by the other. The treaty was signed at Leipsic on the eighteenth of May. Its provisions were not fully known to Frederic until a decade later, but it is not quite correct to say that he was taken by surprise. Many circumstances made him suspect, on the contrary, that the engagements between Austria and Saxony went far beyond the terms of the union of Warsaw, and he regulated accordingly all his plans and movements.[1]

The hopes which Frederic had cherished of Russian or English aid to extricate him from his perilous situation were reluctantly abandoned about the same time. No help from Russia. He himself says, indeed, that Prussian gold kept Russia inactive.[2] If by this he meant that it kept her from taking up arms against him, the statement is at least careless; for the money which was paid in 1744, and that which was tendered as late as March, 1745, had in view positive support, military or diplomatic, or both, from the empress.[3] But either because her ministers were

---

[1] Carlyle, iv. 66, says : " Friedrich was far from suspecting the rages that lurked in the Polish Majesty." But Frederic, writing to count Beess, 13 April, 1745, says : " Sur ce qui est de la nouvelle que vous me mandez des mauvais et pernicieux desseins des Saxons, je n'en ai jamais douté." And in the Œuvres, vol. iii. p. 87, the king speaks of the Saxon intentions, " qui étaient connues à toute l'Europe." The full text of the treaty is in the Recueil des déductions du comte de Hertzberg, Berlin, 1790, vol. i. pp. 28–30 ; Adelung, iv. Beilage IV., etc.

[2] Œuvres de Frédéric, iii. 93.

[3] The second payment was to be one hundred thousand thalers each to Bestuschef and Woronzof. A graduated scale of compensa-

implacable, or because they failed to overcome her own scruples, Elizabeth finally refused to undertake the mediation.[1] "The treason of Russia," Frederic called this decision, and thus enriched the vocabulary of legal science with a new definition. An invitation to send a corps for the defence of Silesia was also declined, on the ground that, although Russia had guaranteed the treaty of Berlin, it was a guaranty only against attack, while in the pending war Prussia was the aggressor. No bettter success followed the effort to have Russia dissuade Saxony from an attack on the Prussian territory. The empress remonstrated only against an invasion of the inherited dominions of the king, thus tacitly excluding Silesia and Glatz.[2] The explanation of all this is that Russia and Austria had made their peace in the affair of the marquis Botta, while Bestuschef, in spite of Mardefeld's gold, was still the bitter enemy of Prussia, and the most powerful person in the councils of the empress. Not only did he thwart all of Frederic's efforts to obtain active assistance, or even a friendly mediation; but he also had a rival plan of his own, vast, audacious, and directly hostile to Prussia. His aim, according to Tirawley, the English ambassador, was to conquer the province of Preussen for Poland, in return for which the Polish districts of Pleskau and Smolensk were to pass to Russia. It was hoped to persuade the empress to this step by appeals to her religious feelings.[3] Russia having thus failed, Frederic was reduced to a narrow alternative. He still had two resources, he wrote, one of which was the negotiation with England; the other, the valor of his troops.[4]

---

tion was proposed for such services as they might render, in case they could not earn the maximum amount by a full compliance with the royal desires. Frederic to Mardefeld, 26 March, 1745.

[1] 23 April, 1745.　　　　　　　[2] *Polit. Corresp.*, iv. 121.

[3] Tirawley, 8 October, 1744, apud Raumer, *Beiträge*, ii. 200, 201.

[4] Frederic to Podewils, 26 April, 1745.

The final failure of the English mediation was not wholly due to England. Lord Harrington did not indeed show much alacrity in helping Frederic out of the difficulty which his own rashness had created, for it appeared less necessary than in 1741 or 1742 to pacify Prussia at any cost. But the minister, being less audacious and sanguine than Carteret, and more open to the influence of the cautious Pelhams, saw clearly that the armies of Frederic were still dangerous to the cause of the pragmatic sanction, and vastly useful to France. Hence, after much solicitation on the part of the Prussian envoy, Harrington presented the points of a treaty of peace which he was willing to submit to the queen.[1] The scheme proposed the simple restoration of the status quo, as established in the treaty of Berlin, and a pledge on the part of Frederic to support the grand-duke for emperor.[2] The additional morsel of Austrian territory, for which the king had pleaded so earnestly, was thus denied. For this reason the English proposals seemed of course defective. But Frederic decided, after only a few days of reflection, that they must be accepted, and orders were sent to Berlin and London to close the transaction.[3] The fate which the propositions would meet in Vienna seems not to have been discussed at the time.

English mediation.

Yet if the urgent appeals of Robinson had proved so often fruitless with the queen in the gravest crises of the first Silesian war, could she be expected now, in deference to far less earnest representations, to forego all the advantages of her position, and leave her baffled assailant unpunished? As days and then weeks elapsed without any affirmative answer from Vienna,

Inflexibility of Maria Theresa.

---

[1] But not to recommend, at least very warmly. On the contrary it appears that Harrington regularly communicated the Prussian notes on the subject to the ministers of the queen. Arneth, iii. 32.

[2] *Polit. Corresp.*, iv. 98.

[3] Frederic to Podewils, 2 April, 1745.

the absurdity of this view gradually dawned upon the king.
The active military movements of the Austrians and
Saxons finally made the situation clear ; and on the nineteenth of May Frederic's conviction was announced that
the issue of the sword had once more to be tried.[1]   Orders
were at the same time given to forward to the king of
France the suspended request for subsidies.

As Frederic thus saw vanish, one after another, the
schemes of peace which he had so fondly nour-
ished, his mind took on a serious, sombre, almost
melancholy tone, yet one from which echoes a
voice of unshaken resolution.   The jaunty, flippant, sarcas-
tic air of the young man who marched into Silesia in 1740
has disappeared.   If lofty maxims of morality and an
elevated sympathy with humane ideals are not revealed,
there is at least no cynical persiflage ; the gravity of the
crisis is felt ; the responsibility of the ruler finds inspir-
ing expression ; and the somewhat violent phrases of a
desperate determination are not unworthy of a philosophical Roman patriot.   " I have made it a point of honor,"
he writes, " to contribute more than any other to the
aggrandizement of my house ; I have played a leading
part among the crowned heads of Europe ; these are so
many personal engagements which I have taken, and
which I am resolved to fulfil even at the cost of my fortune and my life." [2]   And again : " Farewell, my dear
Podewils ; try to become as good a philosopher as you
are a politician, and learn from a man who never hears
the sermons of Elsner, or any other, that it is necessary
to oppose an iron front to all the misfortunes that
arrive, and to learn to despise riches, honors, and all
the attractions of vanity, which cannot follow us after
death." [3]   The king was also required at this time to meet

*Frederic
prepares for
the worst.*

[1] Frederic to Eichel and to Podewils, 19 May, 1745.

[2] Frederic to Podewils, 27 April, 1745 ; cf. Valori, i. 219.

[3] Frederic to Podewils, 29 April, 1745.

a keen personal loss in the death of the amiable and accomplished Jordan. It has often been said, and is widely believed, that Frederic had no friendships. He had none indeed which he put above the interests of the state, and few which he would not sacrifice to an epigram. But he was capable of strong attachment to men who interested him, and in the early years of his reign the most attractive side of his nature is revealed in his intimate correspondence with his friends. One of these was Jordan ; and the death of Jordan, coming at a time when Frederic was overwhelmed with public cares, and peculiarly sensitive to mournful impressions, evoked from him a manifestation of grief not the less genuine because it took a poetical form, and in sufficiently crude verse lamented the untimely loss of a favorite literary companion.[1]

While Frederic was laboriously intriguing to find a peaceful escape for himself, he had not the less earnestly pressed upon the French the lesson of energy, vigor, and audacity. But in Germany a fatal lethargy, or a not less fatal incapacity, seemed to paralyze all their movements. The retreat from the Lahn was the first step backward ; and a change of commanders, by which prince Conti superseded Maillebois, brought no relief. The peace with Bavaria set free a formidable Austrian army, which, first under Batthyany and then under Traun, successfully baffled the not very skilful or very active dispositions of the French. The invasion of Hanover proved a fruitless scheme. *Maillebois and Conti.*

To this failure a striking contrast was, however, offered by the splendid campaign of marshal Saxe in Flanders, culminating on the eleventh of May in the great victory of Fontenoy. The battle was brought *Battle of Fontenoy.*

---

[1] La mort de ses ailes funèbres,
  Vient de couvrir de ses ténèbres
  Mon tendre ami, mon cher Jordan.
          Œuvres de Frédéric, xvii. 286.

about by a desperate attempt of the duke of Cumberland and marshal Königsegg to raise the siege of Tournay, and arrest the triumphant progress of the enemy. With the many stirring and heroic incidents of the engagement history, liberally aided perhaps by fiction, has made the world familiar. Few battles have been so hotly contested; few have reflected such justly balanced credit upon victors and vanquished. The duke of Cumberland missed his Malplaquet because the French were served and saved by the genius of Maurice. But the defeat of the allies, though dearly bought, was complete. Their army retired; Tournay soon afterwards fell; and the French pressed vigorously forward.

The report of this battle reached Frederic at a time when he greatly needed exhilarating news. Hitherto, indeed, he had steadily opposed the plan of the French to throw their principal energy into the Netherlands, and only the week before had had with Louis a sharp exchange of views on the subject. What the common cause needed, he wrote, was victories in Germany, not in Flanders. The capture of Tournay by the French, a descent on the Canary Islands by the Spaniards, and the siege of Babylon by Thamas Chouli Khan were equally useless so far as concerned the war in Bohemia or Moravia.[1] But after reflection he began to perceive that the victory might, by disposing the English and Dutch to peace, prove highly advantageous in the end. It would show the world that France and Prussia united were invincible. If prince Conti would gain a similar battle on the Rhine; if Prussia could have such a day as Fontenoy; if lord Harrington would now hold his head lower, and Chesterfield show a better spirit; if this or that would happen, envious neighbors

---

[1] Réponse au mémoire du roi de France, 16 May, 1745. *Polit. Corresp.*, iv. 166–168. This whole paper well deserves perusal, as also Frederic's marginal comments on the French memorial. *Ibid.*, pp. 158 et seq.

would take a different tone, and a glorious peace would be assured.[1] But all such speculations were soon cut short by a peremptory challenge from his own antagonists.

In the latter half of May the pandours and hussars of the Austrians began once more to push through the mountain passes into Upper Silesia. The Prussian cavalry sent against them proved always superior as fighting soldiers, when sabres clashed in open combat. Under the fiery and impetuous Winterfeld, who combined the daring of a scout with the method of a trained soldier; Zieten, whose uncombed locks waved at the head of every charge ; and Seydlitz, who as captain of horse began a career which now fills a large place in the military annals of Prussia, they showed what ready pupils they were in learning to conduct themselves on the field of battle. In the looser tactics of the flying column or the dashing raid the Prussians never, indeed, reached the proficiency of their masters.[2] But the impetuosity with which they charged, and the fierce obstinacy with which they fought, made them admirably fitted for the work which now fell upon them, — the work of covering the retreat of the garrisons and other detachments scattered throughout Upper Silesia. For Frederic had decided to evacuate this province, and leave it temporarily

The Austrian reoccupy Upper Silesia.

[1] See the rapid series of letters 21 to 26 May, 1745, which, aside from their general interest, are extremely useful to a biographer of Frederic. Thus, to Podewils, 22 May : " Comme je suppose que le prince de Conti pourrait avoir remporté une victoire sur les alliés," etc.; to Beess, at Dresden, 23 May : " Je ne crois pas que les Saxons m'attaqueront. Quel effet aurait produit la bataille de Tournai ? " To the ministers of foreign affairs, who had advised against the recall of count Otho von Podewils from the Hague, 26 May : "Mais, mon Dieu, que l'on m'obéisse du moins une fois dans ma vie. Si je ne puis être maître des grandes affaires, je veux du moins l'être de celles qui me sont particulières."

[2] See the excellent treatise of colonel Denison, *A History of Cavalry*, London, 1877, chs. xx. and xxi. ; also Orlich, ii. 146–153 ; and *Œuvres de Frédéric*, iii. 106.

to its fate. He made no attempt to guard the passes. The length of the frontier rendered this difficult; and in the circumstances it seemed good generalship to entice the enemy through the mountains, and away from their supplies, into a region where a victory over them would be at once easier to win, and more important in its results. It was in pursuance of this plan that Upper Silesia was stripped of its troops, and nearly the whole available force of the Prussians concentrated, toward the end of May, about the town of Neisse. The order to forward to Paris the request for subsidies was dispatched on the seventeenth. Four millions were solicited, and the royal letter reached Chambrier on the last day of the month.[1]

In the mean time the Hungarian light horse, left unopposed, hastened to seize the most important posts in Upper Silesia. The strong fortress of Cosel on the Oder was betrayed to them by the joint treachery of a fugitive Prussian ensign who acted as guide, and sixty soldiers of the garrison who opened the gates; and the whole province was soon in their possession.[2]

The main force of the allies executed with equal ease their part in the preliminary plan of operations. The Austrians under prince Charles, setting out from Königgrätz, and leaving the fortress of Glatz in their rear, entered Silesia near the village of Schönberg. At Landshut on the thirtieth of May they were joined by the duke of Weissenfels and the Saxons. The united forces, then seventy-five thousand strong,[3] pro-

Advance of prince Charles.

[1] Frederic to Podewils, 15 May, 1745 ; Droysen, V. ii. 479. The autograph letter to Louis, thus finally forwarded, was dated 30 March, 1745.

[2] Orlich, ii. 157, 158.

[3] Ranke's figures, if I understand them, make a total of 100,000 troops of the line, and 15,000 irregulars, the latter including Servians, Albanians, and Dalmatians. *Sämmtliche Werke*, xxix. 157. But these are much higher than any other author gives, and Cogniazo, *Geständnisse*, ii. 124, seems to intimate that there was a deficiency of irregulars.

ceeded on the first of June to Reichenau, where Nadasdy reported the discovery of the Prussian camp near Schweidnitz; and the next day pushed on toward Baumgarten, which offered a secure position on a line stretching from Quolsdorf on the right to Bolkenhain on the left. The outposts were advanced to the heights near Hohenfriedberg. The prince had been deceived by false reports as to Frederic's plans, fully expected him to retire under the walls of Breslau, and took few precautions against an attack.[1] The next day, the third, in full obedience to this conviction, the allies even descended, and formed a new line still nearer the Prussians, but on lower and less advantageous ground. The left, which reached beyond Pilgramshain, was held by the Saxons. The Austrians had the centre and right, the latter resting on Hohenfriedberg.

No sooner had the enemy fixed themselves, thoughtless of danger, in this position than Frederic prepared to give them battle. In the silent hours of the night, while the unsuspecting Austrians were sleeping calmly under a mellow June sky, the Prussian army was put in motion toward Striegau, and by two o'clock in the morning it was drawn up in fighting order between that village and the hamlet of Stanowitz. The formation had been carried out with mathematical exactness. Valori, who followed in his carriage, reports his surprise at not meeting a single straggler on the way.[2] As soon as the last arrangements were completed, the king assembled the officers for his final instructions. The general plan was to attack the enemy's left, that is the Sax-

Frederic prepares for battle.

[1] Frederic pretended to accept the services as spy of one Schönberg, whom he knew to be already employed by the Austrians in the same capacity. This fellow, a dupe when he thought he was duping others, was instructed to return to the Austrian army, and send the king the earliest tidings of its approach, in order that he might have time to retire under the walls of Breslau. Prince Charles fell promptly into the trap. *Œuvres de Frédéric*, iii. 104, 110.

[2] *Mémoires*, i. 228.

ons, in oblique order by brigades; and then, after rolling up their line, to make a combined assault upon the flank and front of the Austrians in the centre.

At four o'clock in the morning the roar of the Prussian guns broke the silence of the drowsy valleys, and gave the signal for opening the drama. General Dumoulin promptly put the advance guard in motion. The Saxons, aroused by the cannon, or carrying out some movement of their own, had already thrown forward a few companies of grenadiers; but these were swept away before they could be reënforced, and fell back upon the principal line. By this time the Prussian horse of the right wing, under general Buddenbrock, had overtaken the advance, and were launched in two successive columns upon the enemy. Rothenburg, with twenty-six squadrons of cuirassiers, gave the first shock. General Stille followed with an equal number of dragoons. The Saxon horse held their lines firmly at first, and even gained some little ground. The fighting was close and desperate; but in the end the superior weight and discipline of the Prussians broke regiment after regiment of the enemy, and drove them in fatal confusion from the field. The flight of their cavalry left the infantry of the Saxons exposed to a flank attack, which cost them the loss of their first line. But they fell back to a stronger position, covered by ponds, swamps, and thickets, and there, behind deep rifle-pits, they received the assault of the Prussian foot. This followed in due order about six o'clock, prince Dietrich of Anhalt-Dessau and count Truchsess leading the first column and general Blankensee the second. Heavy fighting again ensued; Truchsess was instantly killed by a cannon-ball; the Prussians found it necessary to send forward brigade after brigade before they succeeded in dislodging the stubborn foe, and finally forced their way through only by the use of the bayonet. When at length the Saxon officers could no longer hold their battalions

Battle of Hohenfriedberg, 4 June, 1745.

together against the unerring rifle and the inflexible bayonet, they beat a reluctant retreat, and their infantry fled to join the cavalry in the inaccessible mountains.

Their retreat left another open flank, that of the Austrians of the centre, now become the left wing. Here, and along the whole line, tardily formed by prince Charles, who had long supposed that the fighting about Pilgramshain was caused by a successful Saxon attack upon Striegau, the struggle was renewed. The Austrians made up the larger part of the allied army, and were still nearly intact. They had some advantage of ground. The preoccupation of the Prussians at the other end of the field, and the dislocation of troops required by the engagement with the Saxons, left at least one important gap in their line, which in the opinion of military critics offered the Austrians a chance for an effective attack. But their delay in forming lost them the opportunity, and in the interval the thoughtfulness of the Prussian general Gessler turned the dangerous gap into a tactical advantage. For while the renewed fight was raging along the Austrian centre this officer, who was in the second formation, suddenly charged through the front line with a heavy body of horse, and struck the enemy with a momentum which carried everything before it.[1] Prince Charles and his officers made desperate efforts to rally their men, but they succeeded only in preventing a panic. It was too late to save the fortunes of the day. Under the cover of their artillery the Austrians slowly retired, and by eight o'clock the field of battle was in full possession of the Prussians.

Toward evening of the same day the two wings of the defeated army met at Reichenau, and late on the fifth reached Landshut. Here, not being energetically pursued, they ventured to take a day's rest. A muster of the regiments showed about twenty-five thousand missing, of whom, according to the most authentic

Retreat of the enemy.

---

[1] Valori, an eye-witness, i. 231–233 ; Orlich, ii. 179 ; Cogniazo, ii. 132.

estimates, about ten thousand were killed and wounded,
seven thousand prisoners, and the rest stragglers or deserters. The allies lost, in addition, some sixty pieces of
field artillery, and a large number of battle-flags. The
Prussian loss is given at a little over four thousand killed
and wounded.[1]

This striking victory put an end, of course, to all im-
Lessons of   mediate danger from an Austrian invasion of
the victory.   Silesia. But it also had some incidental effects
scarcely less important. It was for one thing the first
battle which Frederic had fought according to his own
plan, carried out strictly in all its leading details; and,
since the issue vindicated his tactics, the army perceived
that it had in its king a skilful general, and not merely a
lucky soldier of fortune. As a minor consequence too,
the efficiency of the reorganized Prussian cavalry was fully
established. Frederic himself laid great stress upon this
circumstance, and many years afterwards wrote that the
battle of Hohenfriedberg was the day on which the cavalry finally reached the point of efficiency, so long desired
and thenceforth maintained.[2]

From Landshut the allied army continued its retreat
The armies   through Glatz, and finally took up an unassail-
in Bhemia.   able position near Königgrätz. Frederic followed slowly ; but, being unable to dislodge the enemy,
he was forced to form a mere camp of observation, and
await the development of affairs. The ambiguous character of his relations with Saxony was, however, corrected.
His envoy at Dresden was recalled ; the Saxon agent at
Berlin received his passports ; the Old Dessauer was sent
to the frontier in command of a second army, as in 1741 ;[3]
and the two courts practically recognized a state of war.

[1] Droysen, V. ii. 495, and Arneth, iii. 77, agree substantially in
their statements of the losses ; cf. also Cogniazo, ii. 135.

[2] Droysen V. ii. 494.

[3] First at Gottersleben, and afterwards at Wiskau, near Halle.
He had about 30,000 men.   Orlich, ii. 210.

THE HISTORY OF PRUSSIA

To the Accession of Frederic the Great.

By HERBERT TUTTLE,

PROFESSOR IN CORNELL UNIVERSITY.

With a Map.   Crown 8vo, gilt top, $2.25.

———◆———

From the Frankfurter Zeitung, July 8, 1884.

. . . The longing to enrich themselves by an acquaintance with foreign peoples and their histories has produced, even among the Americans, where on account of the youth of their nationality it was least to be expected, a number of historians who have succeeded beyond all others in the thoroughness with which they have studied, or at least the clearness with which they have presented the history of European States. The Ferdinand and Isabella and the Philip II. of Spain are the best we have. Motley's History of the Netherlands enjoys the same credit. To these his countrymen Herbert Tuttle's "History of Prussia" makes him a worthy associate. . . . He has made not only his own people, but us Germans likewise, no insignificant present; he has succeeded, like Lewes with his biography of Goethe, and Seeley with his Stein, and far better than any German, in unfolding a clear, luminous, and comprehensive picture of an important period of our history. If anybody doubts that an American is capable of this, that we can learn to know ourselves in the judgments of a foreigner, in the mirror that he holds up to us, he ought without delay to read this instructive work.

From President C. K. ADAMS, of Cornell University.

The volume is everywhere marked with a thoroughness of scholarship and a sobriety of judgment that will commend itself to every historical student. The author's knowledge of the sources of information is very complete, and by a long residence in Berlin he was able to avail himself of such knowledge. Perhaps the most striking feature of the book is its impartiality. The author's judgments always incline to severity; but even when the reader is not able to accept his conclusions, he will not fail to admire the candor and fairness with which they are presented. The style is good, perhaps a little too stately to be popular, but one that from the first conciliates confidence in the author's desire to reach the truth and clearly present it. The work is a substantial addition to our literature, and one for which every person interested in the growth of Prussia should be grateful.

From the Christian Register, Boston.

It keeps quite in line with the new method of historic writing, and it gives a history of the people more than of the monarchs who rule them. Much space is properly devoted to the growth of Prussian institutions, arts, and literature. The accounts of the wars are quite full enough, but they occupy less room than in most histories; and the narratives of diplomatic changes are brief and concise. They give the needed facts, that is all. For an understanding of the character of the Prussian people and their wonderful development in recent years, this volume is of great value. It is calm, serious, dignified. Its insights are clear, and its opinions are just. The interest is unflagging to the end, and the literary style is pleasant as well as forcible.

From the Deutsche Rundschau for June, 1884.

. . . It is the history of the formation of the Prussian State, the preparatory work, noiseless but filled with statesmanlike thoughts, of the electors and kings down to the time of Frederick the Great, which Professor Tuttle's book relates. With perfect command of his materials, he is a trustworthy guide, for, never led astray by isolated details, he keeps steadily before us the organic unity of the whole, and describes wars, treaties, dynastic schemes, and territorial accretions only from that point of view. The style is not brilliant, but clear and exact; it is a thoroughly substantial and useful book. So far as we know there does not exist in our own language a similar concise sketch, adapted to a large reading public, of early Prussian history ; and we should not think it inappropriate if this work were made accessible to German readers by means of a translation.

From Prof. RODOLPH GNEIST, *of the University of Berlin, author of an elaborate work on English Constitutional History.*

. . . I can only express the heartiest recognition of the skill with which you have used such stubborn and difficult materials. Their treatment is indeed in one sense facilitated by the numerous German monographs, but is in another sense made more trying, since those special histories often overlap one another in a way extremely confusing to the reader, and make it difficult for a foreigner to decide between Austrian and Prussian, between Protestant and Catholic, and the multitude of other questions which characterize German political history. I think you have succeeded in presenting an intelligible picture of the formation of the Prussian State, and have been able to work your material into a form which will command the interest of the English public.

From the Revue Historique, September 1, 1884.

In the department of modern European history, we have an excellent history of Prussia, from the earliest times until those of Frederick II., by Mr. Tuttle. It is a very solid piece of work, devoted especially to the development of the political institutions of the country, but the author has not neglected the other aspects of its history, and the territorial formation of Prussia is carefully traced. Without pretending to be the result of original research, the work is based on a careful study of the best authorities.

From the Hartford Courant.

It is a careful and thorough piece of work. It is history in the old sense of recording dates and events and names, but it is new history, too, — a social study, sketching the changes of life and pointing out the influences and causes that have come in to affect results. It is amply indexed and makes a very valuable as well as readable history.

From the Hon. GEORGE BANCROFT.

It bears all the marks of conscientious and successful labor, and teaches how Prussia grew to be the formative principle of the German Empire, a needed lesson for all not yet initiated.

From the Philadelphia American.

He has some admirable qualities as a historian, the ability to take pains and get at the bottom of his subject; and a power of detachment from the notions and ideas of his age and country, which is of great value in a historian.

HOUGHTON, MIFFLIN AND COMPANY, *Publishers,*

BOSTON AND NEW YORK.